International Karate Association

KARATE-DO

A WAY OF LIFE

A BASIC MANUAL OF KARATE

by
Mark
Grigorian

EMPIRE Books
P.O. Box 491788, Los Angeles, CA 90049

Disclaimer
Please note that the author and publisher of this book are NOT RESPONSIBLE in any manner whatsoever for any injury that may result from practicing the techniques and/or following the instructions given within. Since the physical activities described herein may be too strenuous in nature for some readers to engage in safely, it is essential that a physician be consulted prior to training.

Published in 2009 by Empire Books.
Copyright © 2009 by Empire Books.

All rights reserved. No part of this publication may be reproduced or utilized in any form or by any means, electronic or mechanical, including photocopying, recording, or by any information storage and retrieval system, without prior written permission from Empire Books.

Library of Congress Cataloging-in-Publication Data
Editor: XXXXXXX
Action Photography: XXXXXXXXX
Interior & Cover Design: Mario M. Rodriguez,
MMR Design Solutions

INTERNATIONAL KARATE ASSOCIATION. INC.
WORLD HEADQUARTERS
3301 NORTH VERDUGO ROAD,
GLENDALE, CALIFORNIA 91208 – USA.
TEL: (818) 541–1240; FAX: (818) 246–0063

E-mail: karatekubota@earthlink.net
Website: http://www.ikakarate.com

Dedication

Traditional karate-do has been a special interest of mine for more than thirty years. I welcome this opportunity to express my gratitude to those who have taught me most of what I have learned. In particular, I am indebted to Soke Kubota for his continued guidance and spiritual support.

This book is dedicated to the entire IKA Family.

ON THE "WAY" OF KARATE

The "Do" aspect of karate-do frequently is touched upon in this and other books on traditional martial arts. While the public is somewhat familiar with the physical attributes of karate training, in general, it is unaware of the more beneficial, non combative aspects of the practice. Long-term practitioners of traditional karate not only feel and benefit from the offerings of the art but also strive to pave the way for others to follow. The way of karate includes both learning and teaching at all levels of proficiency. The meaning of the way, or the path, is neither philosophical nor ambiguous. It is real and tangible.

Most societies are familiar with mainstream faith-based paths, such as the Christian or the Buddhist way or health-based paths, such as a diet and exercise way, etc., all of which are meant to generate well-being and a higher quality of life. The way of karate is just another long-term strategy designed to improve quality of life, in all its forms, for the practitioners as well as the society at large, and it does so by building character, instilling emotional stability, and encouraging good conduct and citizenship.

The selection of a way of life or a combination of lifestyles is not something to be forced upon anyone. It is an important yet critical personal choice that could profoundly affect one's future. To realize what it takes to walk along the path of the "empty hand" the reader is encouraged to study the five cardinal rules of karate practice or the precepts of the dojo elaborated elsewhere in this book. Karate-do purposely emphasizes moral abilities, rather than physical skills that are in turn viewed as martial virtues. Without the path, karate is only a skill. The Samurai, Shaolin monks and traditional karate-ka gain mental and spiritual strength through martial arts practice mainly for the protection of society and higher aimes in life. Gladiators, ninjas and prize fighters employ their skills for entertainment and personal gains only. In summary, the gift of life presents us with many choices and opportunities, including the chance to select a meaningful way of life that is most compatable with our specific abilities and personal traits. How it may affect our personal lives and the society at large is perhaps best contained in the essence of the following old Chinese poem:

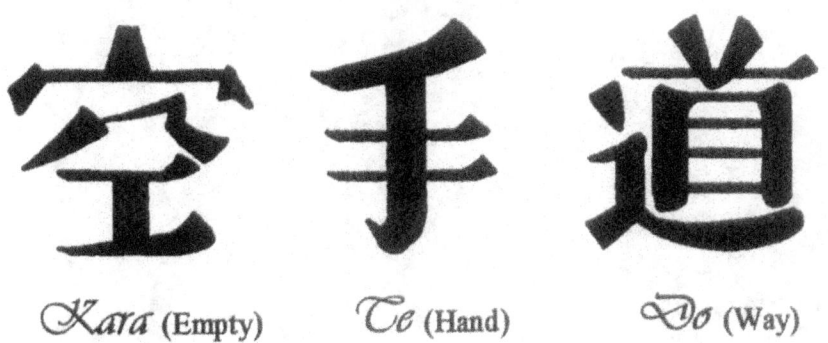

Kara (Empty) Te (Hand) Do (Way)

If there is truth in the way,
There will be light in the soul.
If there is light in the soul,
There will be beauty in the person.
If there is beauty in the person,
There will be harmony in the house.
If there is harmony in the house,
There will be order in the nation.
If there is order in the nation,
There will be peace in the world.

Grand Master Takayuki Kubota
IKA PRESIDENT and WORLD CHAIRMAN

ACKNOWLEDGMENTS

I am the first to admit that my writing abilities are not as good as my karate skills and that I am as hopeless with the typewriter as I am helpless with desktop publishing. Despite these and numerous other deficiencies, the spirit of karate-do helped me overcome the somewhat arduous task of writing a book on martial arts. Having recognized my shortcomings, I relied on the assistance of a large number of very talented and knowledgeable friends—mostly IKA members—to complete the preparation of this book. While it is not possible to acknowledge everyone who has contributed in some way to the completion of this book, I appreciate the help of those without whom this manuscript would never have materialized.

Sincere thanks are due to my teacher and mentor, Shihan Gordon Pfeiffer, for his continued support, valuable suggestions and thorough revision of the manuscripts. I gratefully acknowledge the valuable advice and encouragement of my teachers Shihans Val Mijailovic, Tatsuo Hirano, Boban Petkovic, and George Sinani.

I also appreciate the efforts of my good friends and fellow karateka Shihan Rod Kuratomi, Sensei Ernie Caballa, and Dr. Mark Weissman for their part in proofreading and commenting on some chapters of the first edition of the book.

I especially recognize the benevolence of my good friend and sparring partner Johnny Otero, Yudansha-Kai, for respecting the use of my right hand as an instrument of writing, rather than blocking. I am grateful that he allowed me to use my face and body to shield his left Gyaku-tsuki during the preparation of this book.

I am deeply indebted to Dr. Gayle Randall for contributing the section entitled "Basic First Aid for IKA Karate."

Thanks also are due to So Shihan-dai Kengo Isamu Manako for the use of his inspiring pamphlet, "Guide to Becoming a Better Karateka," which he prepared for IKA long before I joined the headquarters dojo.

Despite my many concerns, the first edition of this book was praised and greeted by the entire IKA family. The few thousand original copies of it became extinct only two years after publication. I am pleased that it met and surpassed most of the goals and expectations outlined in the preface to the first edition. All the praise aside, I believe the book could have been prepared more professionally and for a wider readership.

Nevertheless, I reiterate my added thanks and gratitude to my mentors and fellow karateka who previously were recognized for being so instrumental in the materialization and subsequent success of this effort. I have received many words of advice and encouragement from a large number of readers and well-wishers. Soke and my fellow Shihans kept reminding me that, in order to promote high level karate, the pen should not be underscored by the punch.

Soke Kubota wishes the book to eventually become an authentic manual on IKA karate and training. But this is a different story. We all love and respect him a great deal, and will try to fulfill his wishes in the near future, provided his creative mind gives our tired hands time to rest. However, Soke introduces new ideas and teaching tools faster than anyone can digest them, let alone write about them.

At some intermediate stage in the development of this edition, when I thought I had finished putting the book together, I was informed that Soke had introduced a number of new teaching aids for IKA karate training, and that he also was experimenting with some new ideas. It did not take me long to realize that these were fifteen magnificent new little katas, each one a unique masterpiece on its own. Naturally, I had to stop all work so I could learn and understand these new forms before I could write about them. The book would have looked naked without comments on the novelties of Soke's new kihon katas.

The idea that I might write a sequel or a second volume on IKA karate became apparent the day I finished writing the first book. Karate in general and IKA karate in particular are naturally-evolving phenomena that are growing rapidly in membership and recognition. Such outpouring of information and expansion of ideas requires the test of time to be digested by masters before mere mortals can write about them. I recognize the fact that I am only a humble student of karate-do, not an expert, not even a good writer. However, I felt morally obligated to fulfill the task that I had taken upon myself.

The original version of this book, "The Spirit of IKA," was published in 1995, and the main body of the work was completed in 1990. The world has changed dramatically between then and now, and of course it will continue changing forever, hopefully at a slower pace. And IKA has grown and leapt forward in all directions.

Soke Kubota, as usual, has taken the teaching of karate to new heights worldwide. Karate has become the world's most popular and fastest growing martial art. While not aging as gracefully, I have learned a lot about karate-do and its inner workings—from Soke, from life itself, and from other learned karateka around the world.

With my large share of setbacks and injuries, I still manage to train a couple of times per week. Perhaps the spirit of karate has kept me going all this time. My own life has been enriched by three grandchildren and a black belt daughter-in-law who has turned our house into a mini dojo. At home, I either write or fight. With so much encouragement, inspiration, and perspiration, I simply had to bow to the demands to upgrade the contents of the original manuscript to those presented in this new book.

Because of my travels, I meet and train with many IKA members outside the U.S. I enjoy their friendship and treasure my karate moments with them. I am proud and fortunate to be a member of the IKA. I acknowledge the moral assistance received from IKA members all over the world. I appreciate their spiritual support. I specifically wish to thank my good friend Shihan Grikor Mikaelyan, 7th dan, the president of the Armenian National Karate Federation and IKA's representative in the region, for his support during my extended stays in Armenia. He generously allowed my to use his facilities and train with members of Team Armenia, the outstanding Kubota World Cup Champions for the past ten years.

The late Miss Irene Jashidian worked many hours typing and organizing the manuscript. Her patience is appreciated as much as her dedication to this work. I thank Sensei Judy Rao, 2nd Dan, for voluntarily proofreading the new version of this book.

I am greatly indebted to Soke Kubota for his invaluable advice and suggestions. He contributed whole sections from his private files to certain chapters of this book, which were reprinted directly without any modifications.

And I acknowledge the valuable advice of my fellow instructors at the headquarters dojo. Their continued support made the preparation of this book an enjoyable experience.

Mark Grigorian
International Karate Association

Table of contents

Dedication	iii
On the Way of Karate	iv
Chinese Poem	v
Acknowledgments	vii
Contents	x
About the Author/A Note to the Reader	xiii
Why this Book?	xiv
Preface	xvii
The Insignia	xx
Messages from Soke Kubota	xxiii

CHAPTER 1 - THE ESSENCE OF KARATE-DO — 1

What is Karate-do	5
A Martial art	6
A Creative art	6
A Combative sport	7
A Method of Self-defense	8
A Way of Enlightenment	8
An Athletic Pursuit	9
The Science of Unarmed Combat	9
A Way of Life	10
On "Do" and "Jutsu"	10

CHAPTER 2 - IKA CURRICULUM AND BASIC REQUIREMENTS — 13

Karate Studies	16
Karate Training	17
Physical Fitness	17
Spiritual Growth and Mental Development	18
Karate-do, Instincts, Intuition and Emotions	20

CHAPTER 3 - AN OUTLINE HISTORY OF KARATE-DO — 23

Philosophical Background	23
Historical Background	26
Historical References	26
Contemporary References	27
Historic Schools	31
The Shotokan Style	32
Gosoku-ryu Karate	33
Internationalization of Karate-do	37
Adaptation for Practical Use	37
Improving the Training System	38

CHAPTER 4 - DOJO ETIQUETTE AND RULES OF CONDUCT — 41

The Dojo	42
General Protocol	43
Attire and Equipment	44
Training Session Formalities	45
Contest Protocol	47
Opening and Closing Formalities	49
The Starting Meditation and the Opening Address	49
The Ending Meditation and the Closing Address	50
Administrative Requirements	54

CHAPTER 5 - IKA TITLES AND RANKING SYSTEM — 57

IKA Ranking	59
IKA Titles	60
Other Titles	60

CHAPTER 6 - IKA KARATE TRAINING — 63

Fundamental Karate Training	63
Advanced Karate Training	63
Tournament Training	63
Promotional Training	64
Law Enforcement Training	64
Self-defense Training	64
Weapons Training	64
Kubota Ju-jitsu	65
Way of Meditation	66

CHAPTER 7 - KARATE-DO BASICS: KIHON — 69

Learning the Basics	70
Basic Philosophies	71
On the Components of Basics	73
Basic Rules	74
Strength and Flexibility	75
Bending of the Knees	75
Hand and Arm Techniques	75
Foot and Leg Techniques	75
Pivoting and Planting	75
Sliding and Sepping	76
Bending of Joints	77
Activation of Joints	77
Hip Rotation	77
Hands and Fingers	78
Relaxation and Breathing	79

Kime and Kiai	79
Hanmi and Hikite	79

CHAPTER 8 - VOCABULARY AND TERMINOLOGY — 81

General Terms	82
Basic Commands	83
Orientations, Spaces, Actions, and Positions	83
Counting and Numbers	84
Useful Phrases and Terms	85

CHAPTER 9 - SKILLS AND CONCEPTS — 87

Basic Techniques: Waza	88
Mechanical Principles	89
Mental Principles	89
Spiritual Principles	89
Basic Posture	90
Basic Stances	92
Heisoku-dachi	92
Musubi-dachi	93
Heiko-dachi	93
Hachiji-dachi	93
Uchimata-dachi/ Gyaku-hachiji-dachi	93
Kiba-dachi	93
Shiko-dachi	94
Zenkutsu-dach	94
Fudo-dachi / Sochin-dachi	94
Kokutsu-dachi	94
Sanchin-dachi	95
Neko-ashi-dachi /Ushiro-neko-ashi-dachi	95
Renoji-dachi / Rei-dachi	95
Hangetsu-dachi	95
Jiyu-dachi / Ju-dachi	95
Miscellaneous Stances	96
Tachi-kata	96
Technical Aspects of Standing Forms	98
Foot and Body Movement / Theory of Footwork	100
Suri-ashi	101
Oi-ashi	102
Tsugi-ashi	102
Yori-ashi	102
Kezami-ashi	103
Miscellaneous Steps	103

CHAPTER 10 - BODY PARTS AS MEANS OF DEFENSE AND OFFENSE — 105

Parts of the Hand	106
Parts of the Foot	107
Parts of the Head	108
Parts of the Torso	108
Categories of Karate Techniques	109
Basic Defensive Techniques	111
Philosophy of Defense	111
Basic Offensive Techniques	114
Philosophy of Offense	114
TE WAZA - Hand Techniques	115
KERI WAZA - Foot Techniques	117
ATAMA WAZA - Head Techniques	119

CHAPTER 11 - KARATE-DO AND BASIC SCIENCE — 121

Definitions of Basic Scientific Terms	122
Analysis of a Basic Combination	127
Kokoro	128
Dachi	129
Hanmi	129
Ashi-sabaki	129
Hikite	129
Waza	129
Kime	129
Kiai	130
Target	130
Jiki	130
Ma-ai	131
Balance	131
Kokyu	131
Mechanical Components of Oi-tsuki	132

CHAPTER 12 - KATA — 135

Bunkai	138
Omote-bunkai	138
Ura-bunkai	138
Okugi-bunkai	139
Kenka-bunkai	139
Sutemi-bunkai	139
Sonota-bunkai	139
Karate-do Maxims and Kata	140
First Principle of Kata: Courtesy	141
Second Principle of Kata: Nonaggression	141
Third Principle of Kkata: Perseverance	142
Fourth Principle of Kata: Perfection	142
Ultimate Aim of Kata	143
Personal Development	143
Physical Conditioning	143
Mental Development	143
Spiritual Development	144
IKA Kata	146
The Shotokan Kata	146
Heian-Shodan	149
Heian-Nidan	150
Heian-Sandan	151
Heian-Yondan	152
Heian-Godan	152
Tekki-Shodan	153
Bassai-Dai	154
Hangetsu	155

Kanku-Dai	156
Kanku-Sho	157
Empi	158
The Gosoku-Ryu Kata	159
Gosoku-Ryu Kata Classification	160
The Elementary Forms	160
The Basic Forms	160
The Intermediate Forms	*162*
The Advanced Forms	*162*
The Essence of Kihon Katas	162
Kihon Ichi-No kata	164
Kihon Ni-No kata	165
Kihon San-No kata	166
Kihon Yon-No kata	166
Kkihon Go-no kata	167
Kihon Roku-no kata	168
Kihon Sichi-no kata	168
Kihon Hachi-no kata	168
Kihon Ku-no kata	169
Kihon Ju-no kata	169
Kihon Ju-ich-no kata	170
Kihon Ju-ni-no kata	171
Kihon Ju-san-no kata	171
Kihon Ju-yon-no kata	171
Kihon Ju-go-no kata	171
Kihon Sonota kata	172
Intermediate Katas	173
Uke-no kata	173
Ni-no kata	175
Kime No Kata	177
Gosoku kata	179

CHAPTER 13 - KUMITE   183

Prearranged Sparring	*184*
Basic One-Step Sparring	*186*
Basic Two-Step Sparring	*187*
Basic Three-Step Sparring	*187*
Semifree One-Step Sparring	*188*
Freestyle Sparring	*189*
Tournament-style Sparring	*190*
Basic Sparring Principles	*191*

CHAPTER 14 - TEACHING AND INSTRUCTION   195

Do's and Don'ts of Teaching	197

CHAPTER 15 - FITNESS, LEARNING AND PHYSICAL CONDITIONING   201

Learning and Practice	203
Supplementary Conditioning	206
Preparatory	207
Meditation and Mental Preparation	208
Warming Up	209
Stretching	211
Generic Preparatory Exercises	213
Long-term Conditioning	214
Cardiovascular Endurance	*215*
Muscular Endurance	*218*
Muscular Strength	*220*
Sample Weight Training Program	*221*
Flexibility	*223*
Strength of Character and Toughness	223
The Makiwara	224
Tameshiwari	226

CHAPTER 16 - TESTING AND CERTIFICATION   229

Examples of Interview Questions	231

CHAPTER 17 - TOURNAMENTS   237

Rules and Regulations	240
IKA Divisions	240
Kata Competition	240
Sparring Contests	242
Other Terms	243
Partial WKF Kumite Rules and Regulations	244
Kumite Scoring	244
Prohibited Behavior	245

CHAPTER 18 - BASIC HEALTH AND FIRST AID   248

ABCs of First Aid	248

APPENDICES   256

A1 – On Soke Kubota	256
A2 – References	258
A3 – Schedule of Classes	259
A4 – General Teaching Schedule	260
A5 – IKA Affiliated Dojos	261

ABOUT THE AUTHOR

Shihan Mark Grigorian's many years of experience in martial arts include formalized training, research, and study of the Kan Zen-ryu, Shotokan, and Gosoku-ryu styles of traditional karate-do. He is a senior instructor at the headquarters' dojo and is a member of IKA's black belt holders association. He has presented many lectures and seminars on IKA and Gosoku-ryu karate outside the United States. He has been very instrumental in bringing many new members into the IKA family, including individuals, teams, and countries.

Mark Grigorian, 6th-dan, won the first place trophy of the Kubota Cup World Championships in the sixty years old plus division in Canada in 2003. Three generations of his family, including his grandchildren are all active members of the IKA.

He also is a consulting earthquake engineer practicing in Glendale, California. He is the author of several technical books and scientific publications. He holds a Ph.D. degree in structural engineering from Oxford University, U.K.

A NOTE TO THE READER

The purpose of this book is to provide background information on Karate training and its objectives. Karate cannot be learned from books, periodicals, and movies. Learning only can be achieved in a dojo environment under highly qualified instructors over a long period of time. Karate is not about hurting or subduing people and smashing objects. The martial arts training and physical fitness exercises described in this book may be too strenuous for some individuals. All readers and interested parties are advised to acquaint themselves with all aspects of karate practice and consult a physician prior to training.

All interested individuals should train under the supervision of IKA qualified instructors. Soke Takayuki Kubota, the author, the publisher, and the International Karate Association, Inc., are not responsible in any way whatsoever for injuries and inconveniences that may occur as a result of following the material or instructions presented in this book.

WHY THIS BOOK?

Why this book on Gosoku-ryu? Indeed, why Gosoku-ryu when a number of well-established styles of karate already exist, with many followers all over the world? Gosoku-ryu is not a new style of karate-do. It is an evolutionary advancement and reblending of several traditional methods of empty-hand combat. It is a rejuvenation of the old. The foundations for advancement of karate-do were laid down clearly in Grand Master Gichin Funakoshi's indispensable book, Karate-do Nyumon:

"Since Karate is ever-advancing, it no longer is possible to speak of the Karate of today and the Karate of a decade ago in the same breath...

Karate in Tokyo today is almost completely different in form from what was practiced earlier in Okinawa...

Precisely because it has its own life, 'Do' is subject to the inevitable cycle of growth and decline. It is ever-changing, but only in its outer form. The basic nature of Do remains the same."

Gosoku-ryu is the forecasted advancement. It simply is an upgrading of an old idea. This is why the contemporary Gosoku-ryu is taught in parallel with the classical Shotokan style at all IKA dojos, where the old and the young learn the old and the new side by side.

Nowadays, more people are practicing martial arts than any other form of major sport. Karate is the fastest growing martial art in both hemispheres. Though not an Olympic sport at this time, it enjoys the support and enthusiasm of many educational institutions, sports organizations, law enforcement agencies, armed forces, the entertainment industry, and the general public. Karate-do is being promoted vigorously by all interested parties as an adjunct to a better life. It is a rapidly expanding phenomenon that only can benefit the practitioner and the society at large. It has surpassed all cultural boundaries.

Millions of people engage in the formal practice of karate on a regular basis in all four corners of the world. It therefore is not surprising that its followers enjoy such an abundance of literature and audiovisual aids on various forms and styles of the practice. Presently, there are more books, magazines, and sources of information on karate than any other popular sport. The volume of karate-related literature still is on the rise and is increasing in proportion with the growing number of participants. There are numerous excellent books and periodicals on karate and related subjects and many more that were produced for commercial enterprises or personal promotion with little or no instructional value for the user.

Most of the outstanding books on the subject are style-specific, and are illustrated with hundreds of professional sketches and photographs that depict karate-related body parts, techniques, and sparring scenes, as well as complete sequences of certain katas with their applications.

A large proportion of these depictions are supplemented with additional descriptions and technical discussions. Some of these publications also contain other useful information on karate and its practice. Literature of this kind is of greater value to the followers of its own specific style rather than others. What makes a few of these books stand out and become as instructive as they can be is the amount and depth of conceptual, historical, and philosophical material provided to complement the illustrations and texts.

Understandably, every one of these publications, distributed universally, was produced based on its own unique style of karate and trend of thought. This does not in any way detract from these publications or their producers; it just could not be done any other way. Every old-timer and advanced practitioner with thirty or more years of experience in the art knows that, while the modes and methods of different styles of karate look different at the beginning, their results converge at advanced stages, giving rise to the idea that the final results may be the same near the summit.

Beginners and newcomers have a hard time with this concept. All they really care for is to learn the basics of a new sport associated with a selected "Ryu" or brand name. No beginner can think three decades ahead. Most beginners are inquisitive about their own style and wish to find out all about it and what makes it different from others. This group of enthusiasts needs style-specific literature to complement their physical training. There are also a number of well researched texts and magazines with minimal graphics that deal essentially deal with non combative and non technical aspects of the practice. They are, of course, of great interest to academics and higher ranking followers of the art.

It would be ideal to produce an all-encompassing volume on karate and related topics that covers all aspects of all forms of empty-hand combat with all their trimmings and complete sets of sketches and illustrations. While not totally impossible, such an effort would require overcoming many political, logistical, and economic challenges over an extended period of time. Practically speaking, there is neither a great demand nor use for such a book at the present time. Such an undertaking could become viable only if and when all major world karate organizations forgo their differences and work under a united directorate for a common purpose. This is unlikely to happen soon.

There are no major publications on Gosoku-ryu and IKA Shotokan styles of karate practice. *Karate-do: A Way of Life* is the only book of its kind that carries no elaborate sketches or illustrations. As one reader commented once, it is more mental than visual. This concise publication is targeted at the IKA membership that receives first-class training from first-class instructors in well equipped dojos where actions speak louder than words and pictures, particularly when Soke Takayuki Kubota is present. The inherent message of the book, directed especially at younger students, is condensed in the old adage:

"Daily Life Is Your Dojo"

This means you should live by the precepts of the dojo and aim higher in life and in karate practice. It reminds us, amongst other things, that in daily life:

Today's lesson is tomorrow's aptitude
Today's aptitude is tomorrow's knowledge
Today's knowledge is tomorrow's expertise
Today's expertise is tomorrow's wisdom
Today's wisdom is tomorrow's awareness.

And that in karate-do:

Today's practice is tomorrow's ability
Today's ability is tomorrow's skill
Today's skill is tomorrow's proficiency
Today's proficiency is tomorrow's mastery
Today's mastery is tomorrow's awareness.

A notion clearly inherent in Musashi Miyamotos' golden principle:

"Today is victory over yourself of yesterday."

PREFACE

Karate-do is a martial art developed in Japan at the beginning of the last century after thousands of years of evolution in the Orient. It is a way of life designed to enrich modern man's life in a variety of ways. What we know about the noncombative aspects of karate-do is much less than what remains to be discovered. Even though contemporary karate-do is almost a century old, there are major gaps in our understanding of its inner workings and the way it affects the lives of its practitioners.

Karate-do: A Way of Life is for those who sincerely wish to discover the true meaning of karate-do. There is a great deal more to karate-do than meets the eye. Discovering karate-do is synonymous with understanding yourself and gaining insight into your abilities and shortcomings. It can be achieved only by living the "karate way," a voyage of self-discovery open to anyone. In other words, an understanding of personal limitations could help one make better judgments, thereby increasing the chances of success and reducing the likelihood of harm to all.

Karate was and still is one of the best methods of self-defense. However, times have changed, and the likelihood of karateka hurting themselves during practice or otherwise is much greater than being assaulted by an adversary lying in ambush. Even so, karateka are taught to avoid conflict and refrain from violent response, unless it is a matter of life and death. Perhaps it is more appropriate to look upon karate-do as a method self-protection from invisible adversaries rather than misguided souls. The invisible adversary only can attack from within the person, and sometimes with more devastating effect than a straight punch on the nose. These adversaries come in all shapes and forms, the most common of which are: addictions, negative sentiments, evil thoughts, depression, chronic stress, muscular atrophy, and diminishing immunity due lack of movement. Karate-do is not a cure-all magic, but it somehow protects its long-term practitioners from such ills and their effects. It does, in fact, offer a holistic way of life.

Practitioners of the art neither glorify nor underrate karate-do. True karateka maintain the notion that "While karate-do is not everything, it is part of everything else in a student's life." In fact, a majority of karate practitioners experience some degree of self-recognition and awareness through practice of the art. Another popular argument holds that the universe and individual are one. Parts of everything also are parts of the universe. Good and bad are intertwined and are part of each other. Consequently, for those who follow karate-do, or the way of good intentions, all things still are part of each other, but they influence and interact each with the other in a positive sense. All good deeds generate positive sentiments for all. A single bad deed could adversely affect an entire community.

Karate enables students to recognize their belonging and oneness with their surroundings through instinctive awareness and intuitive knowledge of the environment. Therefore, a real karateka is a person whose life is in perfect harmony with all things.

Karate-do is a multifaceted endeavor that benefits many. The practice of martial arts enriches the lives of its practitioners and supports good citizenship in society at large. Karate-do promotes well-being in many more ways than traditional sports and athletic pursuits. The precise way it fulfills the mental, spiritual, and physical needs of a person remains a mystery. How much an individual benefits from karate-do has a great deal to do with his/her personal traits and degree of sophistication.

While one karateka may find the study of a *Bunkai* as mentally stimulating as scholastic work, another student may find the mental aspects of freestyle Kumite as rewarding as a challenging game of chess. While one practitioner may find the physical aspect of a practice session as invigorating and exciting as a tennis match, another may find it as exhilarating and demanding as a long-distance run. While an advanced student may seek spiritual awareness through performing Kata, a new practitioner may discover spiritual calm through Makoto, a form of short-term meditation performed before and after a training session. This multitude of benefits and diversity of personal experiences are the primary reasons for the myriad of sentiments and interpretations regarding karate-do. However, one thing is certain. Karate-do, like most martial arts, has as its ultimate aim the transcendence of purely physical skills through the development of the spirit and the perfection of character. The International Karate Association, Inc. (IKA) is a world-renowned organization seeking to promote good citizenship, personal well-being, and self-improvement. Grand Master Soke Takayuki Kubota founded the IKA to introduce and advance the cause of traditional karate-do outside Japan. He is one of the all-time karate greats and is regarded as a living legend in his own right.

IKA membership now comprises many thousands of men, women, and children of all ages, from all walks of life, with different social and ethnic backgrounds, each one pursuing karate-do for a different personal reason. Given the diversity of the membership of the IKA and other world-class organizations, which ranges from novices under six years of age to shihans sixty years of age, it is easy to see why the noncombative aspects of the art often are overshadowed by the excitement of physical training and tournament type events. I am but one of the many thousands of Soke's grateful students whose life has been affected profoundly by the way of karate. I undertook to upgrade the contents of the first version of this book, *The Spirit of IKA*, with a new title, *Karate-do: A Way of Life*, for several reasons, most importantly the following:

- To promote Gosoku-ryu, the "hard-fast style" karate, and encourage others to join the IKA family so that they, too, can discover the joy of self-fulfillment through practice of the art, and to propagate the idea that IKA truly is an international organization.
- To compile a concise source of information on IKA and its activities that will form the principal component of an authentic manual on basic karate-do.
- To bring together some of the supplemental reading material required in the IKA curriculum.
- To reflect on Soke's views on the essence of karate-do and to present an introduction to the elements of Gosoku-ryu karate.
- To explain the interrelationship between routine karate training and such esoteric concepts as the "mind-body-spirit" connection, "the state of Zen," "self- improvement and self-recognition," and so on.
- To bring to paper material that seldom is discussed in a dojo environment.
- To help instill the notion: "Today is victory over yourself of yesterday."
- To express my gratitude to Soke Takayuki Kubota for guiding me, my family, and thousands of others along the path of karate-do.

It is too much to expect that the first printing of a book of this nature will be entirely free from error. I sincerely hope that my peers, as well as my fellow karateka, will find this contribution sufficiently interesting and worthy of attention to help correct any defects that may exist and suggest ways to improve future editions of the book.

May the spirit of karate-do empower those who wish to remain in harmony with all things through tolerance, self-worth, and awareness.

Mark Grigorian, Ph.D.

The Insignia

This universally recognized insignia was developed and registered by Soke Kubota as the official emblem of the IKA in the mid 1950s. The dojo sign, or *Kamban*, is more than a commercial trademark. It characterizes the spirit of the organization it represents through simple lettering and expressive graphics.

Originally, the traditional Japanese Kamban included either the coat of arms of the master of the house or the family emblem of the chief instructor of the school. It was displayed on the main gates of the premises. To separate the domestic affairs of the house from the activities of the dojo, the family emblem gradually was replaced by an official trademark and was removed from public view.

The Kamban appears on all official IKA documents and products and is worn proudly by IKA members on their karate uniforms. All members are required to use and display the insignia as required by IKA rules.

This simple yet meaningful symbol reflects the fundamental ideas that form the essence of IKA and Gosoku-ryu karate-do. In physical terms, Gosoku-ryu refers to the hard-fast method of empty hand fighting. Philosophically it implies emotional stability and quick thinking.

The insignia consists of three different but related parts. Every element of each part conveys several important messages in connection with its own image and its relationship to other elements of the emblem.

The first part of the insignia consists of Latin lettering that defines the nature of the insignia and conveys propriety, belonging and ownership. This unique combination of unfamiliar Japanese ideograms and common English words portrays the introduction of an ancient Oriental way of life to Western cultures.

The second part, which depicts the front view of a clenched hand with oversized foreknuckles, symbolizes the art of empty hand combat. It is an unarmed hand turned into a fist. The fist, a natural weapon, is the universal symbol for karate-do.

The form of the fist, or *Seiken*, which displays the basic punching technique in karate, is intended to generate a feeling of deliberation, fortitude, power and skill. The oversized knuckles pertain to certain personal traits associated with karate practice, such as persistence, continuity of purpose, experience, unyielding commitment, and resistance to hardship.

The third part of the insignia appears as the letter K turned on its side and contains two sets of Japanese ideograms.

The first set, consisting of three characters placed within the inclined wings of the insignia, reads from left to right as Buto-ku-kan, or martial virtues or center for martial virtues. The concept of martial virtues is a direct reference to the Samurai code of ethics and social behavior.

The essence of the traditional warrior, the Bushi, was related to seven distinct virtues: justice, courage, benevolence, courtesy, honesty, loyalty and honor. The samurai had to develop these martial virtues along with martial skills to achieve victory in war and perfection in life. The ethics of modern karate-do are related to these virtues and are part of the Dojo-Kun, or precepts of the dojo.

The second set of ideograms, consisting of five Japanese characters placed within the horizontal base of the insignia, reads from left to right *Kokusai Karate-do Kyokai*, or the International Karate-do Association. The combination of the two sets of ideograms implies that IKA is a center for the study and promotion of martial virtues. In a broader sense, the physical aspects of karate-do are considered part of martial virtues rather than martial skills.

The appearance of the words *Gosoku-ryu* and *Butokukan* on the same emblem suggests that Gosoku-ryu karate, despite its young age, is considered a traditional martial art. It upholds all traditional values associated with karate practice as preached by the founders of the modern karate-do.

The prime goal of IKA is upholding the spirit of Butokukan through the practice of Dojo Rules, both in the dojo and in daily life. The overturned letter K embracing the Japanese ideograms symbolizes the traditional Samurai helmet, or Kabuto, with its distinguished horn-like features.

This particular feature, the *Kuwagata*, suggests the capital letter V Soke explains; this inter-cultural form was selected because it symbolizes:

"Victory of good over evil as well as the victory over self."

The initials I, K and A are contained within the line diagrams of the insignia. The sound of the letter K brings to mind the three K's of the *Kokusai Karate-do Kyokai*, the first initial of Soke's name, Kubota; and the initial letter of many terms that define the fundamental concepts of karate practice: ki, karate, kumite, kata, kihon, kiai, kokoro, ken, kime, kubudo, kokyu, kyu,etc.

Soke's gift to mankind is the introduction of Gosoku-ryu karate, a uniquely Japanese martial art. Soke Kubota is the creator and driving force behind this great idea. IKA is the medium through which this noble concept is being realized. IKA members are the messengers of this important humanitarian notion, which now has believers in some 60 nations worldwide.

A MESSAGE FROM SOKE KUBOTA

In *The Spirit of IKA*, the headquarters dojo was referred to as my house and the home of the IKA family. My students are referred to as disciples of the art and messengers of the way of karate. If this is the case, then *The Spirit of IKA* should be regarded as the first official manual that discusses IKA's philosophies and approaches to karate training.

Being head of a household that is 15,000 strong and communicates in 60 different languages has moments of delight but also equal shares of linguistic and cultural problems. *The Spirit of IKA* presents a wonderful opportunity to facilitate communication and strengthen spiritual ties between IKA students and anyone else who might be interested in following the way of karate-do.

It is a great pleasure and an honor to serve a truly international organization whose goal is the promotion of peace and well-being. It is very gratifying when I see my students uphold and promote the spirit of IKA. The collective effort needed to produce this book is a vivid example of my students' belief in the way of karate and what it can accomplish for them and the public at large. I am particularly pleased to see that the importance of mental and spiritual development—in addition to physical training—is addressed frequently throughout the book.

Unfortunately, due to lack of promotion, Western societies have remained less than receptive toward the noncombative aspects of karate-do and martial arts. IKA is one of very few Western martial arts organizations that has succeeded in improving the image of karate-do in the West. We have succeeded by promoting the mental and spiritual values of karate on an ongoing basis.

The production of this book is yet another step taken by IKA to promote good will and share our ideals with anyone interested in benefiting from this noble way of life.

Since their creation in Japan in the early 1950s, both the IKA and Gosoku-ryu karate have received extensive coverage in martial arts and sports media worldwide. Gosoku-ryu karate and my different weapons techniques have been the subject of many technical articles in martial arts journals. A few of my students have produced some very good texts on practical karate-do in English and other languages.

My own book, which now is out of print, deals mainly with the technical aspects of Gosoku-ryu karate. My other books also deal with purely combative aspects of karate-do. *The Spirit of IKA* and other IKA publications complement each other.

The Spirit of IKA is a significant and timely contribution to the literature of karate-do. It is unique in that it emphasizes the importance of physical training and promotes the noncombative aspects of the art in a balanced and subtle manner. This effort reflects a lesson learned well from the study of empty hand combat.

Although Shihan Mark humbly refers to the first edition of *Book One* as a supplementary aid to karate training up to the Shodan level, I feel it contains a great deal more, in depth and in concept, about karate-do than most commercially available publications.

I strongly urge my students, especially the black belts, to read and promote this book and, as requested by Mark, to contribute to the content of future editions.

— Soke T. Kubota, 1995

•••

Almost fifteen years have passed since I first asked Shihan Mark to compile a simple introductory booklet on IKA karate, mainly for internal consumption at the headquarters dojo. Instead, he produced the two-hundred-page, well-organized *The Spirit of IKA*, which still remains the closest work to an all-encompassing manual to IKA martial arts.

The book was a great and timely addition to IKA literature. It was so successful that it became extinct shortly after it was made available to all. Since then, I have been receiving repeated requests from all over the world for additional copies.

More than half of the original copies were distributed among IKA clubs, sister organizations, and public libraries that had asked for it. A large number of copies were awarded as trophies to karate champions at various events and tournaments.

However, instead of reprinting the book, I asked Shihan Mark to upgrade it to a newer version with a view toward more advanced studies and a larger circle of readership, even beyond the IKA family.

As I see it, the upgraded version of the book, *Karate-do: A Way of Life*, contains a great deal of new information. It truly is the best published work on IKA karate that I have come across during all these years. This is the only book on karate-do that discusses the mind–body–spirit connection in a clear and tangible manner.

I advocate the teaching and practice of the elements and the rules of the basics, as emphasized repeatedly in various sections of the book. I especially welcome the addition of the new chapter on teaching and instruction. This book is a must for every student of karate to read. Every member of the IKA family should be familiar with its contents and recommend it to anyone who has an interest in martial arts. I enjoy the book every time I look at it.

I personally am so occupied with my organizational, teaching, research, and acting duties that I hardly have any time for writing, social events, and appearances. I have no time to correspond with friends and associates.

But I do realize that decimation of information and the need to remain in contact with all IKA members and sister organizations is as vital as daily training.

Our web site at *www.ikakarate.com* does its best to introduce IKA to the rest of the world. Our electronic news letter does an excellent job of keeping us informed about each other via the Internet. These IKA publications together have taken IKA's image to new heights worldwide.

I specifically like and endorse the idea that: "Proper learning of the elements of kihon not only aids us in executing effective techniques during kata and kumite, but also brings about the mind–body–spirit togetherness that is central to the practice of karate-do, and perhaps is the best way to perceive most things in life."

I find the new section on the "Grammar of Karate Practice" highly appropriate, useful, and instructive.

I reiterate the sentiments and essence of my previous message and wish that everyone will help promote the ideals of IKA through this book.

— Soke T. Kubota, 2008

CHAPTER 1

The Essence of Karate-Do

The Spirit of IKA was and still is an indirect reference to the heart and soul of Grand Master Soke Takayuki Kubota, founding father of the International Karate Association, Inc., and Gosoku-ryu karate. In a sense, the new book, *Karate-do: A Way of Life*, reflects his views on the essence of karate and martial arts training. Soke's biography, as part of the history of modern karate-do, appears in the third chapter of this book.

The mission of this book is to explain Soke's thoughts about essential aspects of karate practice. Karate-do is a modern, philosophical concept based on man's oldest and most natural way of self-defense. In its traditional context, it embraces all standard methods of unarmed combat in a single category: the art of empty hand combat. The contemporary version of karate-do has been resynthesized as the "Way of Empty Hand."

Karate-do is a modern term coined in 1933 by Grand Master Gichin Funakoshi to establish the rebirth of karate in Japan. The literal meaning of *Kara-Te* is empty hand, or unarmed, seeking peace. Do or doh is derived from the Chinese word Tao and means a path through life. It is used to symbolize the path by which an ideal is accomplished. When do is used in conjunction with a discipline, such as Sho-do, the way of calligraphy, or Karate-do, the way of empty hand, it implies that the endeavor incorporates higher aims, such as the self-perfection of the individual, rather than mastery of the discipline alone. Consequently, the English translation of karate-do has been paraphrased as "The Way of Empty Hand Fighting."

While Japanese and other Oriental proponents emphasize the do nature of karate, Western enthusiasts encourage mainly the physical aspects of the art. In Japan and other parts of Asia, karate is respected because most people understand what it is and what it stands for.

In the West, most people associate karate with spectacular feats of subduing opponents or breaking boards and other objects. There is a common misconception in the West that karate is a violent and destructive sport. In fact, karate is a revered, nonaggressive, and spiritually oriented martial art that has been serving mankind in the cause of justice and human welfare for hundreds of years.

This book tries to dispel misconceptions that karate-do is merely a system of self-defense or a combat sport. It describes how karate also promotes good citizenship and good health, and helps its students understand and come to terms with themselves and the world around them.

There are many myths about karate and many stories that can be understood only by the experienced and highly skilled practitioner. Nevertheless, true karateka, or those who pursue the art faithfully, do develop the proficiency needed to master the legendary abilities of the art, but only when they acquire the necessary spiritual power. It is this union of skill and spirit that empowers karateka to avoid violence and physical conflict. Karateka may commit themselves to many years of work in perfecting the art, yet actually may refrain from using it, a choice that may seem incomprehensible to those people not trained in the way of karate-do.

Unfortunately, Western cultures as a whole have displayed little interest in the nonphysical aspects of the art; as a result, they have denied themselves the opportunity to gain insight into spiritual and other important aspects of karate. This is due to cultural doctrines that differentiate the basic philosophies of the Orient from those of the rest of the world.

The notion that the study of karate can lead to personal awareness and spiritual enlightenment, though intriguing, is at best confusing to the Western mind. It is a complex notion difficult to comprehend from a pragmatic or non-philosophical point of view. The same, however, is not true of Oriental cultures, where the various martial arts often have been a part of their religions and their belief systems. Since this is not a social problem but a cultural issue, it may be resolved most effectively by attempting to understand the philosophical environment surrounding the world of karate-do and martial arts.

It is common knowledge that the highly stressful and materialistic lifestyle of the modern world eventually leads to a lower quality of life and diminished contribution to society. Experience has shown that the ills of society increase as it moves toward greater affluence and a materially centered lifestyle.

Perhaps the least recognized and even less promoted benefit of karate-do is its ability to improve people's lives and their attitudes toward life through physical exercise and spiritual development. There is sufficient evidence that the practitioners of karate-do are less affected by stress and better equipped to deal with the hardships of modern life. They also, as a general rule, tend to provide better service to society in their particular trades, as well as in their daily encounters with other people.

In a free society, the individual is at liberty to choose his or her way of life and ethical values, with the proviso that the freedoms of others are not infringed upon. However, there are no set rules or guidelines as to how the individual best improves his or her quality of life and standard of contribution to society.

Martial arts in general and karate-do in particular offer one of the most productive and practical means of fulfilling this need in any community. To pursue karate-do is not the question for the dedicated karateka. The issue is how to maximize the benefits of the pursuit in favor of the individual and society at large.

True karateka are blessed with the ability to maximize the fruits of their efforts by integrating their physical talents with perseverance and spiritual focus.

This book seeks to identify the processes that are essential to achieving spiritual growth through the methodical practice of empty hand combat. Soke believes that with positive exposure, it is only a matter of time before karate-do will become an accepted and viable method of personal fulfillment. "After all," he says, "it has taken many years for karate to spring out of obscurity and become the world's fastest growing and most popular martial art."

The origins of karate are traced to the ancient Orient, and to Rome, Greece, and Egypt. The downturn of occidental civilizations resulted in the early demise of the martial arts in many regions. In the Orient, however, the methods of empty hand combat developed and flourished. In no other part of the world did they develop to the heights they did in China, Japan, and on Okinawa. Karate was revitalized in Japan at the beginning of this century, where it remained an elitist activity until the end of World War II.

Every step of karate as we know it today has been synthesized methodically by great thinkers of the past who inherited the art from the great masters who came before them. Only an individual with incredible and unique talents can hope to further develop karate-do, thereby adding to the progress of *The Way* through the combined efforts of masters over the ages. By creating Gosoku-ryu karate in 1953, Soke Takayuki Kubota made a significant contribution to traditional karate and also added a new dimension to the world of karate-do.

The International Karate Association, Inc., was established in Tokyo in early 1953. Ten years later, the American branch of the IKA was inaugurated in California. The primary goal of the IKA since its creation has been the worldwide promotion of both the

Shotokan and Gosoku-ryu styles of karate-do. The merging of these two styles has created a new school of karate practice whose effectiveness probably is unsurpassed anywhere in the world.

IKA looks upon karate-do chiefly as an effective way of improving an individual's quality of life and gaining spiritual awareness through systematic practice of the art. This does not imply that IKA overlooks the significance of physical training in favor of mental or spiritual development. On the contrary, Soke teaches that all three aspects of karate training are equally important. In fact, the union of mind, body, and spirit in specific ways is common to all martial and creative arts. The parallel development of mind, body, and spirit is encouraged constantly throughout this book and is deemed essential to meaningful progress both in life and in the pursuit of perfection in karate-do.

While the emphasis of this book is on the informal introduction of the noncombative aspects of the art, it also provides a complementary teaching aid and a concise reference manual on basic karate practice in IKA, leading to the rank of Shodan—or first degree black belt in the Shotokan and Gosoku-ryu styles of karate. Advanced karate training and related subjects are beyond the scope of the present volume.

The present volume is not meant to be a textbook on karate practice. Neither is it meant to be a philosophical and intellectual interpretation of karate practice. It does offer pertinent and interesting thoughts on various aspects of the practice of the art. The approach adopted in this book tends toward introduction and guidance rather than instruction and teaching. It will be of little value to those who believe naively that they can learn and master karate-do on their own.

The best approach to gaining proficiency in any martial art, especially the *Way of Empty Hand Fighting*, is to train under qualified and experienced instructors in a dojo environment. A book such as this only assists the understanding of the intricacies of "The Way," which may help a student become a better karateka.

The book begins with an introduction to the IKA curriculum and its requirements, followed by an outline of the history of karate-do, including a brief account of the development of Gosoku-ryu karate. The main body of the text is concerned chiefly with explanations, comments, and interpretations of the basic rules and elements of karate practice.

An entire chapter has been devoted to fitness, learning, and physical conditioning. Chapter 16 contains pertinent information on scheduled tests that must be taken to fulfill curriculum requirements.

Unlike most standard texts and manuals on the subject, this book does not contain elaborate illustrations or diagrams that depict the human anatomy, karate action, or fighting scenes. This choice was made deliberately in the hopes of stimulating the reader's imagination and thought processes through reading and visualization.

This book is limited in scope and is intended as a simple treatise on the elements of basic karate-do. The present volume is not meant to condone or challenge the contents of any of the many excellent books that already have been published on karate and martial arts. It merely looks at karate-do from a slightly different point of view and should be regarded only as a new addition to the already rich literature on the subject of basic karate training.

To uphold the traditional image of the art, an effort is made to make constant reference to the Japanese words and phrases used in karate practice. To this end, several hundred Japanese terms, their meanings, and areas of application have been compiled throughout this book.

Although the book is influenced strongly by IKA philosophies, it does not promote a style of karate different from that of the other references. Instead, it focuses on the strengths and positive similarities that exist among all traditional systems of empty hand combat. It should, therefore, be equally informative and beneficial for all students of traditional karate, regardless of their preferred style or school of training.

WHAT IS KARATE-DO?

Karate-do is designed to fulfill the mental, spiritual, and physical needs of modern humankind in a variety of ways. Although a wide range of benefits is attributed to the systematic practice of karate, only a few of them have been recognized and are being utilized by the general public.

The precise way a karateka benefits from the art is a matter of personal interest and sophistication. A breakdown of IKA membership into age groups reveals a range of interests and perceptions with respect to the pursuit of karate-do.

Parents want their young children to train and are motivated chiefly by the developmental, disciplinary, ethical and protective nature of the art. Most parents believe strongly in the positive effects of karate-do on the physical well-being and development of self-esteem in their children.

Children, by nature imaginative and playful, find karate a natural and instinctive activity. They take immense pleasure in the mock fighting drills and play-like movements of karate practice. Given the choice, many children would rather pursue karate than engage in school-type athletic activities.

Older children and teenagers generally are attracted to the combative aspect of the art, as well as to the joy of movement inherent in karate training. Despite engaging in high school sports and similar activities, these students often pursue karate as their favorite athletic endeavor.

Younger adults are drawn into training because of its sporting, recreational, and competitive aspects, as well as the combative nature of the art. A large number of young adults who have been pursuing karate-do for many years, and have been forced to leave the practice for personal reasons, tend to come back as soon as conditions become favorable.

Middle-aged adults find the physical fitness benefits an added bonus to the mental relaxation and the protective capability gained from self-defense training.

Older adults and senior students who have been training for many years find the spiritual aspects of the art as rewarding as its mental and physical benefits. It is not uncommon to see men and women of all ages and degrees of proficiency train side by side at IKA dojos. In fact, many parents and children, young and old, participate regularly at mixed group sessions, thereby strengthening their family ties and values.

As karateka grow older, wiser and more skilled, there is less emphasis on the physical and more emphasis on the mental and spiritual aspects of the art. At some point, the ability to defend oneself becomes a given, and a lesser priority. Regardless of age or profession, those who can endure the training for the first few years grow to love it and tend to pursue it for as long as they can.

A different breakdown of IKA students, this time by profession, reveals that the systematic practice of karate makes positive changes in their lives and tends to improve their quality of work and outlook toward society and life in general. This diversity of benefits is the primary reason for the many terms and expressions used to define and interpret the inner nature of karate-do.

Because karate-do is difficult to describe fully and accurately, many advocates of the art tend to simplify their explanation and interpretation of karate-do. Some of these descriptions are as follows:

A Martial Art: This is the most common and accepted term used to describe karate-do. It is a direct translation of the Japanese word Bu-gei, which refers to the so-called Jutsu forms. The suffix Jutsu, as in karate-jutsu, signifies the technical form of the fighting art. All Japanese Jutsu or Bu-gei were developed systematically from the tenth century onward, while karate-do is a product of the present century.

Karate-jutsu is the technical form of the art of empty hand combat. The jutsu provides the warrior with the necessary physical and mental training for the act of combat. On the other hand, Karate-do, which is an outgrowth of Budo, draws upon the same talents and skills in order to avoid confrontation and physical struggle.

A Creative Art: Since the education of the Bushi, or traditional warriors, consisted of a dual emphasis on Bu, the study of martial strategy and combat, and Bun, the study of the literary and fine arts of Japan, martial artists, mostly at the level of master, also were creative artists. For example, the Japanese art of calligraphy, Shodo, is considered a vital part of martial arts training.

The graceful and dance-like movements of karate exercises add to the impression that karate is a creative and performing art as well as a martial art. The existence of karate-like movements in many of the postures of Oriental classical dances further reinforces the notion that karate also is an art form. This perception stems from the understanding that both karate kata and dance are choreographed patterns that are performed to impress and entertain the public. This is not necessarily a misconception, but it is so limited in depth and meaning that it does not do justice to the skills and concepts that support each of these art forms. The fundamental difference between the martial and the creative and performing arts is that while showmanship and display of expertise are the prime purposes of the creative and performing arts, they are contrary to the spirit of karate-do. Furthermore, martial arts and karate-do emphasize control of emotion and systematic pursuit of long-term goals for the individual. The creative and performing arts aim principally at generating spontaneous emotions and short-term entertainment for the masses. Karate-do teaches us to appreciate each art form for its own merits and within its own context.

A Combative Sport: Karate is a physically demanding and highly combative endeavor, but its aims and applications are remote from the actual sporting purpose. Since it lends itself well to sporting enterprise, it has been exploited as a competitive and spectator sport. Fighting to win is contrary to the spirit of karate-do. Karate-do should not be compared to professional boxing, wrestling, or any other combative sport in which the objective is to hurt or incapacitate the opponent.

However, regulated sparring has been used very effectively to further the cause of karate-do through championships and media events. Taking part in tournaments and demonstrations to promote the ideals of karate-do is considered a noble act. One of the important purposes of sports is the establishment of better records or championship performances. However, true karate-do places no emphasis on competition, record breaking, or championships. Instead, its focus is on the ultimate aim of individual self-improvement.

To paraphrase Grand Master Funakoshi; "The ultimate aim of karate-do lies not in victory or defeat but in the perfection of the

characters of its participants." Winning in more traditional sports usually means proving one's physical superiority over others. The goal in karate-do is to overcome oneself. It is feared by many that too much emphasis on the competitive aspect of karate-do might weaken the art and deviate from The Way.

A Method of Self-Defense: This is an accurate but limited reference to one of many beneficial aspects of karate-do. A well-trained karateka should be able to defend him/herself and others in the face of danger. Goshin-jutsu, or practical self-defense, is part of the IKA curriculum for all students, and it is practiced regularly at IKA headquarters and affiliated dojos. Although karate-do also is a highly developed and effective method of self-defense, its primary goals are distanced from training for self-defense and active combat. The aim in practicing self-defense is to develop sufficient personal and spiritual strength to avoid violence and situations in which self-defense may be the only way to resolve a conflict.

A Way of Enlightenment: Although this is the ultimate aim of all traditional martial and creative arts, it is neither a requirement nor is it formally taught as part of dojo training. Rather, students are encouraged by way of example and guidance to find their own path to personal fulfillment through the practice of karate-do. Attaining awareness and spiritual enlightenment, or Satori, is a matter of personal choice. It is a unique personal process that requires many years of hard work, patience, maturation, and contemplation. According to Lao-Tzu, "Knowing others is wisdom. Knowing yourself is enlightenment. Everything else is just knowledge." One way of approaching enlightenment through karate-do is to recognize your own minute accomplishments in the art while never losing sight of your tremendous shortcomings. Furthermore, karateka (like any Budo stylist or student of a martial way) are supposed to add spiritual training and mind control to their study, while developing an all-round global vision of the environment, or Tsuki-kokoro, thus producing a wider field of perception of both oneself and the world at large. The Zen approach emphasizes the cultivation and achievement of the Satori, which is defined as a state of oneness with nature and the universe, attained through contemplation and practice.

An Athletic Pursuit: In the past twenty years, karate has become the world's fastest growing athletic pursuit, in large part because the public has become increasingly aware of the ills of sedentary life and the benefits of regular physical exercise. Unfortunately, not all sports are suitable or affordable for those who wish to indulge in some kind of regular sporting activity. Karate-do is an all-encompassing activity that also is an athletic endeavor and an excellent way to attain and maintain physical fitness. It is a natural sport open to all people of all ages and sexes, regardless of their social status and physical disposition. It is one of the few sports that does not require special talents or physical prowess of its new students. Preselection or discrimination of any kind is contrary to the spirit of karate-do. It is meant to be a lifelong pursuit of human ideals that does not require expensive equipment or facilities; does not preselect only the smartest, strongest, biggest, tallest, and fastest; and offers both physical and psychological benefits. Most advocates of karate-do refer to it as an athletic endeavor or recreational pursuit, rather than a competitive sport.

The Science of Unarmed Combat: This is a pertinent but incomplete definition of the nature of karate-do. There are many credible arguments that support the notion that karate-do is the science of unarmed combat. Whether discovered by trial and error or deduced through science, all karate movements can be validated by the principles of physics and applied mechanics, and have been optimized for maximum effect and least expenditure of energy. Karate training also is based on comprehensive knowledge of the human anatomy and its vital points in order to prevent accidents and injuries during practice. Atemi-waza, or knowledge of the exact location of vital points and how to strike them, generally is reserved for masters and higher level karateka. The healing points of the Japanese healing art, or Shiatsu, are the same points targeted in

Atemi-waza. Perhaps the most intriguing association of karate-do is its connection with Katsu, the Japanese art of emergency first aid, and the Japanese healing art, Reiki. The ability to injure the body and the capability to heal it are seen as complementary processes.

A Way of Life: This is the sentiment or definition most favored by karate masters and higher level students who have devoted major parts of their lives to the practice, teaching, and understanding of the martial arts. Master Anko Itosu first coined the expression "Karate-do is a way of life" almost 100 years ago. Higher level karateka do not judge themselves by how many men they can defeat or how many trophies they have won. Rather, the test is how well they comprehend the meaning of karate-do and how efficiently they impart their knowledge to others. It is indeed an enriching way of life. Soke Kubota recommends practicing the samurai code of ethics, as well as his unique *Kubokido* meditation method, because these methods will help the student focus on the important aspects of life and thus become a more developed human being.

Lack of focus is the primary reason most of us do not make the most of our mental and physical abilities. Living the karate way enables the followers to bring to bear a higher degree of concentration and focus on the task on hand, thereby maximizing their given abilities. The path of understanding karate-do does not end in the dojo. One must live the karate way in order to experience its fullest rewards. In other words, if a person can master strategy in karate-do, he/she can, with the understanding gained from living the karate way, maximize its applications in all aspects of life. Perhaps this is the most desirable function and the most accurate definition of the endeavor that is karate-do. Despite philosophical differences, these are all legitimate descriptions of a growing phenomenon developing at varying speeds throughout the world. Karate-do is an evolving phenomenon that embodies a wide spectrum of concepts and interests, ranging from a playful pastime to a combative sport to a way of achieving enlightenment.

ON "DO" and "JUTSU"

Although the terms karate and karate-do are being used interchangeably all over the world, as well as in this book, they are, in fact, quite different in nature and purpose. By the same token, the Bugei, or martial arts, are not to be confused with the Budo, or

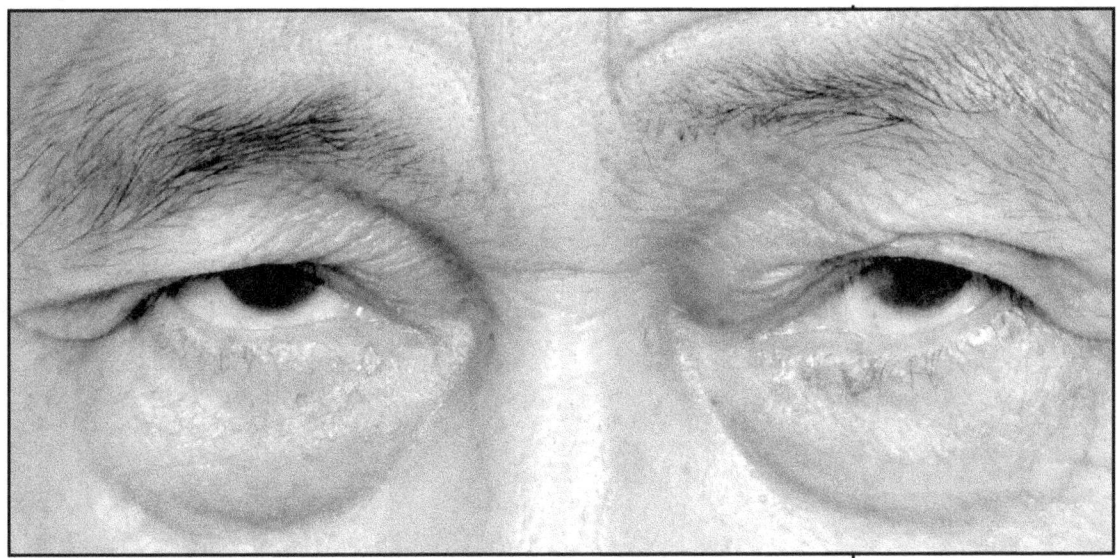

martial ways. Perhaps the following explanation will clear the confusion.

Karate is the collective name of several methods of unarmed combat that have been synthesized into a unique system of self-defense. In reality, it comprises all types of weaponless martial arts, including regular boxing and wrestling. Regardless of their national origins, all systems of empty hand fighting, such as Russian Sambo, and French Savate, etc., are variations of the same concept.

Karate-jutsu is that form or aspect of karate that was developed exclusively for warriors, as a martial art, to defend and protect the group or individual cause. It was and still is available to all. It includes all possible ways and means of subduing the opponents.

In general, jutsu implies a craft, skill, or profession. It does not carry the implication of self-perfection that is the essence of the Do. It does not imply less quality or skill. A person using karate, such as a professional fighter, engages in karate-jutsu, which seeks only the attainment of fighting skills, devoid of the mental and spiritual goals that characterize martial ways. Karate-do, on the other hand, advocates the utilization of the same physical approach to attain self-perfection through the martial way. Karate-do, which is a martial way, has emerged from karate-jutsu, which is a martial art. All "Do" forms originated from Jutsu forms.

However, since the basic physical formats of the Do and Jutsu systems are the same, once the philosophical differences are understood, they may be referred to interchangeably without loss of meaning or context. Nevertheless, neither the above nor more extensive and eloquent descriptions can explain fully and correctly the true nature of karate-do.

Genuine enthusiasts are left with the challenge of discovering the true meaning of the art from their own perspective by pursuing it with diligence, conviction, and an open mind.

CHAPTER 2

Curriculum and Requirements

The International Karate Association offers its students a wide range of opportunities to achieve self-improvement and personal satisfaction through karate-do and other martial arts.

To get the most from their IKA membership, students should recognize and seek the lifelong rewards of practicing karate-do, rather than approach it merely as a short-term indulgence or temporary hobby. However, many practitioners forced by circumstances to end their regular training programs eventually return to karate as soon as conditions improve.

While there is no harm in trying karate for a short period of time, potential students are encouraged to enrich their lives with a long-term commitment to the study of the art.

The practice of karate-do is not an event, not even a chain of events, but a process of learning and enlightenment that requires many years of hard work and practice. For many practitioners, karate-do is indeed a way of life.

For children fortunate enough to start karate-do in the early stages of their lives, it becomes a lifelong treasure and a means of reaching higher levels of mental and spiritual satisfaction. Such a sensation is experienced only by those who attain the pinnacle of perfection in any human endeavor. The way of karate is a self-imposed privilege and an indulgence in personal commitment.

To achieve personal development and self-awareness through karate-do, IKA requires students to dedicate themselves to several years of committed learning and physical training. The IKA curriculum includes, but is not limited to, reading suggested texts, viewing recommended video tapes, attending lectures and seminars by Soke

and his advanced students, participating in scheduled practice sessions, and taking part in tournaments, demonstrations, and other events.

IKA students are urged to develop the power of their minds and the strength of their bodies through systematic study of the art of empty hand combat. Soke teaches his students that training the mind is as important as developing physical skills. For this reason, the IKA offers balanced amounts of mental and spiritual studies in conjunction with physical training.

The essence of the IKA curriculum is based on Soke's wisdom, knowledge, and expertise. It has taken Soke more than sixty years of devotion and contribution to martial arts to achieve the status of Grand Master, or So-shihan, and to earn the red belt, or Aka-obi, which signifies that the wearer has attained the rank of 10th degree black belt, or Ju-dan, the ultimate level of proficiency in karate-do.

Soke claims he still is a student striving toward perfection. Soke's humility is part of his greatness. Greatness in karate-do leads to humility and human perfection. Soke is a role model for thousands of karateka worldwide. His experience embraces a wide spectrum of karate activities, including teaching, research, competitions, and demonstrations. He also consults for law enforcement agencies, the movie industry, institutions of higher learning, and the martial arts media. Soke's personality is reflected in every aspect of the IKA curriculum.

The IKA is one of the most popular and best known karate organizations in the world. Its truly international character has brought together all kinds of people from all over the world. This has enabled dissemination of some of the most effective and efficient methods of training to affiliated dojos in more than sixty countries.

IKA membership is divided into three main age groups: adults, juniors, and children. Children under a certain age are grouped together in specially scheduled classes. The IKA pays special attention to children's training and education. To quote Soke, "We teach children that the first two priorities in their lives should be their families and their studies. Everything else must come after that." Unfortunately, there is a common belief that martial arts training can turn children into bullies. Nothing could be further from the truth.

True martial arts training teaches discipline, respect, and responsibility. It also teaches children to concentrate and achieve goals. These skills are transferred easily to the child's everyday life. Far from teaching children to become bullies, an education in the martial arts helps prepare a child to become a useful and honorable citizen.

Karate training for men and women is divided into three levels: beginners, intermediate, and advanced. This division is somewhat arbitrary and has been designed to maximize the training efficiency and learning ability of each group. The general overview of the curriculum presented in this section is applicable equally to men and women of all ages in all three levels.

The ongoing beginner's class is organized to accommodate new students at any time and at any stage. Novices are given special attention and training to help them progress in the beginner's class. In all three divisions, students progress through learning and learn through progress. Newly-ranked students often are given the opportunity to work and train with peers and higher-ranking students in order to familiarize themselves with their future programs, as well as to measure progress toward the next level of learning.

Truly committed karateka often schedule daily training and practice programs under the supervision of qualified instructors. The IKA recommends a minimum of three training sessions per week for beginner and intermediate level students.

IKA-scheduled classes emphasize training rather than practice. Training is defined as that aspect of learning that deals with the psychological and physiological conditioning of the student. Practice is the mechanical repetition that helps the student memorize the neuromuscular skills acquired through training. Training teaches mental and physical skills. Practice imprints neuromuscular responses into the student's memory. More practice makes perfect. For this reason, the IKA urges its students to maximize precious training time by warming up individually for at least thirty minutes before each class.

The IKA philosophy reflects a deep respect for traditional karate-do while embracing new concepts and encouraging an open-minded attitude. The IKA curriculum includes both the teaching of the traditional Shotokan style of karate-do and the more practical and contemporary Gosoku-ryu karate originated by Grand Master Soke Takayuki Kubota. The Shotokan style is introduced first. The Gosoku-ryu principles are taught at the intermediate stage. The two styles blend and interact with each other seamlessly. IKA students achieving Shodan in karate-do take great pride in reaching the same degree of proficiency in two styles of karate at the same time.

The IKA curriculum is directed toward five distinct disciplines of guidance and learning: karate studies, karate training, physical fitness, mental development, and spiritual growth. To achieve the first level of proficiency in karate-do, traditionally recognized as Shodan, practitioners are required to follow parallel paths of physical training and related studies. These areas of learning are grouped under the five general disciplines described above. Each category contains approximately ten different, but related, sections.

Achieving Shodan in karate-do signifies the completion of the basic phase of learning and prepares the student for advanced studies. Advanced studies begin with the refinement and perfection of basic skills while reading new materials, learning new techniques, combinations, katas, mental skills, and higher levels of spiritualism. A detailed description of advanced studies is outside the scope of this book. The purpose of this book is to provide an introduction to the basic requirements of the curriculum. The curriculum never has been confined to a rigid framework. Like anything else in life, it has evolved through time and experience. Soke is continuously producing new ideas and teaching tools, some of which have not yet found their places in the curriculum.

Karate Studies

This part of the curriculum has been designed to help increase the student's general knowledge of karate-do and its philosophies. Reading about martial arts is a must in the IKA and is encouraged at all levels. Students become familiar with these theoretical studies as they progress through their physical training programs. A great deal of emphasis is placed on self-study and individual reading. The most important branches of study in this category are:

- Introduction to the philosophy of karate-do
- Introduction to the history of karate-do
- Soke, our founder
- IKA, our school
- The Shotokan style of karate
- The Gosoku-ryu style of karate
- Etiquette and rules of conduct
- Administrative rules
- Basic vocabulary
- Technical aspects of karate-do
- Testing, certification and ranking
- Rules of tournaments
- Scientific aspects of karate-do
- Karate-do and physical fitness
- Miscellaneous karate studies
- Basic first aid (optional)

Trying to learn karate-do from textbooks alone is an exercise in absurdity. However, reading about karate-do—its ideals, development, history, and philosophy—is almost as enriching as its practice. IKA students are urged to complement their physical training with as much recommended reading as possible. Although this volume is not a source book on karate studies, it does provide some background information on most of the topics listed above. A list of approved literature, books, and periodicals for further reading is provided in Appendix A2.

This list is by no means complete but is meant to serve as a starting point for IKA students interested in additional reading and karate studies.

Karate Training

Except for first-time students, the IKA curriculum follows a floating format in which students are taught new lessons as they progress through their training program. The fundamental concepts of empty hand combat are grouped in the following general categories of basic karate skills:

Basics and their components	KIHON
Basic stances and standing forms	TACHI KATA
Basic postures and body forms	GAMAE
Basic defensive techniques	HAN GEKI / UKE WAZA
Basic offensive techniques	KO-GEKI/UCHIWAZA/ TSUKI WAZA
Basic footwork and body movements	ASHI SABAKI /TAI SABAKI
Prearranged formal exercises	KATA
Sparring	KUMITE
Basic self-defense	GOSHIN JUTSU
Basic breaking techniques	TAMESHI WARI
Makiwara training	MAKIWARA
Teaching assistance	SHUDO

Physical Fitness

Good health, physical fitness and karate-do all are part of the whole. Good health and physical fitness are the foundation of karate practice. Although no formal physical conditioning classes are offered at IKA, the following physiological attributes are developed systematically in conjunction with karate skills and formal studies:

- Strength and power
- Agility and quickness
- Stamina and endurance
- Acceleration and speed

- Flexibility and suppleness
- Toughness and resistance
- Stability and balance
- Muscular control
- Breathing and rhythm
- Mobility and range of motion
- Coordination and dexterity
- Relaxation and rest

IKA members, especially those who cannot attend dojo training more than twice a week, are urged to complement their karate training with some kind of supplemental conditioning, including stretching, aerobics, and moderate amounts of weight training. The importance of maintaining sufficient levels of cardiovascular capacity and muscular strength is discussed in Chapter 15.

Spiritual growth and mental development

Regular, serious training is essential to success in karate-do. The discipline of training develops the student's physical, mental, and spiritual capabilities. Spirituality in karate-do has no religious connotation; it mainly is a reference to emotional stability. Students are taught to make the art of empty hand fighting a part of their life style, rather than just a lesson learned. Only then will the mind, body, and spirit work in perfect unison. As discipline is developed, the repetitious movements cease to be tedious and become instead sources of mental energy.

Before karate became a martial art in feudal Japan, it used to be part of the religious training and rituals of the Shaolin Temple in China. Shaolin monks used to meditate several hours before, after, and during each practice session until they became proficient in the basic techniques of the art. They had discovered, through the teachings of Lord Buddha, that the integration of intuitive knowledge, or Zen, with martial skills could elevate their fighting abilities to new, unprecedented heights. It is because of the miraculous applications of this belief that the now famous phrase "Karate and Zen Are One" was coined by the nineteenth century masters of the art. The same belief still is being upheld by the majority of contemporary experts, who are convinced that spiritual training always should be part of regular karate practice. They maintain the notion that without emotional stability, the practitioner is only a skilled fighter.

Zen training enables the student to sense and see all that is relevant while not thinking of the one thing that constitutes the eventual goal. It teaches the student to visualize and feel the process without thinking of the outcome of the effort at the same time. It allows the practitioner to see and embrace the path while ignoring the purpose. It puts the emphasis on perfecting the techniques rather than concentrating on the aim. Zen is an ancient notion. Since the thirteenth century, students of Kyudo, the Japanese art of Zen archery, have been forbidden even to aim at a target until they perfect their drawing and firing. They are taught to have no feelings about what happens to the arrow. In karate, students are advised not to look at the hands and feet of the opponent during kumite. Instead, they are trained to develop an intuitive sense of anticipation regarding the sparring situation. Most advanced karateka are able to sense and react to an opponent's technique when he initiates his attack. Like Zen archery, karate students are trained not to have any emotions during empty hand practice or in any other type of encounter in which they have to rely mainly on their own senses and abilities.

Beginners and intermediate level students are guided indirectly toward spiritual growth and mental development through systematic training in karate. From time to time, instructors will discuss the mental and spiritual aspects of karate-do in connection with a specific lesson, technique, kata, or combat situation. However, no formal coaching in mental and spiritual training is offered to *Mudansha*—pupils who have only Kyu grades—until they become *Yudansha*—holders of a black belt. Nonetheless, taking part in any IKA training session is a spiritual experience in and of itself. Without spiritual development, karate is only a sport. Traditional sportsmen may master their techniques but may not necessarily master themselves. The spiritual aspect of karate-do helps the student achieve and maintain the calm and self-control considered essential for developing desirable spiritual qualities.

Certain sections of this book are designed to familiarize students with some of the mental and spiritual aspects of karate-do. While a comprehensive discussion of these aspects are outside the scope of this book, it may be instructive to know that almost all advanced katrateka eventually share the same great spiritual attributes, such as courage, benevolence, tolerance, confidence, and patience. Similarly, most of them develop the mental abilities for better judgment, timing, planning, anticipating, memorizing, and comprehension. In the absence of information, people trust their gut feeling, which is the same as relying on their natural instinct and intuition. The relationship between such inherent phenomena and karate-do are discussed in the next section. The first spiritual lesson of karate-do deals with respect and humility. The remaining chapters of this volume are dedicated mainly to that idea.

Instincts, Intuition and Emotions

All things interact with each other and share the same global environment. Humans and all living things are exposed continuously to new conditions and environmental effects. They include such a variety of things as the ultra-violet rays of the sun, the singing of a bird, and lava flow in a distant volcano. Humans and all other living things continuously encounter such global and near environmental effects as physical actions, invisible signals, and many other bits of information, and respond to them both physically and psychologically. Such cause and reaction may be so insignificant that a person may not even feel it. Under other circumstances, it may result in extreme reactions.

The response to any event or incoming information may vary from person to person, and depends solely on personal traits and sophistication. While one person may keep cool and not panic during a catastrophic event, another may become hysterical from upsetting news. The type and the quality of a person's response to any event, news, or information are related directly to that person's degree of preparedness, which, in this context, implies being informed and trained for similar situations. One's degree of preparedness depends on many things, including the amount and quality of past experiences as well as current physical and mental abilities. For example, soldiers are trained for warfare, paramedics are trained for emergencies, and karateka are trained to defend themselves. All trained and experienced people usually handle their respective tasks with skill and confidence. However, if the same people were totally unprepared but were compelled to perform the same tasks, they would have no choice but to resort to their instincts and intuitive knowledge.

Almost all people are blessed with natural instincts and some degree of intuitive knowledge. Instinct and intuition are inherent preprogrammed response systems designed to help people handle new situations to the best of their abilities. The actual and spiritual components of any response or behavior manifest themselves as physical actions and emotional expressions, respectively. While animals depend mainly on natural instinct and intuition, i.e., prearranged responses, humans rely more on learned behavior and acquired knowledge. Responsive actions and emotions are not separate from each other, but their type and quality differ and depend largely on personal background and spiritual stability. To reiterate the important message of this section: "The value of a response is related directly to the extent, diversity, and degree of personal training, education, and experience." All training, especially karate-do, tends to sharpen the natural instincts and enrich the intuitive knowledge of the practitioner, resulting in greater emotional stability and strength of character. The culmination of technical prowess is mastery. The summit of intuitive "know-how" is unity with the surroundings. Zen is the integration of mastery and unity with nature.

The theory and mechanism behind building character through karate-do are not too difficult to explain. It requires only that the practitioner commits him/herself to the process. The process gradually will improve the practitioner's inherent instincts and self-confidence. Since the process is part of human nature, nature rewards the practitioner with better health and heightened senses. This, in turn, further improves instincts and intuition. The cycle is endless. Humans, like all living things, have been and still are natural hunters and territorial fighters. Since they became civilized, they lost their inherent hunting skills and began buying food from supermarkets. At the same time they gave up their natural hunting and fighting abilities in favor of long range firearms. Over thousands of years of inaction, this has caused their natural instincts, intuitive knowledge, and other natural abilities to decline to the extent that these cannot easily be reinstituted back to normal.

Karate practice is the closest phenomenon to hunting and empty hand fighting. Long-term practice invigorates the senses and rehabilitates the neurological systems that control all inherent abilities, including instinct and intuition. It is interesting to note that no living entity except humans has lost so much natural ability throughout their normal lives. Civilization tends to tip the balance between "learned behavior and acquired knowledge" and "natural instinct and intuition" in favor of the former, which perhaps is a small price to pay for the contemporary lifestyles of the present times. However, instinct and intuition work best when reinforced with knowledge and experience. Without knowledge, natural behavior and civilization could cross paths and get into conflict with each other.

The schedule of training sessions offered at the IKA Headquarters' dojo is presented in the appendix. This schedule is subject to change without prior notice. A graphic chart of the IKA karate training material, divided into two groups, General and IKA specific, also is presented in Appendix A4.

CHAPTER 3

An Outline History of Karate-Do

PHILOSOPHICAL BACKGROUND

Karate-do is a martial art developed in Japan at the beginning of this century after hundreds of years of evolution in the Orient. It is an art, or way, that requires of a great deal of intellectual and physical discipline of its students. It is considered one of the finest forms of combined physical and spiritual training available today.

For the true karateka, karate-do is a means of achieving mental tranquility, spiritual fulfillment, and physical proficiency through the art of weaponless combat. The unique union of mind, body, and spirit requires the unyielding support of mind and body to achieve spiritual serenity. Similarly, the continued support of the spirit and the body are needed to assure a compatible state of mental development.

The systematic practice of karate, as a way of life, can bring together the essential abilities through which karateka may reach unlimited intellectual, physical, and spiritual heights, in life and in practice.

To emphasize the significance of the noncombative facets of karate-do, the need for intellectual awareness is repeated frequently in all sections of this book. The basic philosophical idea promoted by the IKA is that karate-do and fighting are totally different and diametrically opposed concepts. It therefore is vitally important that new students and the public understand the difference between fighting and karate-do. New students should learn at once that karateka do not engage in fighting, either in the dojo or anywhere else. Students also are taught that the purpose of karate-do is to avoid conflict

and refrain from fighting unless there is no alternative. Fighting is a physical struggle against an enemy for the resolution of conflict by way of violence and force. In karate-do, there are no enemies, and conflicts either are avoided or resolved by reason. Philosophy aside, there are sound psychological reasons why karate training brings about nonaggression through confidence. People who know how to protect themselves can maintain a calm spiritual attitude that usually is reflected in their approach to daily life.

Individuals who are proficient in the techniques of self-defense develop a feeling of personal security and self-confidence through experience and familiarity with real combat situations in the dojo. It is this feeling of personal security and self-confidence that leads to the handling of danger in a nonaggressive but decisive manner. In other words, people who can take care of themselves in the face of danger are less likely to run into trouble than those who tend to panic and resort to violence.

Technically, fighting is the intended but instinctive use of limbs and body to control, hurt, maim, or kill another person or living object. Fighting of any kind, with or without weapons, instinctive or otherwise, generally has been banned from civilized society. However, fighting and hunting used to be the sole means of subsistence and survival for primitive man. Instinctive fighting is how all living things except humans subsist and survive.

Karate, on the other hand, refers to a combination of methods of unarmed combat that evolved and developed in the Orient over a period of a thousand years. Only in the past fifty years has karate become known in the Western Hemisphere.

Unlike instinctive fighting, karate is an organized blend of several indigenous fighting arts, some of which still exist and are being practiced in their original forms in Asia. To fully appreciate the difference between instinctive fighting, karate, and karate-do, it is important to become familiar with the environment surrounding karate practice and gain a basic knowledge of its origins and historical development.

The material presented in the next few sections describes the strictly regulated and highly spiritual relationships that exist in a dojo, where every act is related to virtues of gratitude, sharing, humility, and respect.

A typical karate session is conducted by a Sensei, or teacher. *Sen* means before, and *Sei* means born. The literal meaning of the Japanese word Sensei is "one who is born before." This refers to spiritual birth rather than chronological age. Some of the best IKA teachers are much younger than their students. Soke began his teaching career when some of his pupils were twice his age. The person whose spirit has touched enlightenment and has demonstrated a certain level of proficiency in the art can be the teacher of the person who seeks to become the *Seito*, or student, regardless of age, sex, race, or social status.

The process of learning in karate-do is an ongoing phenomenon. In fact, the concept of the teacher learning from the lesson is basic to all meaningful karate instruction. This is why the practice hall is referred to as the dojo, or the place of the way, the place of enlightenment. In this context, enlightenment means getting to know oneself. Therefore, if karate-do is the way to enlightenment, then karate is the vehicle leading to the way. The martial arts began to develop this emphasis on personal and spiritual growth in the sixteenth century when the need for combat skills in the Orient began to diminish. It also was known that the spiritual strength derived from karate practice made the practitioner a better karateka and more skilled in the art.

In karate-do, actual fighting is replaced with kumite. Kumite, or freehand sparring, is a method of practice performed with or without a partner. The partner, or opponent, is a fellow karateka and helps with the process of learning. Kumite is a mutual process of sharing knowledge and experience. If there is a conflict, the opponent at best reflects the mirror image of that conflict but does not help to resolve it. For this reason, there are no winners or losers in kumite. There is only mutual learning and sharing of experience. If there were losers, they would be the real victors because they had learned from the winners. Conversely, the winners would not be the real victors because they had not shared the experience of the losers.

As in all traditional Japanese ways, the object of karate is the development of the individual through systematic training of the mind, body, and spirit to the height of human potential. Karate-do is manifested in movement and thought. Its methods are contemplation and the disciplined use of the mind and body. Its means are the defensive movements of blocking, striking, punching, kicking, throwing, grappling, etc.

Meditation and contemplation are inseparable parts of karate training. Several simple methods of meditation have been designed to augment karate training. Karate's premises of self-discovery and spiritual renewal aim to reduce the stress that people encounter in daily life. For this reason, karate-do is not only a form of self-defense; it also is a method of self-awareness.

The complete mental control required to master the physical movements, and the effort and discipline put forth to achieve harmony of mind and body, lay the foundation for the development of good citizenship and strong character. Karate-do is an endeavor that can benefit all. The need for personal and spiritual growth never can be overemphasized. For this reason, karateka worldwide reaffirm their pledge to the cause of karate-do before and after each training session. The ethics of modern karate-do are contained in the Dojo-kun, or precepts of the dojo, which urge karateka to seek perfection of character, to be faithful, to endeavor, to respect others, and to refrain from violent behavior.

The Dojo-kun, as recited at IKA and other traditional schools, is derived from Tode "Karate" Sakugawa (1733–1815), known as the first Okinawan teacher of karate. The Dojo-kun contains precepts designed for a lifetime of use, applicable both in the dojo and outside as well. Such is the way, or path, of karate-do. It is karate-do, not karate alone, that provides the opportunities for individual progress and spiritual growth, both in life and in karate practice. The "do" is too precious to ignore or to miss.

HISTORICAL BACKGROUND

Although this section is concerned principally with the history of karate, the chronological development of empty hand combat and fighting skills is told within the context of the general history of man. The history of weaponless fighting is as fascinating and dramatic as the history of civilization, and as old as the human race.

Fighting methods in general, and empty hand fighting in particular, always have existed as part of man's history. However, fighting methods have changed over the millennia from means of survival and subsistence to military, law enforcement, self-defense, and spiritual applications. It appears that civilization and the need for spiritual growth have advanced together and at the same pace, as if dependent on each other. It is likely that karate some day will become a recognized vehicle for personal improvement worldwide.

From a functional point of view, the history of empty hand combat is divided into seven distinct time periods, as shown in Table 1, which also traces the evolution of karate-do throughout history. There is sufficient evidence suggesting that primitive forms of karate existed in most ancient civilizations, all apparently influenced in different time periods by the ancient Indian fighting art of Kalaripayat. Scholars hypothesize that the collective skills known as Kalaripayat somehow found their way to other contemporary civilizations that were within practical reach of India. This indigenous martial art still is embedded deeply in the social and religious life of the villagers of southern India, as it must have been for thousands of years. Indian fighting arts and certain philosophic concepts centered on meditation and spiritualism were introduced into Greece, Egypt, and China through trade, military campaigns, and religious missions. The following are the most significant references supporting this hypothesis:

HISTORICAL REFERENCES

- References from Buddhist chronicles regarding Kalaripayat of ancient India dating back to 5000 B.C.

- Hieroglyphics from the Egyptian pyramids describing karate-like pugilism, or fist fighting, in 4000 B.C.
- Homer's 23rd book of the Iliad, referring to practice of pancratium in Greece and Crete in 3000 B.C.
- Koji-Ki Japanese chronicle describing the existence in Japan of early Jujitsu around 1000 B.C.

The functional outline presented in Table 1 (page 28) also contains other pertinent and interesting information regarding the historic progress of karate in the Orient and its subsequent adaptation by the rest of the world.

CONTEMPORARY REFERENCES

The following list of selected publications, though not complete, is provided for the benefit of those students who might be interested in further reading.

- Shotokan Karate: Its History and Evolution, by Randall Hassell.
- Original Martial Arts Encyclopedia, by J. Corcoran, E. Farkas, & S. Sobel.
- Spiritual Dimensions of the Martial Arts, by M. Maliszewski.
- Shotokan's Secrets, by Bruce Clayton.
- Shotokan Karate, A Precise History, by Harry Cook.
- History and Traditions of Okinawan Karate, by Tetsuhiro Hokama.
- Karate's History and Traditions, by Bruce Haines.
- Zen and Japanese Culture, by D. K. Swearer.
- The Way of the Warrior, by H. Reid and M. Groucher.
- The Bible of Karate – Bubishi, by P. McCarthy.
- Karate-do, My Way of Life, by Gichin Funakoshi.
- Teachings of a Grand Master, by Richard Behrens.
- Essential Shotokan, by Edmond Otis.

Karate has been part of man's history and life style. Karate-do is the revered name given by the civilized world to man's oldest instincts for protection and survival. At the same time, karate has been influenced by the same civilization it helped form and caused to flourish.

The origins of karate can be traced as far back as 4000 B.C. to India, the birthplace of martial arts, and to ancient Greece, the birthplace of occidental culture. While empty hand combat flourished in the Orient and developed into a modern martial art, it took a downturn in Greece and Rome about the time it was incorporated into the Olympic Games in 648 B.C.

It is believed that the early demise of karate in Greece, Rome, and Egypt is due to declining morals and a lack of spiritualism. These

Table 1:
FUNCTIONAL HISTORY AND DEVELOPMENT OF EMPTY HAND FIGHTING

PERIOD OF TIME	MAIN FUNCTION IN SOCIETY	METHOD OF FIGHTING	GENERAL ORIGIN	HISTORICAL FIGURES
5000 B.C.	Hunting, Subsistence, Survival, Self-defense, Tribal warfare, and Individual fighting	Instinctive Punching, Striking, Pulling, Pushing, Kicking, and Wrestling.	Africa India	Early Man
4000 B.C. 3000 B.C. 1000 B.C.	Military, Self-defense, Religious training, Ritual performance.	Semi-organized empty hand fighting, Boxing and Wrestling, Jujitsu.	Egypt, India, Tibet, Greece, Japan	Indian Nobility
500 B.C.	Religious training, Self-defense, Military.	Formalized empty hand fighting, Wrestling and Chinese Boxing	China, India, Mongolia, Rome.	
500 A.D.	Religious Training, Self-defense, Military.	Mongolian Wrestling, Chinese Kempo, Okinawan Karate, and Japanese Martial Arts.	China, Japan, Okinawa, Korea, Mongolia	Daruma Taishi (Bodhidharma)
1300 A.D.	Spiritual & Religious training, Military & Self-defense, Sport	Karate and Improved Indigenous Methods of empty hand fighting.	China, Japan, Korea, Vietnam, Okinawa.	Chinese Merchants and Okinawan Delegations.
1700 A.D.	Self-defense and ethical values	Beginnings of contemporary Karate-Do. Compilation of Classical Katas	Okinawa, China	Tode Sagukawa (Shuri-te)
1900 A.D.	Competition sport, Fitness, Spiritual and Personal fulfillment,	Organized Karate and Karate-Do refinement of Classical katas	Okinawa, Japan, World.	Gichin Funakoshi (Shotokan)
1950 A.D.	Self-improvement.	Modern Karate-Do & Technical Innovations.	Japan, USA, World.	Takayuki Kubota (Gosoku Ryu)

conditions eventually led to the collapse of these civilizations after decades of war and social unrest.

As kalaripayat traveled from ancient India—through the Orient, Central Asia, the Middle East, and North Africa—to Rome and Greece, it interacted with some of the indigenous combat disciplines that existed in other countries.

A short list of the indigenous fighting arts influenced by kalaripayat and other methods of empty hand fighting is presented in Table 2. This list is by no means complete or 100 percent accurate. It does, however, give some idea of the degree of cultural interaction that may have taken place over the millennia in certain regions of the civilized world.

The most significant event recorded in the history of unarmed combat is the birth of formalized karate-do in the Hunan province of central China.

The creation of systematized karate-do, as we know it today, is a byproduct of the merging of two great Oriental philosophies, Confucianism and Zen Buddhism, between 500 and 550 A.D.

Bodhidharma, or Daruma Taishi, a prominent and highly educated Buddhist monk proficient in the art of kalaripayat, instituted karate exercises as part of religious training for the monks of the Shaolin-Szu, or Shorin-Ji temple, in 520 A.D. He continued teaching Zen Buddhism and perfecting the art of empty hand combat until 550 A.D.

By devising a systematized method of training, Daruma Taishi intended to increase the stamina and self-confidence of his fellow monks and encourage the practice of self-defense and movements that, when performed near perfectly, would generate a feeling of serenity and enlightenment.

While Zen Buddhism contributed the technical and meditative aspects of karate-do, Confucianism provided the philosophical foundations that enrich the mental aspect of the art and promote personal development and spiritual growth.

For many hundreds of years, China—especially Hunan province—played the key role in the development of martial arts. Most of these fighting systems eventually were exported by Chinese travelers and martial artists to other countries in the Far East. As the Shaolin monks traveled further into China and neighboring countries, their boxing system became more sophisticated as they refined its original techniques and acquired new ones. During this time, the number of original movements in Shaolin Temple boxing increased from approximately twenty to more than seventy karate-like techniques. Wing Chun, a style of southern Shaolin boxing, still is practiced today in many parts of the world in much the same way that Chinese monks practiced it at the Shaolin temple hundreds of years ago.

The existing systems of martial arts in Thailand, Malaysia, Burma, Indonesia, Indochina, and Korea, described in Table 2, clearly are related to different forms of Chinese Kempo. In fact, Daruma's fighting techniques became increasingly less associated with the practice of Zen Buddhism and religious training, and eventually became the foundation of Chinese Ch'uan-fa, or the Chinese Kempo, commonly referred to as Kung-fu.

The next major expansion and growth of Oriental karate took place during the T'ang dynasty (A.D. 620–900). Increased political and commercial relations, as well as continued religious and cultural exchanges between neighboring Asian countries such as China, Korea, Okinawa, and Japan, led to further refinement of the methods of empty hand fighting. At this time, systematized Chinese karate had developed into more than 150 movements, postures, and stances. Some historians argue that more than one quarter of these movements were incorporated into karate for ritualistic, rather than practical, combative purposes.

Cultural activities between China and Okinawa reached their peak during the thirteenth century, when the two nations were exchanging students, merchants, missionaries, and military delegations on a regular basis. By the end of the fourteenth century, a fighting system, which later became known as Okinawa-te, was quite well-developed and popular throughout the Ryukyu Islands.

In 1610, Okinawa fell under the rule of Japanese overlords who banned the use of all weapons. As a result, Okinawa-te and other weaponless fighting systems were consolidated and improved over the next few centuries. In Japan, however, for at least a thousand years, martial arts had been approved and encouraged as an official and integral part of the structure of society.

Of all the Oriental nations that interacted with each other, Okinawa appears to have been the most receptive to assimilating Chinese Kempo into its own method of empty hand fighting, known as Tode. The first blending of Okinawa-te and Chinese Kempo is credited to Tode-Sakugawa (1733–1815) who adopted Tode, or Karate, as his first name.

In Okinawa, the methods of empty hand combat were developed to a degree of effectiveness probably unsurpassed anywhere in the world. There were several styles of empty hand combat practiced, including Shuri-te (or Shurinji-ryu), Naha-te, and Tomari-te. These styles were known collectively as Okinawa-te. Official records show that Shuri-te originally was developed and practiced by the samurai of the court, while Nahe-te and Tomari-te were put together and refined by the peasants and ordinary townsfolk of these two cities.

Ironically, banning weapons not only resulted in the refinement and expansion of existing methods of empty hand fighting; it also contributed to the rapid growth of seemingly innocent but deadly agro-combative disciplines, in which agricultural implements were turned into defensive weapons. These included the rice flail, or Nunchaku; rice grinder handles, or Tonfa; the short staff, or Jo; the long staff, or Bo; and the threshing fork, or Sai. The adaptation of the Sai or Sai-Jutsu was perfected to the extent that it became a most effective means of defense against the staff, the spear, and the sword.

Present-day karate and sai-jutsu are two highly complementary methods of self-defense. They use similar hand techniques and identical stances for defense and offense. In fact, the hand and the sai are interchangeable implements in most karate and Sai katas.

The practice of Okinawa-te remained underground until the years of the Meiji Restoration (1868–1912) when the ban on martial arts finally was removed.

Karate eventually was recognized by the ruling authorities as an important method of self-improvement and was incorporated into the Japanese education system at both the high school and college levels.

By 1933, all Japanese universities had dojos for the practice of both karate and judo. About this time, the official name of the art was changed from karate-jutsu to karate-do in order to reflect the true meaning of its purpose.

Okinawa today, as it has been for hundreds of years, is the karate capital of the world. In keeping with national traditions, karate masters are among the most revered dignitaries of society.

The person responsible for reviving and introducing karate into Japan was Funakoshi Gichin (1868–1956), a frail and sickly Okinawan child not expected to live a long and healthy life. He began studying karate at age 11 under the tutelage of Master Yasutsune Azato, who was one of Okinawa's greatest karate experts.

Gichin was urged to practice karate only to improve his health and stamina. In the years that followed, he studied under a number of well-known Okinawan karate masters, most notably Master Itosu Anko. From then on, he devoted his entire life to the study, refinement, restructuring, and promotion of karate as a new way of life. He also was a schoolteacher and enjoyed writing short stories and Chinese poetry.

The official rebirth of karate took place in 1922 when Gichin Funakoshi was invited to introduce and promote karate as a form of Budo in mainland Japan. His major work on karate, entitled Karate-do Kyohan, was published in 1935. An English translation of the book was published in New York in 1973.

Grand Master Funakoshi Gichin died on April 26, 1956. He did not receive dan grade recognition until after his death in 1957, when he was posthumously awarded judan, 10th degree. He is considered the revered father of twentieth century karate-do.

Due to Grand Master Funakoshi's efforts, karate became increasingly popular in Japan, and the *Japan Karate Association (JKA)* eventually was incorporated as an educational body under Japan's Ministry of Education. It steadily gained popularity in the rest of the world as well, and was introduced in the United States in the early 1950s. While still a very young man, Master Takayuki Kubota established The International Karate Association, Inc. (IKA) and opened his first dojo in Tokyo in 1953. The Tokyo dojo also was used as the official headquarters of IKA until it was relocated to the United States in 1964.

HISTORIC SCHOOLS

It has been estimated that there exist more than eighty different systems of Japanese/Okinawan karate, most of which are unknown outside Japan. There also are more than twenty different non-Japanese systems that share the same roots as most mainstream Japanese styles. In fact, all Oriental empty hand fighting systems share the same beginnings as discussed in earlier sections of this chapter.

The heritage of the IKA and Gosoku-ryu karate follow the same lineage as other well-established Okinawan schools of karate practice. Gosoku-ryu was influenced strongly by traditional Shotokan and Goju-ryu karate, as well as Judo, Akido, and jujitsu, practiced in mainland Japan at the beginning of the last century.

Historically, there are only five other internationally recognized and well established Japanese schools of karate-do. These are:

- *Shotokan*, founded by Grand Master Gichin Funakoshi
- *Goju-ryu*, founded by Grand Master Gogen Yamaguchi
- *Wado-ryu*, founded by Grand Master Hironori Ohtsuka
- *Shito-ryu*, founded by Grand Master Kenwa Mabuni
- *Kyokushinkai*, founded by Grand Master Masutatsu Oyama.

The actual differences between these mainstream styles and their offshoots are difficult for the untrained person to sort out. Except for their moral teachings, the end results of all such styles are practically the same.

The important differences lie mainly in minor technical philosophies, means and methods of instruction, repertoire of katas, emphasis on supplementary conditioning, reading, and their views on interpreting traditional values. (See Table 2)

No founder or grand master has ever claimed supremacy of his system over others. The idea is to learn and understand any one system well enough, so that one can appreciate the importance of the others.

The attitude of the teacher and the willingness of the student play a greater role in attaining goals and succeeding in life than any pre-arranged method of approach.

THE SHOTOKAN STYLE

The roots of Shotokan karate usually are traced back to the renowned Okinawan Master Tode Sakugawa, who traveled to China in 1765 to study Chinese kempo and other indigenous methods of self-defense. Shortly after his successful demonstrations at Shuri Castle in 1922, Grand Master Funakoshi Gichin established his temporary dojo in Tokyo, which he named the Shoto-Kan, meaning the house of Shoto, or pine needles. Shoto was the pen name he used to sign his poems and short stories.

The permanent Shotokan dojo, the first of its kind in Japan, was inaugurated in 1938. Grand Master Funakoshi never wished the name Shotokan to be associated with a style, or Ryu. He always referred to the art as karate-do. However, to differentiate between the methods of training used in the Shotokan dojo and other karate schools, which first began to operate in Japan and Okinawa and later all over the world, the name Shotokan, as a style, became synonymous with the name of its headquarters dojo in Tokyo. The Shotokan style remains the most popular and well-known style of karate in the world. Shotokai, Wado-Ryu, and Kyokushinkai are less popular styles that for social, political, and ideological reasons broke away from Shotokan to form their own organizations.

After being adopted into Japan's educational system, karate continued to evolve and develop into many individual styles, some of which did not survive the test of time. There are approximately one hundred different, less significant systems, of Japanese and other karate styles, mostly operating under impressive sounding names and claiming excellence and distant historical backgrounds. It appears that Shotokan karate has been influenced strongly by Judo, another contemporary Japanese martial art that already was popular in Japan. The similarities of the two methods of empty hand combat perhaps are due to the great respect and close friendship that existed between the Judo founder, Grand Master Jigoro Kano, and the Shotokan founder, Grand Master Gichin Funakoshi. Shotokan karate and judo share many common features, notably certain throwing, sweeping, grappling, and joint locking techniques that are inherent in Shotokan and other classical katas. Perhaps the most distinguishing facet of Shotokan is that Shotokan is karate itself, the art that evolved and was improved upon over several centuries by many great masters. Certainly, masters will continue to refine karate for many centuries to come. The greatness of Shotokan lies not in its organization, or in the continual updating of an ancient art, but in the revitalization of its spirit, as called upon in the Dojo-kun, and reflected in the credo: "There is no first attack in karate."

Shotokan karate was introduced to the United States in the mid-1950s by Master Tsutomu Oshima, one of Master Funakoshi's last direct pupils at Tokyo's Waseda University. A brief description of some of the most widely known Shotokan katas as taught and interpreted by Soke Takayuki Kubota is provided in Chapter 12.

GOSOKU-RYU KARATE

Gosoku-ryu is one of the most modern and effective forms of karate-do practiced in the world today. It was created by Grand Master Soke Takayuki Kubota in Tokyo in the years following the end of World War II. The history of the development of Gosoku-ryu runs parallel with the history of the man who conceived, developed, and promoted it worldwide. That man is Soke Kubota, the founding father of the International Karate Association.

Takayuki Kubota was born on September 20, 1943, in Kumamoto, Kyushu, the southernmost island of Japan. He was

Table 2
CHRONOLOGY OF INDIGENOUS METHODS OF EMPTY-HAND FIGHTING

Method of Fighting	Country of Origin	Period of Time	Descriptions, Comments, and Remarks
Vajramushti	India	5000 B.C.	Systematized fist fighting and wrestling.
Kalaripayat	India	4500 B.C.	Ritual form of combat, also empty hand.
Nata	India	4500 B.C.	Dance-combative ritual movements.
Pugilism	Egypt	4000 B.C.	Fist fighting
Tai-chi-chuan	China	2200 B.C.	Modern ritual calisthenics.
Ju-jutsu	Japan	2200 B.C.	Basis of almost all Japanese martial arts.
Pancration	Greece	1000 B.C.	Combined boxing and wrestling.
Free Fighting	Rome	300 B.C.	No techniques barred, free style fighting.
Sumo	Japan	Japan	Sport wrestling, pushing, and throwing.
Ch'uan Fa	China	550 A.D.	Original Shorin-ji kempo, also Kung-fu.
Tode	Okinawa	600 A.D.	Okinawan indigenous martial art.
Tae Kyon	Korea	650 A.D.	Originally influenced by Ch'uan-Fa.
Fushi-testyles.	Mongolia	650 A.D.	Origin of all systematized wrestling styles.
Muay Thai	Thailand	850 A.D.	Kick boxing with hand and foot protectors.
Tae Kwon	Korea	935 A.D.	Advanced form of Tae Kyon.
Mallavidya	India	1000 A.D.	Science of combat, including empty hand.
Okinawa-te	Okinawa	1300 A.D.	Mixture of Tode and Ch'uan-Fa.
Koshti, Kokh	Persia, Armenia	1400 A.D.	Pure wrestling with observance of virtues.
Koshite	Afghanistan	1400 A.D.	Pure wrestling. No striking or throwing.
Bando	Burma	1450 A.D.	General martial arts including empty hand.
Bersilat	Malaysia	1500 A.D.	Combination of weapons and empty hand.
Silat	Indonesia	1600 A.D.	A version of Bersilat.
Capoeira	Brazil	1650 A.D.	Self-defense originated by African slaves.
Escrima	Philippines	1750 A.D.	Also known as Arnis, includes empty hand.
Savate	France	1835 A.D.	Kick boxing including floor gymnastics.
Judo	Japan	1880 A.D.	Mainly throwing and pinning techniques.
Karate	Japan	1922 A.D.	Embraces all methods of unarmed combat.
Aikido	Japan	1930 A.D.	Techniques of reversing opponents force.
Sambo	Russia	1945 A.D.	Combination of all Soviet martial arts.

raised as the second son of a modest family with strong ties to Japanese culture and martial arts. His father, Denjiro Kubota, was a Ju-kendo, or bayonet fighting, legend in his own time. His older brother, Saturo Kubota, already was an accomplished martial artist and later became a prominent bayonet fighting instructor in the Imperial Japanese Army.

During Takayuki's early childhood, the ideas of modern Budo—or way of the warrior—and the revitalized methods of empty hand combat were being promoted aggressively in Okinawa and mainland Japan. The ministry of education was in the process of incorporating several martial arts systems into its educational structure. Judo, Karate, Aikido, and Jujitsu already had been popularized somewhat in Japan but had not been introduced to the outside world. Takayuki Kubota, strongly influenced by his family traditions and the Budo fever of the mid-1930s, was drawn instinctively into the world of martial arts.

The methods of teaching and training were not regulated or customized for the individual martial arts until the late 1930s. Takayuki Kubota began studying several systems of martial arts at the tender age of 4 under the direction of his father and two renowned Okinawan refugees, Tokunaga sensei and Terada sensei, both Tode experts who were given shelter by the Kubota family.

Because of his insatiable desire to learn every aspect of the arts, Takayuki trained many hours each day and studied different styles of each art at the same time. Despite his restrictive scholastic program and grueling training schedule, he managed to complement his martial arts training with additional studies in meditation, history, and other noncombative aspects of the arts. Even as a child and novice, Takayuki Kubota would experiment with new techniques and methods of training. In the years that followed, Master Kubota distinguished himself by earning advanced instructor ratings in Karate-do, Judo, Aikido, Kendo, Iaido, meditation, calligraphy, and several other arts.

He began his teaching career at the age of 14. Within two years, he had reached such a high level of proficiency in Shotokan, Goju-ryu (hard-soft), and other styles of karate-do that he already was thinking of creating a new system that would consolidate the most beneficial aspects of the various arts and karate-ryus into a single, unified system. When he was 18 years old, he opened his first dojo in Haneda, where he was discovered by American servicemen who wanted to learn this "new" method of unarmed combat.

He was invited repeatedly to teach and demonstrate his martial arts at American military bases throughout the region. At 19, he was hired as chief instructor by the Kumamoto Police Department and other local law enforcement agencies. Shortly afterward, Soke's innovative fighting and attitude adjustment techniques were incorporated into the training programs of the Tokyo Police Academy.

His extensive and in-depth knowledge of the martial arts, and his firsthand teaching experience with different groups and individuals, ranging from young children to local law enforcement agencies, prompted him to refine and modernize karate-do to meet the specific needs of contemporary society. His own experience with self-defense and karate training had made him interested in developing modern karate at all levels. Having been a child prodigy himself, Master Kubota was concerned especially with the methods of teaching children and young people. He also gave considerable thought to the promotion and future of karate, especially outside Japan.

With these concerns and ideas, he set out to create the Gosoku-ryu, or hard-fast, style of karate. It took Master Takayuki Kubota several years of relentless work to develop the basic structure of Gosoku-ryu karate and many more years of further research and improvement until it became the most practical and versatile system of karate being practiced anywhere. In 1989, Grand Master Kubota was awarded the title of Soke, or creator, of this new, unique, and internationally recognized style of karate.

Soke Kubota has written several books on martial arts. They include the official "Kubotan" and "T-hold" technique manuals for police use, and the more famous works, *The Art of Karate*, *Kubotan: Instrument of Attitude Adjustment*, *Weapons Kumite*, and *Close Encounters*.

Although a world renowned instructor of the Shotokan style of karate, Soke refuses to discuss or compare the relative merits of the Gosoku-ryu style with other methods of karate practice. When asked which Ryu is superior or the best one to learn, Soke has this advice:

"Karate is karate. Any one style, well-learned, is more effective than dozens of styles half-learned."

Or, to paraphrase the old adage, the longer you practice karate, the more readily you will see the similarities among the various styles. Soke is a very modest and humble person. His sincere feelings of humility and heartfelt respect for tradition are acknowledged by everyone who knows him.

Out of respect for Soke's feelings, no direct comparison of the major styles of karate is made anywhere in this book. However, some of the philosophical ideas and sociological realities that led to the emergence of the Gosoku-ryu school of karate are discussed briefly to provide the reader with historical background on the subject.

Basically, Soke's thoughts are centered on three major areas of concern: universal promotion of the art; adapting karate-do for practical use; and improving the existing methods of teaching and training for all students, especially children and young people. Chapter 12 contains a brief discussion of the essential aspects of Gosoku-ryu katas.

Internationalization of Karate-do

Soke feared that karate-do would suffer the same fate as judo and other contemporary Japanese martial arts if it remained behind closed cultural doors. Except for Hawaii and a few other locations in the United States where large Okinawan and Japanese communities existed, karate and martial arts were practically unheard of in the Western Hemisphere.

Soke believed karate-do deserved universal recognition and could become Japan's gift to the rest of the civilized world. He believed karate associations that had become a part of the Japanese government would not be interested in promoting karate-do outside Japan. For this reason, he created a new organization, which later became known as the International Karate Association. A partial list of IKA-affiliated countries and jurisdictions is presented in Appendix A5.

Adaptation for practical use

Being an accomplished master of several arts, Soke had discovered the value of mixing techniques, or cross-training, in several different fighting disciplines. He also had taught self-defense and police techniques to law enforcement agencies for many years and believed that karate-do should be adapted to meet the practical needs of twentieth century society. He felt that most of the ritualistic postures, symbolic gestures, and techniques adopted from animals and ancient weapons systems were somewhat impractical for use in real life situations.

On one hand, Soke had a great deal of respect for tradition and the monumental efforts and accomplishments of the old masters and did not wish to modify the classical ways. On the other hand, he knew that karate had to be invigorated before it would command the attention of the more pragmatic youth of the postwar era. For this reason, Soke decided to create a new school of karate-do that would remain loyal to the ideals of its forefathers while complementing those concepts with practical innovations. There were several basic ideas instrumental in the development of the new style:

- Exclusion of redundant movements.
- Inclusion of practical techniques.
- Training in close quarters fighting and self-defense techniques.
- Generation of power through speed.
- Adaptation from Judo, Aikido, and Jujitsu.
- Inclusion of Gyaku-te and arresting techniques.
- Added neuromuscular benefits.
- Added mental and spiritual benefits.
- Adaptability for competition training.
- Optimization and efficiency of movement.

- Improved methods of teaching and training.
- Karate specific supplementary workouts.

Soke incorporated these and other ideas into a new system of karate-do called Gosoku-ryu, which literally means the hard-fast style. These concepts are better understood when studying Gosoku-ryu katas or actually practicing karate under Soke or his advanced instructors. The practical innovations of Gosoku-ryu karate, as well as Soke's mastery of the martial arts, have made his school the most sought after organization of its kind.

Law enforcement agencies, the entertainment industry, and institutions of higher education all seek the IKA for training of law enforcement officers and students and for expert advice on martial arts-related issues in the production of television programs and motion pictures. In spite of its young age, Gosoku-ryu is recognized as representing a traditional system of Japanese karate-do.

Grand Master Kubota's talent for creating new and practical methods of self-defense extends beyond the domain of empty hand combat. He is the originator of the little known, highly effective art of Gyaku-te-jutsu, or the method of reverse hands. He also has designed several effective weapons systems for both law enforcement and public use. In fact, the Kubotai, known in law enforcement circles as the ultimate weapon of self-defense, is so effective that these agencies regularly invite Soke to train their members in its use.

Soke also has developed the Kubotan, a method of self-defense that individuals can learn to use to protect themselves against muggers, purse snatchers, and common criminals.

The introduction and organization of Shindo Tsuye Jutsu, or the art of the walking cane, also is credited to Soke Kubota, who, in collaboration with Soke-Dai, Mr. James Caan, refined these techniques into their present form. Katas and practical applications are at the core of the study of Shindo Tsuye Jutsu.

Soke also is the originator of the Kubokido system of meditation. The heavenly sounds of bells and ancient and modern instruments are combined with chanting and the music of nature to create an innovative melody for meditation.

Improving the Training Systems

Gosoku-ryu karate is one of the most powerful and practical styles of karate-do ever developed. Its effectiveness is due in great measure to its fighting techniques and to the way in which it is taught and implemented at IKA headquarters and its affiliated dojos.

The Kihon katas in general and the Kihon-Sonota kata in particular, were devised by Soke to implement his teaching ideas in a dojo environment. Although Gosoku-ryu karate embraces an extensive repertoire of techniques, its teaching philosophy emphasizes the quality of the technique rather than the quantity. The IKA headquarters uses all of Soke's innovative teaching and training ideas as standard methods of practice. His teaching philosophies have received widespread recognition in the karate world. Readers who want to learn more about Soke's special teaching techniques are urged to join the IKA or access some of Soke's other publications and videos.

As a teacher and educator, Soke was well aware of the shortcomings of the older methods of teaching and training being practiced at the time. Soke recognized at once that traditional methods of training had to be revised to meet the demands of the new karate-do and the life styles of prospective students. He saw that the majority of his pupils would be children, students, and working people with limited time for karate and related activities. To assure training efficiency without compromising technical proficiency, he devised specific step-by-step training methods and practice drills that were compatible with both the physical demands of the Gosoku-ryu system and the limitations of his students.

Soke saw the solution to his concerns in the creation of an international organization and a new school of karate-do that would incorporate his high standards of management, teaching, and human values. He founded the International Karate Association in Tokyo in 1953, introducing Gosoku-ryu karate through the IKA to the rest of the world. In 1990, Soke was inducted into the prestigious Black Belt Magazine Hall of Fame in the weapons category. Since its inception, the primary goal of the IKA has been to promote traditional Japanese karate, especially the Gosoku-ryu style. In August, 1964, Soke was invited to the USA by the late Ed Parker, founder of American Kenpo Karate, for a now-famous martial arts demonstration in Long Beach, California. Later in the same year, IKA's headquarters and the main dojo, or Hombu, were moved to the United States, where it attracted talented young students who later formed the core of the IKA's American branch. Soke already was a 7th degree black belt in karate when he first visited the U.S. Since that time, the IKA has grown to more than 20,000 members in more than 60 nations.

To learn more about Soke, his character, and his activities before he came to America, the reader is referred to a historical article by Rene La Plante that was published more than forty years ago. The title of the story is "Karateka Fights Thugs," and is retold in the appendix without modification.

CHAPTER 4

Dojo Etiquette & Rules of Conduct

Rituals and mannerism are integral parts of Oriental cultures. They also are inseparable parts of martial arts training. Protocols or the "Rei-gi" are the traditional rules of conduct that form the foundations of modern karate-do.

The importance of the rei-gi cannot be over emphasized in real life and in karate practice. Proper adaptation of the rei-gi promotes harmony and trust; it conveys respect and humility. Rei-gi is an established framework that projects good manners and mutual understanding. This in turn reflects honor and lack of pretense. Most importantly, it helps avoid conflict, stress, and emotional instability in the society.

Rei-gi is not a familiar phenomenon in the West, but it is not something out of this world either. It can be learned and put to good use at any time. The ordinary handshake, the military salute, rising for national anthems, greeting each other, etc., all are simplified rituals that have become second nature to us. They all serve a purpose and there is nothing unusual about them. The same applies to rei-gi in karate-do.

The "Rei" or the bow implies many things in Japanese culture. It is similar to a handshake with a feeling of humility and respect. A bow always is acknowledged by a bow, which may or may not be the same in depth and attitude. Reciting *Osu* is a verbal sign of recognition and acknowledgement. It is similar to conveying greetings or saying–yes sir, good day, etc. Not returning a bow or Osu is a sign of disrespect and bad manners. Perhaps the best thing about courtesy rituals is that it tends they establish order, reduce stress, and prevent conflict among individuals.

THE DOJO

In a practical sense, a dojo is a training hall where martial arts are practiced. In the spiritual sense, the dojo is "The Place of the Way," the way of life that is the path to personal fulfillment and development. As such, the dojo is quite different from a commercial gym or sports hall. It is not a training camp for prize fighters, nor is it a place for settling personal accounts. If anything, it is more like a shrine. The headquarters dojo is the spiritual fortress of its followers.

The dojo is an arena where combative sides find peace in conflict; where anxiety leads to tranquility; where opponents are friends, not foes, sharing the joys and pains of learning. Opponents help each other reach personal perfection. They show each other respect and gratitude before and after combat.

The process of learning karate-do takes place in the dojo through hard work, patience and devotion. Every minute in the dojo provides an opportunity for learning something new. What a student gains in the dojo can be paid for only with love, tolerance and courtesy.

The dojo is more than merely a place to practice karate-do. It is a place for learning the way of karate and making that way a part of your life. According to a Zen saying: "Nichijo kore dojo" or "Daily life is your dojo."

IKA students are fortunate to be taught and guided by Soke Takayuki Kubota and his disciples. The headquarters dojo, or Hombu, is seen as Soke's house. It is also the home of the IKA family.

The dojo is a classroom for life. It is shared by instructors and students who enrich each other's lives socially, physically, mentally and spiritually. The dojo atmosphere is serene, formal and respectful at all times.

The dojo is a place of high esteem and great respect. It is a simple place free of pretense. The rules of conduct, or Rei-gi, traditionally observed in the dojo are centered on the virtues of humility and respect. These rules are mandatory for all students regardless of rank or degree.

The front of the dojo is called the Shomen and is regarded as the place of honor. It often features symbols of respect such as flags and words of wisdom, the pictures of the highest spiritual or national figure. In the front right corner, a picture of the founder of the school usually is displayed.

Most modern dojos are equipped with simple training aids such as wall mirrors, punching bags, striking pads and boards, weight training implements etc.

IKA encourages its students to use its facilities as much as possible. It also welcomes friends and guests to watch training sessions at IKA headquarters and affiliated dojos. All visitors are asked to observe the traditional rules of conduct presented in this section.

GENERAL PROTOCOL

The primary lessons taught in karate-do are humility, respect and discipline. The oldest Japanese saying about karate is:

"Karate-do wa rei ni hajimari rei no owaru."
"Karate-do begins and ends with respect."

It therefore is appropriate to devote a few words to dojo courtesy. The following guidelines are provided to introduce new students and guests to the customs, official requirements and ways of expressing respect:

- The etiquette surrounding the Senpai-Kohai or Senior-Junior relationship is an important part of Japanese cultural heritage that is strictly observed in all martial arts circles. All karateka are required to respect and pay respect to their seniors and martial arts elders.
- Please bow and recite *Osu* to higher ranking belts and to your teachers.
- Promptly respond and obey orders by your dojo seniors. Recognize their seniority by reciting "Osu" or "Hai."
- Please make sure your shoes are clean and dry before you enter the dojo. If they are not, please take them off and leave them outside.
- Please open and close doors slowly and quietly.
- Please bow as you enter or leave the training floor area. To bow properly, stand in musubi dachi, hands down on your sides, bend forward at the waist, pause briefly after finishing the bend, straighten up and proceed as usual.
- If you wish to enter the training area, please remove your shoes and store them neatly in the spaces provided for this purpose.
- Please bow as you enter or leave the dojo.

- All guests and friends are asked to stay in the designated seating area and remain as quiet as possible during practice sessions.
- Smoking, drinking, eating and chewing gum are not allowed inside the dojo.
- Pets are not allowed inside the dojo.
- Please turn off your cell-phones while in the dojo.
- The dojo telephone is reserved for school business and emergency purposes only.
- All guests and friends are asked not talk with instructors and students during practice sessions.
- Always address and refer to Grand Master Kubota as Soke. Others may be addressed or referred to by their titles, such as Shihan, Shihan-Dai, Sensei, or, if appropriate, by their last name, adding the suffix "-san", as in Norris-san, David-san, etc. Do not, however, add "-san" to your own name.
- As part of their duties, all karateka must help maintain and enforce all dojo formalities at all times.
- If you wish to speak to Soke or any of his students, please contact the administration officer at the front desk.
- All guests and friends are asked to remain seated and observe absolute silence during meditation or when an instructor is addressing the class.
- You are asked to refrain from entering the training floor while the class is meditating, when Soke or an instructor is addressing the class, or when kata practice is in progress.

ATTIRE AND EQUIPMENT

Simplicity, humility and lack of pretense are common virtues reflected in karate-do dress codes. Karate, the art of the empty hand, is practiced with empty hands and bare feet. The same simple uniform is worn in all seasons and for all conditions. All IKA members, even five-year-old novices and Soke himself, wear the same white practice suit. The white color symbolizes purity and cleanliness. Only the colors of the ceremonial belts indicating rank and degree are different. Simple, plain, soft wrist and head bands can be worn during practice.

The following regulations are meant to assure maximum comfort and safety for karate students practicing in IKA dojos:

- All karateka must provide their own training uniforms and equipment, approved by IKA. No shoes or socks are worn during practice.
- IKA-approved attire consists of the traditional karate gi, a plain white jacket, or uwagi, plain white pants, or zubon, IKA identification badges worn on the left chest area of the uwagi, and

IKA-issued ceremonial belts or Obi.
- Athletic cups for men or kin-ate, breast covers for women, and sparring gloves and protective mouthpieces for all students are required by IKA.
- No jewelry–including, but not limited to, hair pins, watches, rings, earrings, chains, bracelets and necklaces–should be worn during practice sessions. Any piece of jewelry that cannot be removed must be covered with tape or protective gear. Fingernails and toenails must be kept trimmed or protected during practice.
- All clothing and personal items should be stored neatly in dressing room racks. IKA is not responsible for lost or stolen items.
- If you tend to perspire a lot, you are requested as a courtesy to your fellow karateka to wear absorbent head and wrist bands during practice.

- All gis must be clean, neat, and free from stains, tears, unauthorized graphics and body odor.
- Karateka intending to practice more than twice a week are advised to own a spare set of clothing and equipment.
- All karateka are advised to carry a small emergency pouch containing adhesive medicated bandages, clean gauze, safety pins, and elastic wrapping bands for minor cuts and bruises.
- The use of rigid protective gear, such as plastic or metal shinguards or elbow guards, is prohibited. The use of soft, padded protection gear, or bogu, is permitted.
- The use of all recording equipment, such as cameras and audio and video recorders, is prohibited, as is the use of personal radios, beepers, and hand-held telephones within the headquarters building.

TRAINING SESSION FORMALITIES

Traditional rules of conduct are observed in all dojos where martial arts are practiced. The following are some of the more common rules of conduct observed at IKA headquarters and affiliated dojos around the world:
- At the beginning of each training session: All karateka must line up by rank, from front to back and right to left, with the highest ranking student standing at the right-hand front corner of the class, facing the instructor.

- At the end of each training session: After the instructor leaves the training area, the most senior student at the front right hand corner leaves the area toward a designated exit. All other students, by descending order of ranks, and in single file, follow the class leader. Do not break ranks for any reason.
- All karateka must learn the standard Japanese and English commands and terminology used in a karate dojo.
- Always acknowledge a command or instruction by replying "Osu" or "Hai" in a loud and clear voice.
- Always bow to higher ranking karateka before addressing them.
- Always bow to your training partner before and after an engagement.
- If you are late for a class, ask the instructor in charge if you still can take part. If the instructor agrees, meditate first either outside the exercise floor or at a designated area and wait for the instructor to invite you into the class.
- If an instructor asks you to move up front, always walk behind the outside right-hand sideline of the class.
- It is improper to chew gum, talk, laugh, complain, argue, move out of place, make unnecessary gestures, pretend to be exhausted, and fake injury.
- All karateka should warm up and complete their stretching exercises before entering the training area for a scheduled class. All karateka are advised to start warming up at least 30 minutes before the scheduled class.
- Karateka wishing to leave the practice session can do so only by seeking permission from the instructor. Once permission is granted, the student should bow and move to the end of the dojo, find a quiet place, kneel, meditate, and leave.
- All gis and belts must look neat and orderly before entering class, during meditation, and before leaving the practice session.
- To tidy up and adjust clothing during practice or before meditation, a student must turn about-face, adjust his/her gi, then turn to face front.
- If you are injured, have an open wound, or are wearing a hard medical brace, support, or cast, you must inform your instructor before joining class.
- Karateka wishing to ask a question should address the instructor by bowing and stating the instructor's correct title, such as Soke, Shihan, Shihan-Dai, or Sensei. When acknowledged, the student asks his/her question while standing at attention. Afterward, the student bows and states, "Thank you." Students address the instructor by stating, "Soke, o-negai shimasu,"

meaning: "Soke, please teach me." Afterward, gratitude is expressed by stating "Arigato gozaimashita." These forms indicate courtesy and respect.

- It is common in dojos for the instructor to ask the class to pay respect to Soke, Shihan, high ranking students, and guests of honor. The instructor simply commands, "Face Soke!" (or Shihan, Sensei, etc.) The class immediately turns toward that person and stands at attention. The instructor then commands, "Soke-ni rei!" (or Shihan-ni rei, Sensei-ni rei, etc.) The class expresses respect and humility by bowing and saying "Osu" at the same time.

- When practicing in pairs and forming two lines to work out with a fellow karateka, students should select training partners of equal size and ability. Both partners should align themselves with the higher ranking pair, standing next to them.

- If the instructor wants to demonstrate a movement or address the class, it is customary for the next highest ranking student to order "Sei-za!" or kneel down in a loud voice. The class turns its attention toward the instructor, and performs sei-za so that everyone can see and hear easily. Once instruction is over, the lead student orders, "Yame!" The other students acknowledge the command by saying, "Osu!" All return to their spots and stand at attention.

- If a karateka whose ranking is higher than that of the designated instructor is present at a scheduled training session, the instructor is obliged, as a sign of respect, to invite the higher ranking karateka to preside over the class and take charge of the training session. If he/she declines the offer, he/she is asked to preside over the class by taking a position under the founder's picture while facing the class and the instructor at the same time. The higher ranking person, at his/her discretion, may accept or decline the offer.

CONTEST PROTOCOL

Rules, regulations, types and categories of events, and scoring systems of karate contests differ from country to country, style to style, and among different schools of the same style, and usually are subject to changes without prior notice.

Contestants and their coaches are advised to familiarize themselves with all rules and requirements several days prior to the announced dates of karate contests and tournaments.

Some of the more important rules and regulations adopted by *The International Karate Association Tournaments, Inc.*, or IKAT, are listed in Chapter 15.

Regardless of the nature of the host organization and the administrative requirements of any tournament, local, national, or international, the following general rules of conduct must be observed by all contestants and their representatives:

- Always complete the necessary paperwork and registration forms required by the tournament organizers. You may be required to pay a nominal registration fee and produce an official identification document and/or membership card. You also may be required to wear a standard tournament badge bearing your official tournament identification number. Memorize your number, because competitors are summoned to specific contest areas by these numbers.

- Rules pertaining to dress code and protective gear already have been described in the attire and equipment section of this chapter. You also are required to provide your own regulation protective cup guard, mitts, and mouthpiece. You may not be allowed to wear arm, shin, elbow, instep, and knee guards. However, you may be required to wear regulation protective headgear.

- You must warm up, stretch, meditate, and be ready at least 20 minutes before your scheduled contest.

- Whether participating in kata or kumite, always enter and leave the contest area, or shiai jo, from the same predesignated location. Never enter a contest area unless invited by the referee, an authorized official, or by request through the public address system.

- Always bow as you enter or leave the contest area. After you enter, wait for the referee to invite you to the starting or contest line. Assume the Yoi position at the starting line.

- You may be required to wear an additional red or white belt – or a red or white ribbon in addition to your own belt – for identification purposes during a sparring contest. After the event, return the belt or ribbon to the ring official, using both hands while bowing and saying, "Osu." It is considered extremely bad manners to drop or throw the identification belt or ribbon as a sign of protest.

- Bow to your opponent, the judges, and other officials, such as timekeepers and scorekeepers, as instructed by the center referee. Always acknowledge the referee's commands by bowing and replying, "Osu."

- Never dispute a referee's decision, even if you believe he or she is wrong. When the referee commands, "Yame!" stop all activity, bow, say, "Osu," return to the starting line, and assume the Yoi position. Never complain about the outcome of your contest to anyone, especially organizers and officials of the tournament.

- If your opponent is injured during the bout and the referee stops the contest temporarily, you should return to the starting line, kneel down facing away from the center and wait for the referee's instructions.
- Do not boast about your victories. Do not show off your medals or trophies. Do not be disappointed by your defeat or feel sorry for yourself. A contest is only another learning experience. The important thing is what you have learned from it.
- It is considered bad manners for coaches, instructors, or friends to yell commands, instructions, or advice to karateka during a contest. Such behavior can result in a cautionary word from the referee and/or expulsion from the tournament.

OPENING AND CLOSING FORMALITIES

Traditionally, most martial arts events begin and end with meditation, or Makoto. In most dojos, the training sessions begin and/or close with the class reciting the Dojo Rules and/or the Dojo Kun, or karate pledge. IKA training sessions all begin and end with meditation and recitation of the traditional thoughts on karate-do.

Crompton's *Dictionary of Martial Arts* defines makoto as: "a feeling of absolute sincerity and total frankness, which requires a pure mind, free from the pressure of events." This ethical concept, which is entirely Japanese, includes a sense of moral purity and physical hygiene particularly relevant to those who participate in the martial arts.

The spiritual message contained in IKA opening and closing addresses reflects the true essence of karate-do as taught and preached by Soke and the founding fathers of modern karate-do.

To be worthy students and achieve personal fulfillment, all practitioners must develop a clear and sincere understanding of makoto and dojo-kun. Makoto performed at the beginning and end of each practice period is not merely a formality but constitutes the most important part of the training session. A true makoto can empower the spirit with great strength and tranquility.

All karateka must learn and memorize the opening and closing addresses of the practice session: the dojo rules and the dojo kun, respectively. These addresses always are recited by the highest ranking black belt present, who at his/her discretion may delegate the task to the highest ranking brown belt present.

The starting meditation and the opening address:

The purpose of the opening address, or salutation, is twofold. Meditation helps the student separate himself from the concerns of the outside world. It also helps him concentrate on the rules of conduct and the aims of karate-do.

Once the opening meditation becomes a natural part of the student's practice session, it begins to serve its purpose by clearing the student's mind of all concerns and leaving him/her with a sense of expected fulfillment.

The spiritual experience of the training session becomes real and the goal of pursuing personal achievement is within reach. The opening ritual is conducted in the following manner:

While the class stands at attention, or Musubi-dachi, the instructor performs Sei-za facing front, or Shomen. The act of Sei-za is the correct sitting position, where one sits in the traditional Japanese manner, on the knees. In this position, the spine is erect, without strain, and the head straight. The hands rest on the knees or thighs.

This meditative posture also is known as Mokuso. In this posture, one relaxes, breathes calmly, and tries to maintain a clear mind, freeing oneself from habitual tensions.

Next, the highest ranking student commands "Sei-za!" The class performs Sei-za.

The opening address is recited loudly and clearly:

"Makoto!"	(meditate with closed eyes) (Class obeys)
"Makoto yame!"	(stop meditation)(Class obeys)
"Dojo rules!"	(class repeats same)
"Each seeks perfection of character!"	(class repeats same)
"Each be faithful!"	(class repeats same)
"Each endeavor!"	(class repeats same)
"Each respect others!"	(class repeats same)
"Each refrain from violent behavior!"	(class repeats same)
"Yame!"	(end bowing)
"Shomen ni rei!"	(class bows while saying "Osu")

The class remains in sei-za until the instructor gives the command to rise. The instructor first commands, "Inhale!" The instructor pauses a moment, then commands "Ichi Kiai!" or a similar command. Immediately after the "Each Kiai!" command, everyone shifts from the Sei-za position into a one-legged kneeling position, with the right knee on the ground and the left foot moved forward and flat on the ground. Simultaneously, everyone performs an outward block, or Soto-uke, with the left arm. Right away, while still in the kneeling position with the left arm in the blocking position, everyone delivers a strong punch with the right hand. The punch is delivered with a strong "Kiai."

The words of humility and respect recited in the opening address are IKA's English version of the Japanese Dojo-Kun, which is recited in all karate dojos loyal to the traditional ways begun in Japan.

As a sign of respect to the author of the Dojo-Kun, Grand Master Tode Sakegawa, the original words of the five karate maxims are reiterated as follows:

"Dojo kun!"
"Hitotsu! Jinkaku kansei ni tsutomuru koto!"
"Hitotsu! Makoto no michi o mamoru koto!"
"Hitotsu! Doryoku no seishin o yashinau koto!"
"Hitotsu! Reigi o omonsuru koto!"
"Hitotsu! Kekki no yu o imashimuru koto!"

The numerical prefix Hitotsu, or one, separates each maxim in meaning, even though their purposes are one and the same: the striving for inner strength and modesty.

IKA students do not have to learn the Japanese version of the opening address but they do need to develop an in-depth understanding of the complete Dojo-Kun. The Dojo-Kun are:

Character and Personality:	Being morally correct and courageous.
Faithfulness and Sincerity:	Being true to yourself and others.
Effort and Endeavor:	Training and trying hard at all times.
Etiquette and Respect:	Being courteous at all times.
Self-control and Restraint:	Having control over one's emotions.

The ending meditation and the closing address:

The closing address helps clear the mind and relax the body after the training workout. It also reaffirms the ideals involved in achieving the goals of performing karate-do.

Once the ending meditation becomes an effective part of the student's training session, it clears the student's mind of all concerns while replacing them with a sense of personal achievement and spiritual fulfillment. If this is accomplished, the practice session has achieved its goal.

The ritual of the closing address is performed in a few simple steps: While the class stands at attention, the instructor performs Sei-za, facing away from the class. The highest ranking student commands, "Sei-za!" The class obeys. The reciter commands:

"Makoto"	(class meditates)
"Makoto yame, sho men ni rei!"	(class bows)

"Face Soke, etc., repeat after me!"	(class obeys)
"Soke!" (or Shihan, etc.)*	(class repeats title)
"Domo arigato gozai mashita."	(class repeats same)
"Soke-ni rei!" (or Shihan-ni rei)	(class bows toward Soke, Shihan, etc.)
"Face front!" or "Face each other!"	(class obeys)
"Otagai ni rei!"	(bow to everyone) (class obeys)
"Dojo kun!"	(class repeats same)
"Koku sai karate-do kyo kai!"	(class repeats same) ("International Karate-do Association!")
"Soke kunji!"	(class repeats same)("Soke's message")
"Hi to tsu!"	(class repeats same) ("One item/Be number one")
"Tsuyo ku!"	(class repeats same) ("Powerfully/with strength")
"Tano shi ku!"	(class repeats same) ("Cheerfully/Have some fun")
"Se kai no karate-do!"	(class repeats same) ("World's discipline of karate-do")

If a person whose ranking is higher than that of the designated instructor is present in the class (but not in charge of the training session), this part of the recitation is omitted from the closing address. Instead, the reciter continues by commanding:

"Face front!" or *"Face each other!"* etc.

The class remains in Sei-za until the instructor tells the students to rise. The instructor first commands, "Inhale!" He pauses a moment and then commands, "Ichi Kiai!" or a similar command. Right away, everyone shifts from the Sei-za position into a one-legged kneeling position with the right knee on the ground and the left foot moved forward and flat on the ground. At the same time, everyone performs an outward block, or Soto-uke, with the left arm. Right away, while still in the kneeling position with the left arm in the blocking position, everyone delivers a strong punch with the right hand. The punch is delivered with a strong, "Kiai!"

Next, the instructor stands up and calls "Yame' or "Tate." Class follows suite and waits for the final command and class dismissal.

Training session is not yet over. The entire class is asked to perform "Soji" or cleaning before leaving the training area.

Soji is part of the training for all karateka regardless of their rank or title. Soji also is a sign of humility and respect for the dojo as well as fellow classmates and the next group of students who are waiting to enter the training hall.

Soji is an act of humility, respect, and belonging. The entire training area, including doors and windows is properly dusted, vacuumed, and cleaned for the next group of users. Refusing to do soji

without good excuse and permission from the instructor is considered poor manners and disrespect to others.

ADMINISTRATIVE REQUIREMENTS

Students must be committed strongly to the rules and regulations governing the daily affairs of their dojos to ensure efficient administration of training sessions and other IKA activities. These rules are practically universal for most international and local organizations. IKA students must comply with the following administrative requirements:

All karateka and/or their guardians must familiarize themselves with the contents of the form regarding "Student Enrollment and Release and Assumption of Risk Agreement" signed at registration.

If you need information, want to make a payment or purchase, seek to register a new student or inquire about special and private classes, please contact the administration desk during regular business hours.

The dojo hours and a schedule of classes are posted behind the glass at the front door.

All karateka must familiarize themselves with information and notices posted on the bulletin boards as well as the IKA newsletters.

All dues and payments must be received on time and immediately upon receipt of notice from the front desk. Monthly dues and fees may be paid by cash, check, or credit cards in the front office.

Payment in full is required regardless of the number of classes missed. There are no refunds for missed classes. A membership card must be presented to be marked paid.

The last person leaving the last scheduled class of the day must make sure that all curtains are drawn; all water, lights, and air conditioning are turned off; check that nothing has been left behind in the dressing rooms, and all exit doors are locked.

All karateka must participate in Soji, or the cleaning and maintenance of the dojo, as directed by their instructors or higher ranking students.

Students must carry their current membership identification cards with them when practicing at the dojo and participating in tournaments or other IKA functions. Loss of identification cards must be reported immediately. The identification card may not be reproduced, loaned, or transferred in any way.

Any action causing disgrace to IKA or its membership will be grounds for disciplinary action and/or expulsion.

If a student is going to miss or arrive late for a scheduled class or meeting, he/she must inform the administration office at least one hour in advance.

In order to avoid inter-dojo problems, all karateka are advised to obtain written permission from the administration office before training at another IKA-affiliated dojo.

Guest karateka are welcome to share training experiences with IKA members during all scheduled classes. However, we ask that they first seek permission from Soke and complete the necessary paperwork before entering the practice floor.

If a student is going to be absent for an extended period of time, he/she must inform the administration office at least one day in advance.

IKA, IKAT, and the Insignia are registered and proprietary items and cannot be used for any purpose without written permission from the headquarters office.

All IKA, IKAT related business, legal, and other correspondence should be addressed directly to Soke Takayuki Kubota at the Headquarters address.

All new teaching aids, material, handouts, and booklets shall be approved by Soke before use and or distribution.

CHAPTER 5

IKA Titles and Ranking Systems

Setting goals entails evaluation of progress at various stages of the process. The question often asked is, "What are the limits and ways of evaluating the practitioners' progress toward their goals?" The answer is difficult to find since there are no limits to human endeavor and achievement. However, for the rest of us less gifted part-time warriors, there appear to be three tangible levels of achievement: becoming technically proficient; acquiring enough knowledge of the art, as well as the maturity to support our skills; and finally, developing a sense of "unity" with our skills and daily life. A simple example of this phenomenon is when you ride your bicycle or play the violin elegantly, effortlessly, and with a sense of satisfaction without even thinking about it. This is when you become one with the action. In the context of karate-do:

"You become the art and you are the action."
This is "Zen" and cannot be measured.

Nevertheless it is easy to grade a student's level of physical proficiency through the ranking system, e.g., a green belt, a second "Dan," etc. It is more difficult to appreciate a senior student's knowledge and maturity with respect to his/her title, such as "sensei," "shihan," etc. It is probably unthinkable for most people to reach a state of oneness with an art. The highest level of skill, though admirable, without knowledge is only "waza."

A high level of skill combined with relevant knowledge is "Mastery." Karate-do is a goal oriented endeavor; the ranking system has been designed to help the students assess their progress toward their martial arts goals.

Ranking is defined as the evaluation of an individual's

progress toward the attainment of human perfection through the practice of martial arts. This evaluation is not based solely on the physical techniques of the art. It encompasses the student's entire physical, moral, and spiritual development.

The Kuydan system was created in the late 1890s by Grand Master Jigoro Kano, the founder of judo. The belt grading system for karate-do was further refined and standardized in 1964 by the Federation of All-Japan Karate-do Associations, or FAJKO. Until that time, grading was left to the collective judgment of each organization.

Altogether, there are twenty major levels of achievement in the IKA grading system, or Kyudan: ten Kyus, or ranks (literally pupil grades) and ten Dans, or degrees. A student's degree of expertise is signified by the color of his/her belt.

Generally, different types of martial arts—even different styles of the same art—use slightly different systems of ranking and colors. In spite of several different ranking systems, a white belt almost always indicates no ranking, while a brown belt indicates a student is approaching the level of black belt.

The IKA ranking system, Kai-Kyu, consists of eight colored belts corresponding to ten Kyus–or grades–and ten Dans–or degrees–for black belts. Traditionally, each Kyu or rank is signified by a different colored ceremonial belt, or Obi, worn by the student. After learning the basic etiquette, the student wears a white belt and is unranked. Kyu ranks generally are considered learning grades. The Dan degrees signify achievement in improving and perfecting skill and character.

The most important and symbolic feature of the ranking order is that the color of the belts becomes progressively darker as the student advances through the kyu system. It usually takes a good student about four years of regular and committed training to progress through the kyu ranks and qualify for the black belt test.

A first degree black belt indicates that the student has achieved an acceptable level of proficiency in the preliminaries of traditional karate-do and is prepared to embark on a long-range program of technical refinement and personal improvement. It also implies that the wearer of the kuro obi is committed to upholding the ideals of traditional karate-do, both in the dojo and in daily life.

Contrary to common belief, the black belt neither signifies complete mastery of karate-do nor implies that the wearer is an expert in all the techniques of the art.

Progress through the dan degrees is a matter of lifelong commitment to karate-do and to personal fulfillment. The term dan, or degree, is used for anyone achieving at least first degree black belt. IKA dan ranks are Shodan, Nidan, Sandan, Yondan, Godan, Rokudan, Shichidan, Hachidan, Kudan, and Judan, or first through tenth degrees.

IKA RANKING

The IKA ranking order and the corresponding belt colors and stripes are summarized below:

Belt	Obi	Stripes	Grade	Kyu
White	Shiro	-	No ranking	-
Yellow	Ki	1 stripe	10th Kyu	Jukyu
Yellow	Ki	2 stripes	9th Kyu	Kukyu
Orange	Orange	-	8th Kyu	Hachikyu
Blue	Aoi	-	7th Kyu	Schichikyu
Purple	Murasaki	-	6th Kyu	Rokukyu
Green	Midori	1 stripe	5th Kyu	Gokyu
Green	Midori	2 stripes	4th Kyu	Yonkyu
Brown	Cha	1 stripe	3rd Kyu	Sankyu
Brown	Cha	2 stripes	2nd Kyu	Nikyu
Brown	Cha	3 stripes	1st Kyu	Ikkyu
Black	Kuro	-	1st Dan	Shodan
Black	Kuro	-	2nd Dan	Nidan
Black	Kuro	-	3d Dan	Sandan
Black	Kuro	-	4th Dan	Yondan
Black	Kuro	-	5th Dan	Godan
Black	Kuro	red stripe	6th Dan	Rokudan
Black	Kuro	red stripe	7th Dan	Shichidan
Black	Kuro	red stripe	8th Dan	Hachidan
Black	Kuro	red stripe	9th Dan	Kudan
Red	Aka	-	10th Dan	Judan

When a kyu or dan grade is conferred, a diploma, or Gaku, signifying its validity, is issued and recorded in a central registry. Although many talented and hardworking teenagers fulfill the requirements of Shodan and are allowed to wear the kuro-obi, their official diplomas often are issued only after their 16th birthday.

IKA black belt holders are admitted automatically into the IKA Yudanasha-Kai, or Black Belt Association.

IKA TITLES

When a practitioner reaches the level of sixth degree black belt, he/she may wear a black belt with a red stripe, the Kuro-Obi, Aka-Suji. A pure red belt, Aka-Obi, marks the ultimate in karate expertise, an eighth to tenth degree level of proficiency. Perhaps fewer than ten karateka in the world have advanced to this level. Soke Takayuki Kubota is the only person in IKA history who has achieved the title So-Shihan, Grand Master and tenth degree black belt.

The Yudansha-Kai members also have courtesy titles. The most senior instructor of a worldwide organization also is known as O-Shihan or Grand Master. Soke, as President and Grand Master of IKA, may bestow the following titles:

Title	Meaning	Minimum Degree
Kyoshi	Self mastery	usually 8th degree black belt and higher
Renshi	Expert Instructor	usually 7th degree black belt & higher
Shihan	Expert/Master	usually 6th degree black belt & higher
Shihan-dai	Deputy Master	usually 4th degree black belt & higher
Sensei	Instructor/Teacher	usually 1st degree black belt & higher
Sempai	Deputy Teacher	usually higher-grade brown belt
Sempai-dai	Assistant	usually a brown belt

OTHER TITLES

Soke also may give honorary titles and degrees to individuals who enjoy the respect of the community by virtue of their character and who have made outstanding contributions toward the elevation of the image of karate-do, upholding and promoting its values in a manner befitting karate's international status.

The practice of karate-do is a goal-oriented activity. The ranking system has been devised to guide progress toward perfection through organized schedules of learning and testing.

Generally, as the student progresses, each succeeding kyu becomes more difficult to achieve and takes longer to acquire. While it may take a beginner only two months of regular practice to obtain a yellow belt, it may take the same student more than two years of hard work to progress from brown to black belt. Training in the dojo is like attending college. It generally is agreed that achieving IKA Shodan is as important as obtaining a degree from a prestigious college or university. Attaining the rank of Shihan in

IKA is perhaps even more significant than obtaining an advanced degree from a well-known university. On the average it takes the dedicated karateka between 30 and 40 years of training and teaching to qualify for the status of Shihan.

Other traditional honorary titles such as Hanshi or supreme mastery at 9th and 10th dan, and Renshi or expert instructor at 6th dan, and Kyoshi or self-mastery at 7th and 8th dans, are well known in Japan. Soke Kubota is one of the very few living Hanshis in the world. They seldom are heard in the West, simply because their holders do not use them with reference to their names and there are not many high ranking personalities amongst us. Kancho is the chief director of a school or organization. It is important for students to measure their progress through testing and certification. However, neither testing nor certification should become important goals in life for karateka, as the path to perfection is as important and fulfilling as perfection itself.

Karate testing and ranking up to roku-dan is practically concerned mainly with striking techniques, standing on both feet, and not wrestling on the ground. This is so because the founders of the art knew that in modern times, unlike the samurai era, no one could devote his entire life to the study of all forms of empty hand combat. In fact, judo, karate, ikido, jujitsu, etc., became separate disciplines all about the same time at the beginning of the last century. In reality all of these fighting methods are highly intertwined and interdependent. In short, karate practice is not limited to only striking and blocking. Even in its present form, karate contains a large number of throwing, grappling, sweeping, joint locking, and other non-striking techniques.

The moral of the story is that it is not a written rule for higher ranking students to master other martial disciplines before they can advance in the ranks, but if tradition has anything to say, it is expected of them to excel at least in one other such form or totally different endeavor, such as calligraphy, painting, music, general arts, sciences, mathematics, medicine, etc.

A brief discussion of ranking requirements, how they relate to the curriculum, and other relevant issues, is presented in Chapter 16.

CHAPTER 6

Karate Training

Broadly speaking, IKA offers eight different but related disciplines of karate and martial arts training. Each area of practice consists of proportional amounts of intellectual and spiritual studies, physical fitness, and technical training. These areas of training are grouped together in the following ways:

Fundamental karate training

This is IKA's most popular and best recognized training program. The contents of this book are related solely to basic karate training at IKA and its affiliated dojos. Several sessions of fundamental training are offered daily at IKA headquarters. This level of training prepares students to satisfy the requirements for the first degree black belt in the Shotokan and Gosoku-ryu styles of karate-do. Fundamental karate training includes both combat as well as sport karate.

Advanced karate training

This is the natural continuation of IKA's basic curriculum and leads to higher degrees in Shotokan and Gosoku-ryu karate. A student must have a first degree black belt to enroll in this program. IKA offers at least one scheduled session a day of advanced karate training and related studies. Advanced level students are expected to be in good physical shape, demonstrate exemplary citizenship, and assist with the daily affairs of the dojo.

Tournament training

Although tournaments and competition training are not the major concern of IKA, special sessions and seminars are held from time to time to prepare participants for local and international tournaments. This type of training includes actual physical workouts, as well as familiarization with the rules and regulations of such tournaments. Special classes also are held to train referees and tournament officials. The tournament arm of IKA, IKAT, is a nonprofit organization dedicated to the promotion of karate-do worldwide.

Promotional training

This type of training is held for advanced students called upon to demonstrate new ideas or generate interest in karate and IKA. This may include breaking techniques, kata, or kumite. IKA also provides training sessions for the entertainment and advertising industries, which need to learn how to stage realistic fighting scenes and sequences.

Law enforcement training

IKA provides special training for law enforcement and security agencies both in the United States and throughout the world. These include advanced Gyaku-te-jutsu, Kubo-jutsu, and arresting techniques that have been developed and adapted for practical use by Soke Kubota over the past thirty years. This type of training is not part of IKA's regular curriculum and is not available to the general public.

Self-defense training

Although basic self-defense, or Goshin-jutsu, is part of IKA's curriculum, additional classes are offered periodically for the general public and IKA members. There are no specific prerequisites for participating in these classes. IKA members are encouraged to enroll in these classes as often as possible.

Weapons training

IKA also offers scheduled classes in the use of traditional weapons, or Kobu-do. Soke himself teaches several of these classes. The traditional weapons systems developed by Soke Kubota include:

Toshin-Ryu (Sword Spirit School): Though not the oldest weapon in Japan, the sword is the central weapon in the martial hierarchy. The sword was all things to the samurai: a divine symbol, a badge of honor signifying his ancestry, a weapon without peer. IKA katana practice includes eight sword drawing katas. Continuing

Japan's illustrious tradition of the samurai swordsmen, Soke Kubota's sword katas were developed originally for feature film action sequences. The katas combine the precision of quick draw and cutting techniques with the extended combat confrontations characteristic of karate forms. Sparring with Shinai, the bamboo sword, and Boken, the wooden sword, are also part of the training.

Kobu-jutsu: Kobu-jutsu, a term borrowed from Aiki-do is parephrased by Soke to introduce a new sport that involves weapons sparring, specifically the Shinai, mentioned above, and Tonfa, or rice grinder handles. The matches are scored much as a karate bout with points and half points. The shinai was developed from the sword as a practical training tool.

The tonfa consists of two pieces of wood: one shaft of hardwood about twenty inches long with a five-inch cylindrical wooden grip projecting at right angles about five inches down from one end of the long shaft.

The tonfa's history goes back to the days when Okinawa was part of feudal Japan. The wooden handle usually was wedged in a hole in the side of a millstone and used for grinding grain. Farmers quickly adapted it for use as a stunningly effective weapon against the swords of their samurai overlords.

The tonfa is the progenitor of the PR-24 police baton and Tiger Hook baton—both developed by Grand Master Kubota. These two weapons now are popular with law enforcement agencies around the world. Also included in Kubo-jutsu's system of weapons study are katas with Tonfa, Bo, and Jo, or wooden staff. IKA repertoire of weapons katas includes two Jo and two tonfa forms.

Shindo-Tsuye-Jutsu: The common walking cane, a most humble and unassuming weapon, has a number of unique characteristics that set it apart from other traditional weapons. The long end can strike like a wooden sword and the hooked end offers limitless offensive and defensive capabilities. IKA cane katas include nine specific forms.

Grand Master Kubota and James Caan refined these techniques into their present form. The study of Shindo-Tsuye-Jutsu is pursued primarily through mastery of katas and practical combat applications. These weapons classes normally are offered only to higher ranking students.

Kubotan: It looks and functions like a key chain, but this six-inch, pencil-like device is a very effective weapon of self-defense. Invented by Soke Kubota and named after him, the weapon was developed for everyday use and has become tremendously popular. With proper training, it can be used to control or devastate an opponent. Demonstrations and seminars are available through IKA headquarters. The kubotan trainng form is known as Kubotai-no kata.

Way of meditation

At the heart of Grand Master Kubota's many disciplines lies one constant: the use of meditation to attain the proper focus needed to gain mastery of mind and body. Kubo-kido meditation is a new study Soke offers his students, but meditation itself is an ancient practice, a discipline many generations old.

With the gift from his students of an ancient Tokugawa Shogun meditation bell, Grand Master Kubota has, in turn, made the healing and energizing sounds of its toll an integral part of his unique meditation instruction. For home meditation, Soke has produced a cassette and compact disc that capture the bell's sounds as part of an original composition combining the tones with a contemporary theme.

Soke recently developed a meditation kata, the *Anso No Kata*, which is being taught by the IKA. This kata is receiving a great deal

of interest and appreciation from the grand master's students and karate experts worldwide.

Kubota-ju-jitsu

This word, coined by Soke Kubota literally means Kubota's ju-jitsu, art, or skills. It is a new mixed martial art that combines the essence of many different fighting systems and draws from the rich repertoires of several well known martial arts forms, such as Aiki-do, Ju-do, Ju-Jitsu, Gyaku-te and others. It is meant to complement the martial skills of advanced karate students. The course, which entails one hour of formal training per week, is conducted directly by Soke at the headquarters dojo. It is open to adult brown belt and higher ranking students who enjoy good health and can demonstrate a certain standard of physical fitness. The course includes a lot of throwing, joint locking, and rolling on the mat. There are only three ranks before obtaining shodan–white, green and brown belts. To increase focus and reduce disturbance during class, all curtains are drawn, doors are locked, and spectators and nonessential personnel are prevented from entering the school.

CHAPTER 7

Karate-Do Basics: KIHON

The process of learning karate-do traditionally follows the same fundamental steps taken when learning any skill, art, or profession. As such, it requires parallel training in different, but related, aspects of the discipline.

The combative aspect of karate-do requires the learning of special fighting skills, preparation of the mind, as well as physical conditioning of the body.

In karate-do, the process of learning begins with the study of the elementary skills of unarmed combat, such as striking and blocking. These fundamentals are studied and practiced first and form the basis for learning the more advanced techniques in the future.

The basics of blocking, punching, and kicking are the essentials of any karate system. Soke Takayuki Kubota reminds his students that impeccable basics, or Kihon, are the foundation of successful techniques. He says:

"The basics must be an unconscious part of every movement."

To attain proficiency in the basics, students must achieve and maintain a certain level of physical fitness and mental alertness. Although highly desirable, the IKA does not expect all practitioners to maintain competition level physical fitness at all times.

A short list of the basic physiological qualities considered essential to the realistic practice of karate-do is given in the third section of the curriculum under physical fitness. The importance of overall physical fitness also is discussed in other sections of this book.

While learning basic skills and improving general physical fitness, karateka also should empower themselves with some of the basic spiritual attributes inherent in the practice of karate-do, including humility, simplicity, sanctity, serenity, and sincerity. The practice of karate-do becomes even more meaningful when students learn some of the basic states of mind, or attitudes, prevailing in a dojo environment, such as confidence, perseverance, devotion, determination, self-control, safety, and sportsmanship.

All karateka should devote proportionate amounts of time and effort to the study of the basic non-physical aspects of karate-do, as described in the curriculum. The practice of karate-do without the benefits of its mental and spiritual attributes reduces the social value of the art to less than school level physical education or commercial aerobics training.

In many dojos, it is common to see advanced students, even Shihans, practicing the basic techniques over and over again. Practice makes perfect. Perfection has no limits. There is a saying in the dojo:

"Just learning how to punch properly is a never-ending search in self-improvement."

The basic physical exercises and the basic attributes of the mind and spirit are practiced frequently and repeatedly until they become second nature to the practitioner. The practice of basics becomes an essential part of the student's workout routine for as long as he or she follows karate-do.

After a while, the practice of karate becomes meditation in action, and meditation becomes part of the practice. This is the time when karate starts to become karate-do. Soke says:

"The main purpose of practicing karate-do is to learn to avoid confrontation."

Unfortunately, confrontations are real and do happen from time to time. In real life, freehand combat may take place in a variety of situations between and among two or more opponents. Fighting may break out between two persons sitting across a table, turn into boxing when up on their feet, and continue with wrestling on the ground. Karateka should be prepared for all situations and combinations of situations.

However, the purpose of karate-do is to avoid confrontation and refrain from being drawn into a fight. Karateka are taught to stay away from confrontation and to subdue any opponent with a single block or strike, if necessary. For this reason, this book focuses on the basic techniques of standing combat only.

LEARNING THE BASICS

To facilitate the process of initial learning, the basic elements of karate-do are intentionally divided into two distinct but related categories, each of which have been described thoroughly in various sections of this book. The first is "Basic Philosophies and Knowledge" and the second is "Basic Technical Skills." There already exists an abundance of literature with picturesque presentations and well-documented technical illustrations. A selected list of such publications is listed in Appendix A2. As intended, the emphasis in this section is inclined more toward the former category than the latter. The most important reason that all martial artists should understand and master the "elements of kihon" is that they all are common to all types of martial arts: boxing, kick boxing, kung fu, taekwon-do, judo, sumo, etc. For example, rotating the hips, keeping the knees bent, remaining calm, using kime and kiai, and so on.

BASIC PHILOSOPHIES

The journey toward becoming a proficient karateka begins with the practice of elements of the basics. As mentioned earlier, there are three fundamental facets to this process: the physical, the mental, and the spiritual. While the mind, the body, and the spirit are not completely separate entities, the student must strive to improve and invigorate the actions that stimulate and bind these entities together and lead to a better life. The goal of attaining benefits from one or more aspects of karate-do is a personal choice. It is not simply a trivial endeavor. To fully benefit from the practice of karate-do, the student should understand and feel the functions of the mind, the body, and the spirit in the context of the art.

Simply stated, the body is the physical framework of the living person. The brain, which is part of the body, is the organ that processes and regulates the physical and mental functions of the human being. Mental functions are processed through data and information that constitute the mind. Evidently the mind is preprogrammed both to regulate the vital functions of the body, such as breathing, sleeping, seeing, etc., and to learn new functions and skills, such as reading, writing, swimming, performing kata, etc. Therefore, the soul is the program or the encoding that runs and governs the operating system of the body.

The spirit, otherwise known as the "essence of life," is the mind set or the encoding that, by acquiring information from the environment, forms our unique personalities and attitudes toward life. It is believed that systematic repetition of meaningful techniques brings about the spiritual traits associated with such acts. Conversely, these spiritual values express and signal their presence through the same gestures. While the mind, the body, and the soul may be considered gifts of nature, their development needs careful planning and personal effort. The development of the spirit is a function of how the mind and the body are treated during one's life, especially in early childhood. Martial artists generally are credited with the ability to attain higher spiritual attributes much earlier in life than others. One of the ways this beautiful concept may work is as follows:

Repeated performance of karate techniques with an understanding and feeling of its applications can inspire and instill sufficient inner strength and belief to create, through imagination, real spiritual values such as self-esteem, confidence, optimism, etc. For instance, if you move your body and limbs in such a way as to block a lower front kick, you will have performed a lower level block or "gedan-barai," which is a basic karate technique or "kihon-waza." Now if you practice lots of "gedan-barai" over an extended period of time, you eventually will improve your physical conditioning and develop a mental picture of a lower block. With more practice, you will acquire the skill to block or divert a front kick or lower level attack unconsciously. Once you feel you know the technique well enough to use it appropriately, you will have established your first basic mind-body connection in the context of karate-do, something you lacked before becoming a karateka.With further practice, your mental picture will become a reality. This will be the beginning of your spiritual growth, when you start feeling better about yourself, with added self-worth, courage, and tolerance. Subsequently, with continued practice, you will start enhancing your immune system and developing a more positive attitude toward life.

It is reasonable to assume that if the practice of a simple technique or "waza" can improve a student's life to any extent, then the practice of many more techniques and combinations should lead to greater enrichment and better life. The question that often comes to mind is: how long and how intensely should one practice to attain all that karate-do can offer? The answer depends mainly on the practitioner's unique character and personality. However, one thing is clear: the extent of benefits gained from the practice of karate-do is largely a function of how truthfully and correctly the basics and their applications are practiced.

Proper learning of the elements of "kihon" not only aids us in executing effective techniques during kata and kumite, but also creates new combinations when needed. Last, but not least, the repetitive cycles of applications of the basics bring about the "mind–body–spirit" togetherness that is central to the practice of karate-do.

Performing repeated Waza (techniques) and Kihon Katas (basic exercises), or engaging in Ippon Kumite (one-step sparring) under the guidance and supervision of an experienced instructor, are among the best ways to practice the basics.

Most karate techniques appear easy to perform. Serious students quickly learn that mastering the basics is by no means a simple task. Most instructors believe it is best to start by practicing the basic skills slowly and correctly, rather than hastily and incorrectly.

Karate-do is an art of patience, perfection, and timing. A single karate thrust or strike easily can maim or kill an assailant. An accomplished student never draws upon the entire arsenal of karate techniques to subdue an opponent. Mastering a single basic block or punch is more effective and valuable than being superficially familiar with hundreds of defensive or offensive techniques. Students are urged to remember Soke's favorite saying:

"After basics, more basics."

Most students eventually discover that the most useful and advanced techniques in karate are the basics.

ON THE COMPONENTS OF BASICS

Martial artists and indeed the human race differ in their masses, skeletal framework, abilities and attitudes, but follow the same laws of nature. The human anatomy is designed for relatively limited action. Humans can jump limited heights but can not fly. They can swim well, but can not live under water. Their hunting and fighting skills, with or without weapons, are all dependant on their anatomical restrictions. Human physical abilities are relatively limited. They can run the hundred meters near 10 seconds but not much faster. They can jump four times their body length but not much longer, they can lift their body weight but not much more.

All karate movements have been designed and evolved experimentally over thousands of years with a special view of human abilities. All motion in karate, whether the whole body, a part of it, or a combination of both, obey the same laws of physics and body mechanics. All motions are energy dependant. The body, being a living entity derives and stores energy in accordance with laws of organic chemistry. The same psychological laws govern all human attitudes.

Being in tune with nature is a positive thing and could lead to a higher quality of life; the opposite is walking towards failure and

eventual defeat. It is therefore reasonable to tune the elemental concepts of martial arts practice in line with the corresponding laws of nature. In other words, knowing exactly what to do and how to approach training for best results. In order to achieve this, a distinction must be made between basics and their components.

By definition, basic techniques are simple movements of body parts used in offense and defense, such as a front kick or an upper level block. Each basic karate technique is composed of several components, e.g. the lunge punch contains at least ten components as described in the last section of Chapter 10 of this book. All techniques are ideally delivered from stable stances and postures. The most optimal or best techniques are those that fully employ all of their components in a smooth and timely fashion. The theory embracing the inner workings of the most common types of these components and ideas is sometimes referred to as the "Grammar of martial arts or the basic rules." These elementary requirements are applicable to all types and styles of martial arts such as judo, karate, sumo, jujitsu, taekwondo, boxing, aikido, wrestling, etc. It is vitally important for all beginners to understand and adhere to correct implementation of the grammar of martial arts.

A large number of beginners, especially children and young adults tend to overlook the importance of first learning the components of a technique in favor of the more elaborate and impressive technique itself. One reason that some karateka cannot perform certain techniques as perfectly as they wish, say, an upper level roundhouse kick or even a mid-level side kick, is the simple fact that they have failed to learn these basic techniques correctly by breaking them down into their simpler elements and trying to master them component by component, as opposed to mimicking their instructors. Even when a student fully understands the intricacies of a technique and commits himself to learning it properly, i.e., component by component, he first must ascertain that his body and limbs are actually capable of performing the task. In other words, to check if the joints are flexible enough and the muscles are strong enough to support the chorography of the technique.

BASIC RULES

A good understanding of the components of the basics or the grammar of karate could not only result in execution of perfect techniques, but also reduce injuries as well as saving time and energy. The most important components of the basic techniques or the basic rules of karate practice are as follows:

Strength and Flexibility: Although it is desirable for a beginner to be athletically capable before joining a karate school, it is by no means an official requirement. Simply stated, if a student cannot perform half-decent splits, then he or she will have a difficult time mastering the technique. By the same token, if he/she lacks muscular strength, it probably will be difficult, even painful, to hold the leg suspended in the air for some milliseconds. It therefore is best to work on one's athletic abilities, especially flexibility and strength, before and after joining a karate school.

Bending of the Knees: Both knees should be bent slightly during kata and kumite, just as much as required by a particular stance. This will lower the body's center of gravity and keep the hips down, resulting in a more stable posture and greater storage of muscular energy in the legs and the lower abdominal region. Stiff knee joints can render the person immobile. All kicks are delivered from a both-knees-bent position. The striking leg knee joint always is flexed again to gain angular momentum.

Hand and Arm Techniques: In order to be most effective, all hand techniques should be executed in such a way as to allow the hands to travel the longest possible distance prior to impact. This can be achieved only by starting the hands from behind the ears or over the hips. All thrusting hand techniques, such as Choku-Tsuki, start from over the hips, and almost all rotational techniques, such as gedan-barai, start from over the hips. This also activates more joint rotations, which in turn adds momentum to the action of the hand.

Foot and Leg techniques: Similarly, all foot or kicking techniques can be most effective if the feet travel the longest possible distance and activate more joints before hitting the target. This is possible only if the knee joint is raised above the hips or near the chest, e.g., a mawashi-geri, ushiro-geri, mae-geri, etc. Learning to flex the toes up and make contact with the ball of the foot are important lessons before attempting any kicking techniques.

Pivoting and Planting: Pivoting, planting, and sliding are elementary components of dachi-kata, used to change body direction and step from one stance to another. They are perhaps the most important basic components that beginners should learn from day one. Pivoting is the act of rotating the feet and the entire leg about a certain point, for instance the center of the ball or the heel of one or both feet. For example, standing on heisoku dachi, the student can keep the heels fixed in position while rotating the toes away from each other by as much as 45 degrees and end up in musubi dachi. In this particular case, the act of rotation is called pivoting on the heels. From musubi dachi, the student can pivot about the balls of the feet in opposite directions until the feet become parallel. The student now is on heiko dachi. Pivoting is used mainly for gentle rotations, not more than 180 degrees. In pivoting, the practitioner never loses contact with the ground and experiences some degree of friction at the bottom of the foot. All moving or stepping techniques, especially those involving kicking, require the supporting foot to be placed properly and anchored to the ground. The orientation of the supporting foot with respect to the line of action of the waza is the single most important component of the basic technique. Planting is the simple act of moving and rotating the feet from any given position to another. The transition may take place by either sliding or stepping into the new position. Planting generally is used for dynamic movements, avoiding friction with the ground, avoiding twisting of the ankle joints, and torsion of the knees, as well as saving precious time and energy.

If an advanced student is asked to take a single step forward with the left foot and deliver a front kick with the right leg in a straight line, then the supporting left foot most probably will be planted either parallel with or at a slight angle, say 15 degrees, with the line of action, conforming to the rear foot orientation of a classical zenkutsu-dachi. If he is asked to repeat the same, but execute an upper level roundhouse kick, he probably will place the left foot between 30 to 45 degrees with respect to the line of action. Finally, if he is asked to do the same, this time performing a side kick along the same direction, he naturally would plant the left foot at 90 degrees to the line of attack. Notice, in all three cases, the student could have planted the left foot in line with the direction of the movement and then pivoted the foot into position, as required. However, this would exert a large torsional strain on the supporting knees and ankles and friction on the bottom of the same foot. The act of correct placement of the supporting foot on the ground is called planting. Planting and pivoting usually are used concurrently for performing spinning techniques, such as a spinning back fist attack or a spinning reverse roundhouse kick.

Sliding and Stepping: There is no regular walking in karate practice. Karateka employ either sliding or stepping techniques to move from one point to the other. Sliding is the act of moving one foot along a horizontal curve, scraping the other, and remaining lightly in contact with the ground, with both knees bent throughout the movement. The sliding foot is not raised and carries no body weight until it comes to rest. The idea is to remain as stable as possible during this transition. Sliding usually is interrupted by kicking. Stepping is the same as regular walking except that one knee is always bent. Stepping is most commonly used when kicking consecutively with both legs or jumping out of position to avoid a strike. For the first case, the kicking foot becomes the supporting foot for the next kick by the other leg. In the second case, the quick displacement of the feet and the entire body resemble a short jump in which both feet become airborne almost simultaneously.

Bending of Joints: All major joints except the wrists always should be kept in a slightly bent position. All joints must be provided with sufficient range to generate and absorb maximal forces about their axis of rotation. These particular joints never should be locked, either before or after executing a technique. Stiff limbs are of little use in karate practice. A slack wrist and finger joints are prone to injury. It is prudent to warm up all body joints, starting from the smallest to the largest, before each and every training session. Locking joints in shadow training is asking for trouble. In hitting air or shadow training, all strikes should be snapped back to prevent injury to the joints.

Activation of Joints: Joint rotations result in angular motions that result collectively in a strong force directed at a target. The larger the number of joints involved, the faster their speed of rotation, and the larger their range of motion, the stronger the resulting force. There are a limited number of joints in each limb. Apparently, the secret in activating more joints with larger angles of rotation is in starting the hands or the feet as far away as possible.

Hip Rotation: The hip joint is the largest and most powerful joint of the human body. It comes into action for every single move in martial arts practice, as well as common sports. It is rotated automatically after each and every step. Its range of motion is magnified when stepping from one stance to another. Its correct use, around the appropriate axis, could result in extremely powerful blocks, strikes, or throws. The musculature of the lower abdominal and hip regions should be strengthened continuously through special stretching and weight training exercises.

Hands and Fingers: Hands are the most important and frequently used tools in karate practice. They are subject to extreme exertions, yet they are anatomically weak and prone to disabling injury. Both hands always are kept high, in a defensive posture, to protect the head and the chest during all exercises. The best way to keep the hands and fingers protected is of course by wearing special protective gear during sparring and kumite practice. Hands, wrists, and fingers, as well as toes and ankles, should be stretched properly and warmed up before any karate practice. It is strongly recommended to keep the hands in either a relaxed fist or arched knife-edge position, with the first joint of the thumbs bent toward the palms. Making a good fist and chopping hands are prime lessons in karate practice.

Relaxation and Breathing: All karate exercises should be carried out in a calm and relaxed way with a heightened sense of the surroundings, i.e., being alert. This would make the training session an enjoyable experience, free of stress and injury. Beginners should pace themselves with the ongoing rhythm of the class and try to breathe as normally as possible until more advanced methods of breathing and relaxation are introduced to them. Periodic cardiovascular training, such as cross-country running or working out on a treadmill, can help increase and normalize breathing habits. It is considered good practice to inhale through the nose before delivering a technique and to exhale through the mouth with an outburst, the kiai, at completion. It is well known that inhaling tends to relax the muscles, while exhaling helps in contracting them. New students should start practicing abdominal breathing, as opposed to chest breathing, as soon as possible.

Kiai and Kime: Kiai and kime are both unique and elemental phenomena that add power and impetus to all karate techniques. The kiai is simply a momentary and forceful exhalation, a yell that tends to direct and concentrate all energies towards the target. Kime, literally translated as focus, is the concentration of all efforts directed at the target at the moment of impact. Together, kime and kiai are the finishing act of a karate technique. A kiai is not a genuine kiai unless the exhalation is imitated from the diaphragm and not the chest; it is a loud sound starting with a vowel. The word" kiai" should never be substituted for the yell. Shouting" kiai" is wrong.

Hanmi and Hikite: Hanmi literally means half-facing. Hanmi, as opposed to full-facing or side facing, is the preferred position of the body when sparring with a partner. Standing at an angle, say 45 degrees, to the opponent, offers many advantages over other postures. It reduces exposure to frontal attack and makes front hand jabbing and blocking easy. It allows for much faster full-body retreat and evasion. It allows for better hip rotation and increases the distance between the target and the striking rear foot and/or fist. This in turn increases momentum at impact. Hikite literally means the pulling hand. It is the motion of the non-striking or reacting hand that resembles a front pulling action or spear hand attack that becomes a back elbow strike upon retraction. The simultaneous, opposing movements of the two hands create twisting forces that add to the power of the attacking punch.

CHAPTER 8

Vocabulary and Terminology

Martial arts in general, and karate-do in particular, are sciences utilizing the human entity—mind, body and spirit—for means of offense and defense. It is imperative that students learn the names of the parts of the body and the techniques associated with these parts.

Learning all the Japanese terminology used in martial arts is neither practical nor required, but IKA expects its students to memorize the meaning of basic terms used frequently in karate practice.

More than 10 million people practice karate-do worldwide, and half of them are followers of the Shotokan style. IKA membership has grown to more than 15,000 members in more than 50 nations.

The true multinational character of the IKA and of the Shotokan and Gosoku-ryu styles of karate-do encourage IKA students everywhere to strengthen their bond through karate-do and the language of karate-do.

IKA students, like those in most other internationally recognized karate organizations, frequently visit each other's dojos both locally and internationally. Without a common language, there can be neither communication nor exchange of ideas. While the soccer ball has different names in different countries and the "Swan Lake" ballet is recognized by its translation, "Kata Heian Shodan" or the "ushiro-geri" have the same meaning all over the world, even if the styles are different.

The same conventions and Japanese terminology are used in all local and international tournaments. Most local and international seminars also use the same vocabulary. Visiting instructors have no choice but to resort to the same means of communication.

Before learning the basic postures, stances, strikes and blocks, it is instructive to become familiar with some of the standard terminology practiced in karate dojos. For this reason, the most common terms and phrases used in karate practice are grouped in the next few sections. These include general terms, basic commands, positions and actions, counting and numbers, parts of the body, stances and postures, names of techniques, names of katas, and miscellaneous phrases and terms. All karate-related Japanese terms and their English counterparts are used interchangeably throughout this book to facilitate their comprehension for the uninitiated.

General terms

These are some of the terms every karateka should know. Most of these terms are used frequently during training sessions

Term	Meaning	Term	Meaning
REN SHU	practice	KUN-REN	learning
KARATE	empty hand	OBI	belt
KARATE-KA	karate practitioner	HAI	yes
KARATE-DO	the way of karate	OSU, OOS	greetings/hello
DOJO	training hall	SAN	friend/respectable
RYU	style/school	TOBI	jump
TE	hand	DACHI	stance
ASHI	foot	GAMAE	posture
SHIAI	contest	SHOBU	match
DO	path, way	KIHON	basic
KUMITE	combat, sparring	SOJI	cleaning
KATA	form, formal exercise	WAZA	technique
MAKIWARA	striking post	TORI	attacker
DESHI	trainee, disciple	KACH	win/win
TAMESHI-WARI	breaking	UKE	blocker
KI	inner power, spirit	IBUKI	breath control
TSUKI	punch, thrust	GERI	kick
SEMEITE	attacker	UKE-TE	defender
BU-DO	martial arts	KA	practitioner
BU-DO-KA	student of martial arts	SHIN	mind/spirit
SHINPAN	referee/arbitrator	AI	coming together
SHIZEN-TAI	natural, basic stance	JUTSU	method/strategy
UNDOO	calisthenics	RENRAKU	combination
ZANSHIN	a state of awareness	YOKERU	evasions
SEN SEI	teacher	KO HAI	junior/younger

KOKORO	heart	SEN PAI	senior/elder
TAMASHI	spirit	YOWAI	weak
FURI-SUTE	whip swing (judo)	TSUYOI	powerful/strong
TSUKAMI-DORI	grab-pull (judo)	SEITO	student/pupil
ASHI-DORI	leg takedown (judo)	TATAMI	straw mat

Basic commands

The following are some of the words used by instructors to communicate with their students during training sessions. All of these terms are used several times during each practice period. All IKA students must learn these basic commands. Understandably, neither the pronunciations nor the translations are absolutely correct. Once again, this list is by no means complete.

Command	Meaning	Command	Meaning
YOI	Get ready, prepare	TSU ZU KE TE	Carry on/continue
YAME	Stop, end, halt	I-MA	Now
		TA ZU KE TE	Get help
YASUME	Relax, rest	KI-O-TSUKE	Come to attention
SEIZA	Kneel down		
REI	Bow with respect	MAE NI	Move forward
		TATTE	Stand up
KIAI	Exhale and yell	NARANDE	Line up
		YO KKURI	Move more slowly
HAJIME	Begin		
MOKUSO	Contemplate/meditate	YO WAKU	Move lightly
		USHIRO NI	Move backward
MAWATE	Turn around		
SHIZUKANI	Quiet	MUKAI ATTE	Face each other
TSUYOKU	Powerfully, with strength	MODOTTE	Go back to your place
KIME	Focus		
HAYAKU	Quickly/hurry up/with speed	SEIRETSU	Line up
		NAOTTE	At ease
SORE-MADE	That is all		

Orientations, spaces, positions, and actions

Karate and martial arts techniques are performed in relation to the position and posture of an opponent. In freehand fighting, the combatants try to control and protect their own domain or immediate space, while attempting to penetrate and disturb the opponent's space or sphere of influence.

The concept of space, or *Ma*, is fundamental to karate practice. The following are some of the Japanese terms used to describe the type and area of execution of a blocking or striking technique. All of these terms are used in conjunction with the names of basic techniques and parts of the body and will be described in another part of this book.

Term	Meaning	Term	Meaning
DAN	level	TATE	vertical/upright
JO-DAN	upper level	JU	soft/gentle
CHU-DAN	middle level	GO	hard/rough
GE-DAN	lower level	SUKI	opening
HIDARI	left	SOTO	outside/outward
MIGI	right	UCHI	inside
SHOMEN	front/forward	GE	lower/inferior
USHIRO	back	MAE	front
YOKO	side/lateral	KE-AGE	rising
FUMI-KOMI	down thrust or stamping	KE-KOMI	with thrust
ISSOKU-CHO	one foot length	TENSHIN	moving
GYAKU	reverse, opposite	CHAKUCHI	landing
MAWASHI	round, semicircular	TACHI-REI	standing bow
NAGASHI	sweeping/flowing	ZA REI	kneeling bow
TANDEN	the center of balance	TSUGI	one after other
HYOSHI	timing	O/OKI	big/great
SUM	angle	KO/SHO	small
OMOTE	above	URA	opposite
KOKO	here	SHITA	below
ASOKO	there	MASSUGO	straight ahead
OTOSHI	descending	JIKAN	time off
KAITEN	turning	HINERI	twisting
MA	space	JIKI	timing
CHIKA-MA	short-range	TO-MA	long-range
HAYASA	speed	CHU-K AN	medium range
USHIRO-ASHI	rear leg (foot)	HANMI	half facing
SORASHI	feint/false attack	O-TAGAI	each other
AWASE	together	MA-AI	distancing

Counting and numbers

Numbers and counting are unavoidable in any disciplined activity. They are used widely in karate practice and terminology. Movements or combinations of movements usually are synchronized, with instructors counting numbers in Japanese. As a minimum, all students must learn to count from one to ten in Japanese. In practice, the numerical count usually is limited to ten:

ICHI, NI, SAN, SHI, GO, ROKU, SICHI, HACHI, KU, JU.

The count of numbers beyond ten is: JU-ICHI, JU-NI, JU-SAN, JU-SHI, and so on. NI-JU is 20. Then NI-JU-ICHI, NI-JU-NI, and so on to SAN-JU, which means 30. KU-JU-KU is 99, HYAKU is

100, SEN is 1,000, and MAN is 10,000. ICHI-NO, NI-NO, SAN-NO, YON-NO, GO-NO, up to JIYU-NO means first to tenth on numbers one to ten respectively. JIYU GO-NO means fifteenth or number fifteen. The following terms describing numerical order also are used in karate and martial arts practice.

Term	Meaning	Term	Meaning
KATA-TE	one hand	YONHON	four-step, quadruple
MORO-TE	twin, two together	GOHON	five-step, quintuple
IPPON	one-step, single	SAN-JU-NO	thirtieth/number thirty
NIHON	two-step, double	REN WAZA	double or repeated technique
SANBON	three-step, triple		

Some useful phrases and terms

The following terms and phrases are provided for the benefit of the interested reader. However, students can show respect and interest, and make a good impression by learning just a few of these phrases and terms.

Students should pronounce every syllable and make intonation rather flat.

Phrase	Meaning
SOJI-O-SHI-MASU	May I clean
ONEGAI SHI-MASU	Please teach me
OHAYO GOZAI-MASU	Good morning
KON-NICHI-WA	Good day
KOMBAN-WA	Good evening
SAYO-NARA	Good-bye
OYASUMI-NASAI	Good night (on retiring)
DO-MO-SUMIMASEN	I am sorry, my fault
ARIGATO-GOZAI-MASU	Thank you (very much)
SHI-TSU-REI-SHI-MASU	Please excuse me
HAI-SO-DESU	Yes, it is; yes, I agree
I-DESU	That's good
DAME-DESU	That's no good
SUKOSHI	A bit, a little
I-IE	No
HAI, HAI	Yes, I am listening
HAI, WAKARI-MASU	Yes, I understand
WAKARI-MASEN	I don't understand
ASHITA	Tomorrow
KARATE-GI-O-KIRU	Wear the karate uniform
OBI-O-SHIMERU	Wear (tie) the belt
DO-ZO	Please
CHIGAI-MASU	No, I disagree
KAMPAI	Cheers, hooray
DO-ZO-YOROSHIKU	Pleased to meet you
DO-ITASHIMASHITE	You are welcome
I-IE-KOCHIRA-KOSO	No, thank you
JACKSON-DES	My family's name is Jackson

CHAPTER 9

Skills and Concepts

Traditional karate training is the principal function of IKA and its affiliated dojos. Basic karate training is the main concern of this book and forms the cornerstone of the advanced training systems outlined in the preceding chapter.

Karate training generally consists of five fundamental forms of learning: waza, kata, kumite, reading, and supplementary conditioning. The first three forms of training take place in the dojo. All five of these training methods are applicable equally to all levels of skill and proficiency. A brief description of each of these methods is presented in a later chapter.

Breathing control and effective meditation also are important abilities in martial arts training. However, no formal training in breathing control and meditation is offered to kyu ranking students until they become the holder of a black belt.

Depending on a particular schedule and the mix of a student's ranking, a typical training session can include any combination of these methods. Each one has its own merits and purposes in training, yet all three are highly interdependent and complement each other. In fact, the merit of one is measured by the degree of proficiency in the other two. The ability to execute a good waza—or technique–makes proper performance of kata more likely. On the other hand, a good kata performer is likely to do well in kumite practice. Good fighting instincts lead to improved waza performance.

However, to attain the rank of Shodan, students must demonstrate a high level of proficiency in three qualities known collectively as Shin-Gi-Tai. These are Shin, or moral and mental worth; Gi, technical skill; and Tai, phys-

ical development. These three qualities are inseparable and must be developed together, harmoniously, with patience, care, and devotion.

To succeed in the dojo, students should commit themselves to additional physical training, such as that discussed in Chapter 15.

BASIC TECHNIQUES: WAZA

The manner in which the body or a body part is used to execute a technique is known as waza, or skill. All karate waza, executed from any stance or posture, whether in a standing mode or in motion, are uniquely designed movements with specific purposes and modes of action in mind.

A technique may be practiced on its own or in combination with other techniques, in slow motion or with maximum speed. The importance of practicing the basic waza is stressed repeatedly in this book.

The basic waza are practiced at the beginning of almost all scheduled classes, regardless of the program planned for that session. It is quite common to see advanced students practicing simple combinations of basic techniques several times during a normal practice session. In fact all karateka, regardless of their rank and titles, practice the basics all the time. Soke says:

"It is more important to master one or two basic techniques than to be only familiar with lots of fancy movements."

Knowing a waza and being able to execute it effectively are two different things. The difference can be measured by the difference in the ranking of two students performing the same technique. Generally there are three different but related methods of practicing waza. These are shadow training, training with striking pads and training with a partner.

Shadow training, as in shadow boxing, is the most popular method of technical training. Students practice selected techniques against one or more imaginary opponents. The emphasis in shadow training is always on the quality of execution rather than the speed or number of repetitions.

Shadow training with equipment may consist of practicing a given technique against a slightly padded surface, such as a punching bag, a hand pad or the makiwara. This type of training is best suited to more experienced students who wish to toughen their hands and feet and improve their striking and targeting abilities.

The methods of training with fellow karateka are discussed in Chapter 11 and other sections of the book. Effective execution of waza requires some degree of proficiency in all aspects of karate practice and is governed by the following principles: Mechanical, Mental, and Spiritual. In reality, these principles are highly intertwined and cannot be separated as different human values. However, experience has shown that the grouping of these principles into three distinct categories, as presented here, greatly facilitates both the teaching as well as the learning of the subject.

Mechanical principles, which explain the choreography of all movements and include all basic body functions, such as:

Hand and foot techniques, including defensive and offensive movements.

Stances and postures, including stationary and moving modes of action.

Body and foot movements, including both slow and explosive types of action.

Mental principles, which define the purpose, strategy, and manner of execution of all actions. These mental principles manifest themselves as practical strategies and must be practiced as such. All judgmental actions, conscious or otherwise, depend on the power of the mind and its ability to respond as appropriately and as quickly as possible. Many such phenomena control all thought processes and neuromuscular actions, including:

- Timing and speed.
- Targeting and distancing.
- Concentration and coordination.
- Tactical and physical control.

Spiritual principles, which empower the mind and body by regulating the flow of vital energy. In pragmatic terms, the spiritual principles are related to functions of:

- Kokoro, the heart (guts), soul, or essence of being.
- Kiai and kime, the coming together of life energy.
- Instinct and intuitive knowledge.
- Awareness and indifference.
- Emotional control.
- Zen.

The nature and application of these principles are explained in some detail in the next few sections of this chapter.

BASIC POSTURES: GAMAE

The way in which a karateka holds or guards the body is known as a gamae, or combative posture. The term also implies a frame of mind affecting one's thoughts or behavior.

Karateka should understand the physiological importance of gamae. Briefly, all body movements are accomplished by muscles that have two functions: contraction and relaxation. Contractions often are voluntary and usually are of short duration, resulting in motion of body parts.

Relaxation normally is a sustained contraction and is reflexive in nature. Relaxation usually causes no motion. The term muscle tone refers to this reflex contraction. Its function is to maintain position or posture. In martial arts, posture implies a state of readiness for action. In karate-do, physical posture and mental attitude are interrelated.

In general, combative postures are initiated from three different body positions: standing, sitting, and being on the ground. The scope of this section is limited to standing gamae only.

Each formal gamae may be held in two different styles: the free, or normal, style; and the classic, or formal style. Each posture may be held toward the left, right or front of an opponent, such as:

Migi gamae	Right side forward; right hand and foot forward
Hidari gamae	Left side forward; left hand and foot forward
Ma-Shomen gamae	Forward facing or front viewing posture

Some of the basic postures encountered in kata and kumite are listed as follows:

Posture	Meaning / Application
Hanmi-no gamae	Half forward facing combative posture
Ma-hanmi gamae	Side facing or side viewing posture
Morote-no gamae	Middle level combative posture/middle
Jodan-no gamae	Upper level combative posture/ upper guard
Gedan-no gamae	Lower level combative posture/ lower guard
Shizen-dach-no gamae	Natural combative posture/natural guard
Ninoji-no gamae	Parallel arm combative posture
Mu gamae	No posture combative form
Birin-no gamae	Fish tail combative posture
Chudan-nukite-no gamae	Middle level spearhand posture

Ryoken-koshi gamae	Fists on hips/kata Heian Sandan
Koshi gamae	Both hands on one hip/kata Heian Nidan
Kage gamae	Hook punch posture/kata Heian Godan
Manji gamae	Kata Heian Godan
Muso gamae	Kata Hengetsu
Juji gamae	Kata Kanku Dai
Ken-mune-mae gamae	Kata Empi
Kaishu-ryowan gamae	Open hands forearm posture
Kaishu-yama gamae	Open hand mountain posture/Hangetsu

In formal training, the postures are related to the axis of body rotation with respect to an imaginary straight line connecting the eyesight of two standing opponents who are facing each other. Formal half facing, therefore, implies an angle of approximately 45 degrees toward right or left with respect to the axis of the forward direction of the body.

During freestyle fighting, the practitioners may adopt different combinations of postures and stances depending on the most useful positions for their bodies with respect to each particular combat situation. For more information on this subject, see the section on body movements later in this book.

Experienced karateka usually can predict an opponent's intentions or state of mind in a combat situation by observing his/her combative postures. Postures are natural and practical configurations of the body suited to particular combat situations and are studied most effectively under the direction of experienced instructors.

While postures define the form of the body with respect to an opponent or imaginary base line, the distribution of body weight and the position of feet are described by classic standing forms, known as Dachi-kata, or stances.

Dachis and Gamae are integral parts of each other. Stances and postures should be regarded as momentary body forms made necessary by combat situations. They are not intended as fixed positions from which techniques may be executed.

The next section is devoted to a brief description of a chain of movements that connect some of the basic stances to each other. It also is a practical summary of the most common stances encountered in karate practice.

BASIC STANCES: DACHI

Stance is defined as the position of the feet and legs needed to assure the optimum balance, stability, mobility, and power for a given combative posture. Dachi kata simply mean standing forms.

Moving from one dachi to another necessitates the rotation of a number of joints, most importantly the ankles, the knees, and the hip joints. Each joint rotation, especially the hip, if properly executed, could result in more effective and enhanced performance.

Mastering basic karate stances and postures is essential for efficient engagement in kumite, effective execution of techniques, and correct performance of kata. Regardless of a karateka's physical attributes, it is nearly impossible to deliver an effective strike or direct a successful attack without a firm base. The techniques will lack power and accuracy. The body will lack balance and stability.

Some of the most common stances practiced in karate-do are shown in Table 3. There are many different stances and postures, and many combinations of the two. From these basic stances, any position of attack or defense can be assumed very quickly.

Table 3 depicts the position of the feet for 15 basic stances with respect to two imaginary base lines. The base lines resemble the inverted letter T. The stem points toward the imaginary opponent. The letter S indicates a distance equal to one shoulder width.

The Dachi-kata are unique standing forms. These somewhat unusual body configurations can be challenging to learn and execute, but they are extremely effective once mastered. Karate stances are learned and practiced best in front of a mirror guided by an experienced instructor.

Stable and well-balanced stances are essential in order to execute effective blocks or launch decisive blows. For this reason, all katas are performed almost entirely from classical stances. However, the actual mechanics, philosophies of karate stances, and their relative merits and applications always are demonstrated most effectively by qualified instructors in a dojo environment.

The philosophical concepts and mechanical properties of each Dachi-kata are unique and have evolved through many centuries for specific training purposes and combat situations. Therefore, it makes sense to learn each stance with patience, awareness, and a sound understanding of its most effective applications. Here is a brief description of the Dachi-katas depicted in Table 3, located at the end of this section. You will find it helpful to look at the sketches while reading the descriptions below.

Heisoku-dachi, or closed feet attention stance. This is the first ceremonial stance taught to all karateka worldwide. It is a position of standing at attention. Feet are held together, toes pointing ahead. The body is straight; the hips and shoulders are in line with each other; the chin is up. Hands are straight down with the palms open. This dachi also is known as the informal attention stance.

Musubi-dachi, or open toe attention stance. The body and the head are held as in Heisoku-dachi. The heels are together but the toes are separated by an angle of nearly 90 degrees. Hands are straight down with the palms open and touching the outside of the thighs. This is the position usually taken before bowing. It also is known as the formal attention stance. All karate events begin and end with this stance.

Heiko-dachi, or parallel feet stance. The heels are held in the same plane as the body, one shoulder width apart. This is a noncombative, natural stance. The body is upright, relaxed but ready. The mind is alert. The shoulders and hips are in line with each other. The weight of the body is distributed equally on both legs.

Hachiji-dachi, or open leg stance. This is a noncombative, normal stance. The body and the heels are held in the same position as in Heiko-dachi, but the toes are turned outward, each making an angle of roughly 45 degrees in relation to the frontal axis of the body. The hands are held down in front of the abdomen with the fists clenched but relaxed. The body is relatively tensed and the mind is alert. All Shotokan katas and most karate exercises begin and end with this stance.

Uchimata-dachi and *Gyaku-hachiji-dachi*, or pigeon toe or inverted foot stance. The feet are held in the same plane as the body, one shoulder width apart, with both toes turned inward, each making an angle of approximately 45 degrees in relation to the frontal axis of the body. The fists are clenched in front of the abdomen. This stance always is assumed after executing Rei. The Gosoku-ryu and Kihon katas always end with this stance. This form of standing also is known as the reverse open leg stance or Gyaku hachiji-dachi.

Kiba-dachi, or horse riding or straddle leg stance. This is a strong combat stance with a high degree of sideways stability. The heels are held in the plane of the body approximately two shoulder widths apart. Feet are parallel with each other and at right angles to the plane of the body. The hips are lowered and the knees are flexed forward and outward. In a perfect Kiba-dachi, the thighs are parallel with the floor and the forelegs are perpendicular to the ground. The shoulders are in line with the hips. The weight of the body is distributed equally on both legs. In spite of excellent lateral and vertical resistance, this stance is weak in frontal direction. It is ideally suited for performing side kicks, side thrusts, and strikes.

Shiko-dachi, or square or sumo stance. This stance is almost identical to Kiba-dachi, except for the direction of the feet, which are turned outward and away from each other. The angle of the feet is approximately 45 degrees with respect to the line of the shoulders. The main advantage of this stance is its capacity to help thrust the body forward and pack direct punches with great power and speed. Because of the low center of gravity and wide spacing of the feet, the entire body is well-balanced against lateral movement.

Zenkutsu-dachi, the front or forward stance. This is the most frequently encountered formal stance in karate practice. It also is one of the most stable and versatile stances utilized in practice and kata. It is the formal adaptation of the natural body posture in a face to face situation. The feet are positioned along the diagonal of a rectangle measuring approximately one shoulder width wide and two shoulder widths long. The body is kept upright and facing almost full front. The hips and shoulders are in line and in the same plane. The head faces front. Approximately 60 percent of the body's weight rests on the front leg, with the remainder on the back leg. The front foot points forward with a slight inward rotation. The rear foot is almost parallel with the front foot. The rear leg is straight. The front leg is flexed with the front knee directly above the front toes. This stance is very strong to the front, relatively weaker to the sides and back. For added maneuverability, the back leg should be slightly flexed.

Fudo-dachi/Sochin-dachi, or the stable or immovable stance. This stance is a modification of the Zenkutsu-dachi described above. The rear leg is bent and tensed in an outward direction, instead of being straight. The feet are almost parallel. The body is facing halfway toward the front. This stance has the same amount of stability and means of executing powerful blocks and strikes as the Zenkutsu-dachi, except that the rear leg also can thrust the body forward and/or sideways. On the whole, it is more maneuverable than the front stance.

Kokutsu-dachi, or back stance. This powerful, yet simple, stance allows the rotation of the hips to amplify the blocking or striking momentum of the hands. It also enables graceful retraction of the front foot for a snap kick as well as forward sliding of the feet for better positioning. Depending on the circumstances, the body could be half-facing, with the hips making a 45 degree angle from the front, or completely front-facing. Approximately 70 percent of the body weight is carried by the back leg. The feet are roughly two shoulder widths apart, front to back. The front foot points forward with a small inward tilt. The direction of the back foot is almost at a right angle to the front foot. The heel of the back foot is almost in line with the long direction of the front foot. The hands usually are held as in the knife edge defensive posture.

Sanchin-dachi, the hour glass or inward tension stance. The basic application of this very strong and stable stance includes performing kata, breathing exercises, groin defense, resisting frontal and vertical pushing forces, and correcting body postures. In this stance, the knees are flexed inward and held approximately one fist distance apart. The toes of the rear foot are in line with the heel of the front foot. The directional axes of the two feet intersect at nearly 90 degrees. The toes of both feet are turned slightly inward.

Neko-Ashi-dachi, the cat or cat foot stance. This is a much shorter and more flexible version of the Kokutsu-dachi, with almost all of the body weight resting on the back leg. Both knees are bent. The front foot barely carries the weight of the front leg and rests on the ball and toes of the foot. This stance is adapted from Kokutsu-dachi by sliding the front foot backward and shifting the weight of the body to the back leg. The back foot is rotated inward to make an angle of 45 degrees with the direction of the front foot. The back and the head are straight and facing front. This enables fast counter front snap kicks and rapid body movements. This highly maneuverable stance also allows quick transition to other stances,

Ushiro-Neko-Ashi-dachi, or the backward cat stance, is the natural variation of the classical cat stance described above. Approximately 80 percent of the body's weight rests on the front foot, which is flat on the ground. The rest of the body's weight is on the ball and toes of the back foot. This stance frequently is used to shift body weight from one foot to the other while remaining in Neko-Ashi-dachi.

Renoji-dachi/Ren-dachi or Rei-dachi, the "L" stance is best described as an upright flat front foot Neko-Ashi-dachi or shortened Kokutsu-dachi. It is a normal standing form with the front foot nearly one shoulder width in front of the rear foot. The front foot points forward, and the rear foot makes an angle of approximately 45 degrees with the axis of the front foot. Approximately 70 percent of the weight of the body is supported by the back leg. Both knees are slightly flexed. This stance is encountered frequently in Gosoku-ryu katas.

Hangetsu-dachi, the half moon or wide hourglass stance. This stance is an exaggeration of the Sanchin-dachi. The feet are positioned at the ends of the diagonal of an imaginary square with each side measuring one and one half shoulder widths. The knees are flexed strongly. This stance is used mainly in performing kata; during breathing exercises; when resisting pushing forces; and when executing powerful punching and striking techniques.

Ju-dachi/Jiyu-dachi, the adaptable or free-fighting stance, is the mobile and more flexible version of the front stance. Approximately

60–70 percent of the body's weight is on the front leg. The front foot is positioned on the front end of the diagonal of a rectangle measuring one shoulder width wide and one and one half shoulder widths long. The rear leg is slightly flexed at the knee. The body is upright and half front facing. This stance allows the practitioner to execute fast movements in all directions.

Miscellaneous stances: The following stances are less commonly incorporated in kumite and combat, but also are encountered in karate practice, mainly during kata

Stance	Meaning
Shizen-dachi	The natural stance
Kosa-dachi	The crossed feet stance
Hiza-dachi	One knee stance
Kake-dachi	Hooked stance
Tsuru-Ashi-dachi	The crane stance
Kuzure-Heiko-dachi	Staggered parallel stance
Han-Mi-Kutsu-dachi	The eight stance
Teiji-dachi	The " T " stance
Sochin-dachi	Diagonal straddle leg stance
Ippon-dachi	One legged stance
Kagato-dachi	On the "heels" of the feet
Tsumasaki-dachi	On the "toes" of the feet
Sokuto-dachi	On the "balls" of the feet
Mage Tsumasaki-dachi	On folded toes

All standing forms or dachi-katas should be studied and practiced in conjunction with standard postures, or gamae, and footwork, or ashi-sabake, described in this book. These standing forms also should be studied in relationship with each other, for instance, going into kokutsu-dachi from zenkutsu-dachi or from zenkutsu-dachi into kiba-daci, and vice versa. Efficient body movements or tai-sabaki depend on quick and smooth footwork.

TACHI-KATA

Students are encouraged to learn a newly developed exercise by Soke Kubota, which he simply calls "Tachi-kata." This formal exercise consists of a large number of standing forms, starting from Shi zen-dachi to Hiza-dachi.

It shows how to move from one dachi to another smoothly and gracefully. Transitions of dachis occur smoothly because they are arranged to follow each other without abrupt footwork or jumping. One or both feet are always on the floor. In other words, all movements are stable and body shifting takes place in such a way as to minimize time and effort.

There are no Geri or Te waza in this exercise. There is no kime or kiai. The first eight movements are performed along a short hor-

Table 3
BASIC STANDING FORMS AND POSITIONS OF THE FEET

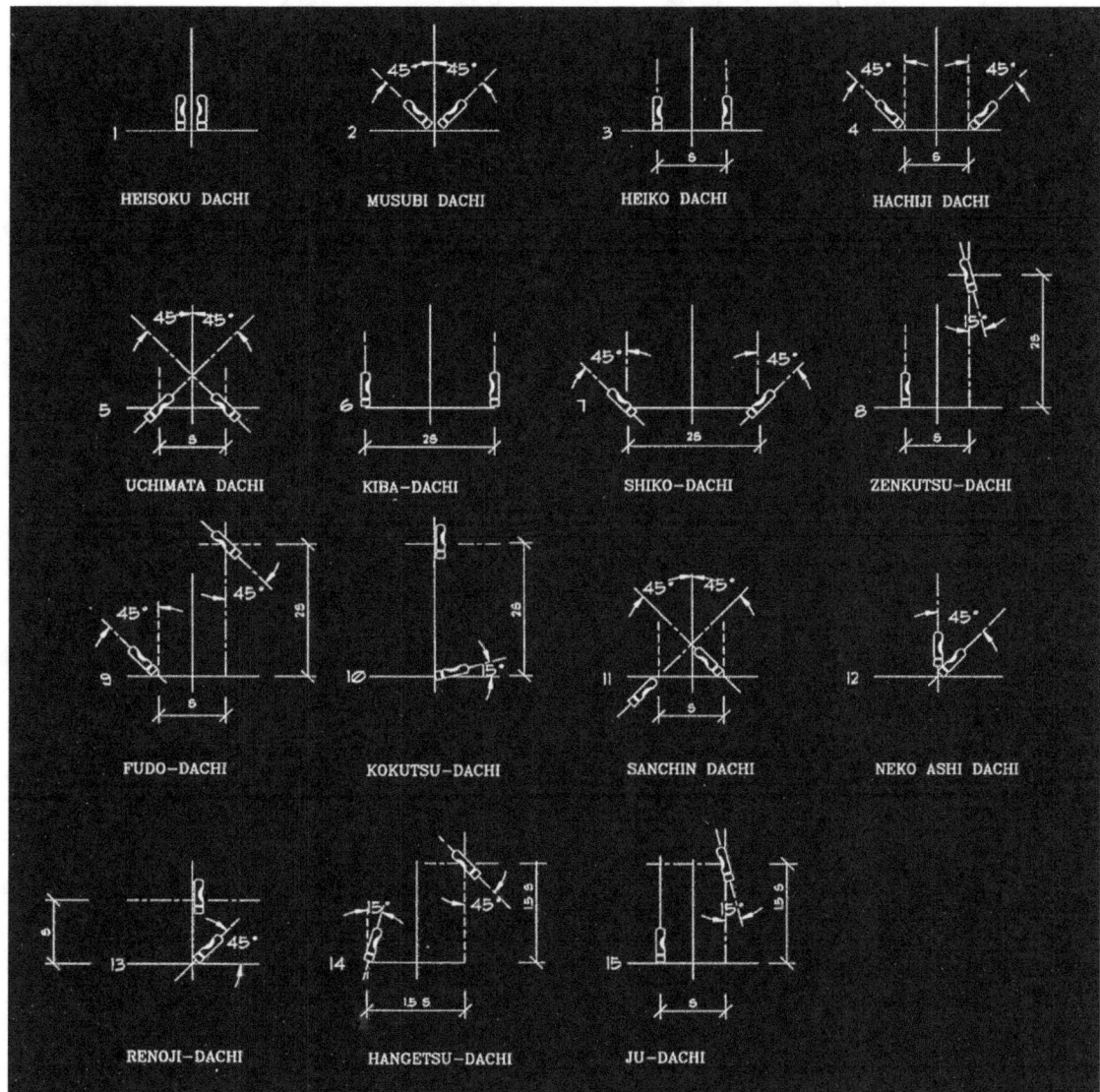

izontal line passing through the heels of the performer at Shi zen-dachi, with both feet rotating on their heels or balls in opposite directions. The order and the grouping of these standing forms, after normal formalities, is as follows:

Group I: Shizen-dachi, Kiba-dachi, Shiko-dachi, Uchi-mata-dachi, Hachiji-dachi, Heiko-dachi, Musubi-dachi, Heisoku-dachi. Here the transition to the next move occurs through Oi-ashi into a front stance.

Group II: Zenkutsu-dachi, Fudo-dachi, Kokutsu-dachi. The rear foot then is dragged next to the front foot into a heisoku-dachi.

Group III: Heisoku-dachi, Ren-dachi, Neko-dachi, Sanchin-dachi, Hangetsu-dachi, Kosa-dachi, Ippon-dachi. Next, the body is shifted through a Suri-ashi followed by a Kizami-ashi into a te-dachi.

Group IV: Te-dachi, Tsumasaki-dachi, Hiza-dachi, Shizen-dachi. End of kata.

TECHNICAL ASPECTS OF STANDING FORMS

Karate is a natural form of self-defense that has evolved over many centuries. All processes of natural development follow the same universal laws of science, including the laws of physics, physiology, and conservation of energy. Natural evolution tends to optimize form and energy for any function or purpose in life.

Karate techniques and stances also are evolutionary phenomena—and these optimized functions of the body are designed to generate maximum effort with minimum expenditure of energy.

Students who wish to study the scientific aspects of these stances are urged to develop a sense of mental and physical appreciation for the constituent components of each and every stance. They will learn that the chief factors in each stance are the supply of power, the maintenance of balance, and the ability to perform efficient techniques. With some practice, students may become aware of the concept of Hara, which defines the unified centers of gravity, spirit, and the immediate space surrounding the body.

With time and practice, students will discover that stances with lower centers of gravity and wider spacing of the feet generally are more stable and can generate more powerful strikes and thrusts than stances with higher centers of gravity and shorter spacing of the feet, even though these stances can generate more speed and reach. Students also will discover that lower centers of gravity combined with closer foot spacing can result in greater maneuverability than higher centers of gravity with wider foot spacing.

The ten most important parameters influencing the characteristics of karate stances are:

- Position of the feet with respect to each other. The spacing and orientation of the feet regulate the stability of the stance. Wider spacing is associated with more stable stances. Feet that are not parallel also appear to enhance the lateral stability of the stance. Neko-ashi-dachi, Kosa-dachi, Tsuru-ashi-dachi, and Ippon-dachi are very versatile stances, but they are not as stable as Zenkutsu-dachi or Kokutsu-dachi.

- The percentage of body weight distributed to each leg. The leg carrying less body weight is better suited to performing a technique than the leg subjected to more body weight. On the other hand, a leg under greater body pressure can propel the body with more power and speed than the lightly loaded foot.

Therefore, each leg should be strong enough to carry the entire weight of the body and to thrust the body in any direction.

- Degree of flex or bending of the knees and other joints. An outstretched arm without elbow flex and a straight leg with no knee bent have little or no potential for developing muscular power. Muscular power is associated with the amount of flex in the joints; the greater the flex, the greater the potential for muscular power. For instance, a sprinter who uses the crouching start, with the propelling leg completely flexed, is able to accelerate more quickly than the sprinter beginning from a standing start, where the degree of flex in the rear leg is minimal.

- Elevation of the center of gravity of the body with respect to the floor. A lower center of gravity is associated with better balance and greater storage of muscular energy for upward movement. It is a little known fact that a good kiai (exhalation or yell) can lower the center of gravity of the body and restore equilibrium. Almost all Tobi waza or jumping techniques performed in Shotokan and Gosoku-ryu katas are accompanied with a loud kiai. Such intense kiai are intended to lower the center of gravity of the performer and stabilize the body upon landing on the floor.

- Inclination and rotation of the body with respect to an opponent. Forward inclination of the body is associated with added momentum for forward movement. The degree of initial twist of the body with respect to an opponent is associated with added power generated by hip and shoulder rotation. The greater the hanmi, or half-facing orientation, the better the possibility of generating a good hip rotation. For optimal results, the hanmi should not exceed 45 degrees.

- Location of the gravitational line of action with respect to the vertical axis of the body. In a correctly held body where line of action of body weight coincides with the vertical axis of the body, little or no tension is exerted on the main muscle groups, allowing the body to relax and avoid undue fatigue. This is what physicians call good posture. In karate, good posture is more than standing straight. It is the result of how the muscles work and respond to action.

- Mobility and maneuverability of the stance. The ability to move from a given stance is of paramount importance in karate. Different types of footwork and body movements are discussed in the next section. Ren-dachi and Ju-dachi are among the most mobile karate stances discussed in this chapter.

- Stability of the body in all directions. The degree of stability in the stance is defined by the ability of the body to recover from the effect of a disturbing force or technique. Depending on a person's build, some stances may be more stable in one direction than in another. As a general rule, Zenkutsu-dachi, Fudo-dachi, and Hangetsu-dachi are the most stable karate stances depicted in Table 3.

- Degree of relaxation or tension of the neuromuscular system. Relaxation is the phenomenon of decreasing tension on the neuromuscular system of the body, without regard to the type and mechanics of a stance, and is controlled by the mind. Tension is the amount of stress sustained by the muscles in performing a mechanical task. Tensed muscles are slower and more energized than relaxed muscles.
- Ability to generate hip rotation. Such ability not only increases the momentum of the body but adds range to the striking hand or foot. As a general rule, the longer and wider the stance, the better the possibility of generating effective hip rotation. However, a well-trained karateka should be able to generate effective hip rotations from any stance. Changing dachis and half-facing guards always augment hip rotation.

FOOT AND BODY MOVEMENT: ASHI-SABAKI AND TAI-SABAKI

Dachi-kata and Ashi-Sabaki are to karate what standing and walking are to normal life. Body shifting is defined as the displacement of the body's weight from one stable stance to another. Stance, therefore, is the motionless state of the body before and after shifting.

Body shifting is the technical equivalent of moving around in karate. Body movement through footwork is an effective way of avoiding an assault and launching an attack in unarmed combat. Evasions and dodging both are methods of body shifting.

The body shifting and footwork techniques of karate are classified under three main groups, depending on the manner of holding the center of gravity through motion.

Sliding, stepping, shuffling, spinning, and turning: in this group of movements, one foot always is firmly on the ground and bears the weight of the entire body until the other foot takes over. The body's center of gravity remains at the same height and moves along a straight horizontal line. This group of movements also is known as the basic steps.

The second group of body shifting techniques is a variation of the first group. The body's center of gravity is raised or lowered to augment a striking or blocking technique. Properly moving the body's center of gravity is especially important when combining techniques or performing them sequentially. With correct timing, body shifting can intensify the power of a technique. On the contrary, if timing is off or shifting is not conducted properly, balance is disturbed and technique weakened.

Jumping, running, dropping, skipping, and falling are part of the

third group of body movements and footwork. In this group, both feet can be momentarily off the ground and the center of gravity can travel in any direction. The second and third groups of movements also begin and end in stable stances.

Here are the general rules governing the correct execution of basic steps while maintaining the same stance:

- The body should move unwaveringly with the center of gravity remaining at the same level at all times, unless it is meant to augment a technique by raising or lowering the body.
- The weight of the body should be shifted smoothly in a horizontal direction along a straight line.
- The knees should remain flexed at all times with strong balance in all directions.
- When moving, the body should be maintained in a defensive posture, relaxed but alert.
- The feet should not be raised off the floor or dragged without control.
- Body movement should not give away an impending technique, unless the practitioner intends either to warn or mislead his opponent.

A description of all known Ashi-sabaki and Tai-sabaki methods, their variations and combinations, is beyond the scope of this book. However, in a broader sense, the term tai-sabaki also implies dodging and evading during sparring or unarmed combat. The most common basic foot and body movements initiated from a forward stance are reviewed below.

Suri-Ashi: This technique, sliding of the feet, is used to cover short distances with agility and speed. Sliding usually is utilized to shift the body forward, backward, or sideways. For instance, to slide forward from a Renoji-dachi or relatively short Zenkutsu-dachi without changing stance, the forward lean of the body and the slight flex of the rear leg are used to slide the front foot and thrust the weight of the body forward by as much as two feet, consequently allowing the rear foot to slide the same distance. When sliding forward, the front foot is raised off the ground just enough to avoid contact with the floor while the weight of the body is shifted quickly to the rear leg. As soon as the front foot touches the floor, the entire weight of the body is shifted to the front foot. The rear foot follows naturally. To slide backward from a short Zenkutsu-dachi to the same stance, the sequence of the foot movement and body shifting is reversed, with the rear leg leading and the front leg following.

Oi-Ashi: Lunge stepping, or karate walking, is used to move in all directions. All the general rules described above are fully applicable to this method of body shifting. To step from Zenkutsu-dachi to Zenkutsu-dachi, the weight of the body is shifted momentarily to the front leg, while the rear foot is raised slightly off the floor, moved in toward the front foot and then moved out along the diagonal of the imaginary rectangle to its stable position. The weight of the body is readjusted between the two legs. Both legs are flexed equally as the feet come together. The in and out diagonal motion of the stepping foot is designed to protect the groin from possible attack, augment hip rotation as well as store enough energy to drive the body forward. Backward stepping from Zenkutsu-dachi to Zenkutsu-dachi is achieved by reversing the sequence of the movements, thereby pivoting over the rear foot and withdrawing the front foot in and out about the diagonals formed by the imaginary front and rear rectangles. The stationary foot is kept solidly on the ground at all times.

Tsugi-Ashi: The purpose of the shuffling foot, or step, is to change the position of the hands and feet in order to avoid an attack or confuse an opponent. This maneuver allows the practitioner to alternate the direction of the stance while keeping the opponent within range for effective blocks or counterattacks. For instance, to shuffle from a right foot forward Zenkutsu-dachi to a left foot forward Zenkutsu-dachi, the weight of the body is momentarily shifted to the rear left leg while retracting the right foot (practically sliding it on the ground) until it is parallel and almost touching the left foot. The left foot is positioned quickly in the forward Zenkutsu stance. The hands are switched simultaneously with the feet. The shuffling step is performed quickly and smoothly. The foot shuffle may be repeated several times or combined with other foot movements.

Yori-Ashi: Literally translated as dragging feet, the motion of the rear foot is more like sliding than dragging. The mechanics of the movement are similar to that of sliding except that the motion is started with the rear foot moving toward the front foot, while the front foot remains stationary and bears the weight of the entire body. The front foot may then be pushed forward, sideways or not moved at all. For instance, when executing a right Yoko-geri from a left forward stance, the weight of the body is shifted momentarily to the front foot. The right foot slides along the diagonal of the imaginary rectangle until it is next to the left foot. When both knees are flexed, a right side kick is executed.

Kezami-Ashi: Kezami-Ashi is for all intents and purposes a two step oi-ashi. It is a shorter oi-ashi followed by a short but dynamic forward step by the same leading foot. It is an effective method of chasing and hitting a retreating target. It is also an effective way of reaching a target when starting from a short stance, say a renoji-dachi or short zenkutsu-dachi. In a regular oi-ashi, going from zenkutsu–dachi to zenkutsu-dachi, the rear foot travels approximately four shoulder widths forward. However if the target is too close, the attacker may decide to advance the rear foot three shoulder widths only. Now, if the target moves back half a shoulder width, the attacker can continue the forward motion, without stopping, by stepping the front foot by the same distance. The transition between the short oi-dachi and the next step is smooth and without delay.

Soke Kubota encourages his students to:

"Use smooth, relaxed and rapid footwork to avoid becoming a stationary target in free style sparring."

In advanced karate, body movement is used frequently to add momentum to a kick, thrust, or block. The Oi-tsuki, or lunge punch, is a good example of a body-augmented thrusting attack. Both Shotokan and Gosoku-ryu katas contain multiple combinations of body movements and footwork. Gosoku-ryu Kihon katas were developed specifically by Soke Kubota to make it easier to learn karate basics with appropriate emphasis on correct and faster methods of body shifting and footwork.

Miscellaneous Steps

The following less common steps also are encountered in karate practice:

Step	Meaning
Okuri-ashi	Slow sliding step
Fumikumi-ashi	Stamping step
Mawari-ashi	Turning step
Kosa-ashi	Crossed leg step
Da-ashi	Snake walking step
Hiraki-ashi	Open leg step
Hebi-ashi	Snake-like, zig zag

CHAPTER 10

Body Parts as Means of Offense and Defense

Karate-do is a means of achieving personal improvement through systematic training of the body (Tai), mind (Shin), and spirit (Kokoro). Processes involved in learning martial arts strengthen the body, develop the mind, and refine the spirit. True karate-do places greater emphasis on the spiritual aspects of martial arts.

From a holistic point of view, the mind, body, and spirit are integral parts of each other. Spiritual strength is accomplished partly through methodical development of the mind, and training of the body as well.

In karate-do, the physical training of the body is achieved through the practice of the art of empty hand combat. In a combat situation, the powers of the mind, body, and spirit combine to transform the individual into an arsenal within a human fortress. The mind plans the strategies, the body provides the weaponry, and the spirit supplies the guiding power or inner energy. The entire body becomes a single, unified weapons system. All parts of the body become the means of offense and defense.

The manner in which a body part is used to block or deliver a strike is known as waza, or technique. Knowing the names of the body parts used in karate is essential for learning the basic techniques encountered in training.

Although the entire body is mobilized in freestyle fighting, the hands and the feet are the principal weapons of unarmed combat. Strategically, an opponent sees hands and feet, as well as arms and legs, as major potential

sources of attack. Karate techniques that make use of different parts of the hands and feet are designed specifically to nullify or minimize damage sustained by these body parts in practice and real combat.

The effective use of the limbs as a means of offense and defense is the result of proper application of scientific principles to the movements of the body. The remarkable psychological and physiological attributes of karate-do are demonstrated best by the art of Tameshiwari. Here, the principles of science and psychology are combined to illustrate higher levels of achievement in karate practice. It is not the object of this book to elaborate on the scientific or practical aspects of all karate techniques. However, a useful section has been provided to illustrate the basic applications of the laws of physics to the elementary combinations of some common techniques.

A short glossary of terms used to describe parts of the hands and feet, as well as techniques incorporating movements of the arms and legs, can be found in the following three sections. This information is provided to supplement what the student learns at dojo practice.

Parts of the hand/arm	Meaning	Basic application
TE	hand/arm	offense/defense
WAN	arm	offense/defense
GAIWAN	outer arm	blocking & striking

HAIWAN	back of arm	blocking & striking
NAIWAN	inner arm	blocking & striking
SEIKEN	forefist/ two knuckled fist	direct punching
URAKEN	reverse punch using back fist	face/temples/ribs
RIKEN	outward back fist	face/temples/ribs
TETTSUI/KENTSUI	hammer fist/ bottom fist	head/hard areas
SHUTO	knife hand/ outer edge	head/neck
KOKEN	back of the wrist	blocking/striking
HAITO	ridge hand/ inner edge	face/ribs neck/groin
IPPON KEN	one finger fist bent forefinger	plexus/head/body
IPPON NUKITE	one finger spear hand	eyes/plexus
NIHON NUKITE	two fingers spear hand	eyes
NUKITE	fingers	direct attack
YONHON NUKITE	four fingers/ spear hand	plexus/ribs/throat
HAISHU	back hand	face
KAKUTO	top side of the wrist	blocking
HIRAKEN	four knuckles half clenched fist	nose/mouth/plexus
KEIKO	bear hand	nose
KUMADE	bear hand	ears
UDE	forearm	blocking/striking
EMPI	elbow	chin/chest/ribs
SHOTEI / SHO	palm	chin/face/plexus
TEISHO	palm heel/ within forearm	chin/face
SEOI / KATA	shoulder	throwing/blocking
SEIRYUTO	ox jaw hand	collar bone
TEKUBI	wrist	chin/blocking
Parts of the foot/leg	**Meaning**	**Basic application**
KANZETSU	joint	to be protected
ASHI	foot/leg	offense & defense
HIZA	knee	ribs/abdomen/face

SOKUTO	knife foot/ outside edge	jaw/armpit/knee
KAKATO	heel	instep/groin/body
TSUME SAKI	toes/tips of toes	armpit/ribs/groin
CHUSOKU	ball of foot	abdomen/chest/face
HAISOKU	instep	groin/body/face
KOSHI	ball of foot	abdomen/temple/jaw
TEISOKU	sole of the foot	sweeping/blocking
KAJI	thigh	blocking
ASHI KUBI	ankle	to be protected
HIZA GASHIRA	knee cap	to be protected
KOBORE	tibia	to be protected

Parts of the head	Meaning	Basic application
CHOTO	nose	to be defended
KEICHU	back of head/neck	to be defended
KUBI	neck	to be defended
ATAMA	head	to be defended/headbutt
MIMI	ears	to be defended
KASUMI	temples	to be defended
TENTO	top of skull	to be defended
MEN	face	to be defended
HICHU	Adam's apple	to be defended
KAMI	hair	to be defended
HITAI	forehead	to be protected

Parts of the torso	Meaning	Basic Application
HARA	abdomen/stomach	to be protected
KINTEKI	testicles	to be protected
KYOSEN	solar plexus	to be protected
KOSHI	hips	to be protected
MUNE	chest	to be protected
KODENKO	spine	to be protected

The short list of items presented above contains only a very small number of body parts referred to in karate-do. Advanced karate-do begins with a better understanding of the human body, its functions, physiology, and a recognition of the vital points as targets of offense and defense.

CATEGORIES OF TECHNIQUES

Karate may be practiced in two different ways: individually and with a partner. Training with a partner, or opponent, is known as kumite and will be discussed later in this book. Training without a partner generally consists of practicing prearranged combinations of techniques, as in kata, or repeating randomly arranged combinations of techniques selected by an instructor for a particular training session. A detailed discussion of individual training forms will be presented later in this book.

A karate technique generally is defined as a unique body movement designed to subdue an opponent with a single decisive action, such as a strike, throw, choke hold, sweep or pin down. However, as with any broad definition, there are many exceptions to, and variations of, the rule. In reality, there are no limitations on the types of techniques, combinations or methods that may be used to subdue an opponent.

In a life and death situation, a simple, decisive blow delivered to a vital body point is the best way to subdue an uncontrollable adversary. A student also may resort to effective grappling or throwing techniques, depending on the situation. In other words, no empty hand technique is excluded from karate.

Gosoku-ryu's powerful and highly sophisticated system of self-defense is based on the idea that all of these individual methods of self-defense are part of the martial art known as karate. Most of these tactical elements of combat are inherent in Gosoku-ryu's repertoire of kata and self-defense systems.

Traditionally, and for the sake of simplicity, the following karate techniques have been grouped into several basic categories, including but not limited to those highlighted below.

Method	Name	Example
Hand techniques	TE-WAZA	a punch
Foot techniques	ASHI-WAZA	a kick
Crushing techniques	ATE-WAZA	a knee strike
Throwing techniques	NAGE-WAZA	a shoulder throw
Joint twisting and bending	KANZETSU-WAZA	an arm lock
Techniques of vital points	ATEMI-WAZA	a temple strike
Break fall techniques	UKEMI-WAZA	a forward roll
Pinning techniques	OSAE-WAZA	a pin down
Strangulation techniques	SHIME-WAZA	a choke hold
Grappling techniques	KATAME-WAZA	a body hold
Freeing techniques	TOKI-WAZA	from a hold
Stabbing technique	SASHI-WAZA	a spear hand

Thrusting techniques	TSUKI-WAZA	a reverse punch
Striking techniques	UCHI-WAZA	knife hand strike
Blocking techniques	UKE-WAZA	an upper block
Sweeping techniques	HARAI-WAZA	a leg sweep
Stopping techniques	TOME-WAZA	an "X" block
Dodging techniques	KAWASHI-WAZA	leaning sideways
Rolling techniques	KAITEN MI WAZA	a cartwheel
Reverse hand techniques	GYAKU-TE WAZA	a hand twist
Sacrificing techniques	SUTEMI WAZA	protecting heart
Flying or jumping techniques	TOBI WAZA	jumping kick
Secret techniques	KAKUSHI-WAZA	
Misc techniques	SONOTA-WAZA	

Each technique in each group of waza has its own merits and specific applications in empty hand combat. For instance, the ushiro empi uchi, which is an ate-waza, is suited to close quarters fighting or when the body is held from behind, the kezami tsuki, which is a te-waza, is better suited to defending yourself at a normal distance. All of these waza are very powerful and highly effective means of offense and defense, but they become even more effective and powerful when used in combination in a naturally occurring sequence of actions.

The scope of this section is limited to the introduction of the terms defining offensive, or Ko-geki, and defensive, or Han-geki, movements of the Te-waza and Ashi-waza categories only. However, students should know Soke's thoughts on the variety of karate waza:

"Karate is not only kicking and punching. Your kicks and punches might be strong, but choke holds and other waza in self-defense give you even more power."

For help in proper application and correct execution of these techniques, students should seek advice from Soke or one of his higher ranking instructors. The variety and complexity of karate waza indeed are overwhelming. Not many individuals can dream of reaching proficiency in more than a handful of categories of techniques. However, there are those who have devoted most of their lives to the study of the art and have reached complete mastery of most karate waza. Soke Kubota is one of very few persons in the history of modern karate-do whose mastery of the art has surpassed the limits of the categories discussed in this section.

BASIC DEFENSIVE TECHNIQUES: HAN-GEKI

Philosophy of defense

In karate-do, as in all martial arts, students are taught to value peace over conflict, defense over offense and to divert an assailant's attack rather than maim him. Graceful but effective blocking is preferred to inefficient striking.

Karateka never deliver a first strike unless the assailant is armed or uncontrollable. IKA rules are very clear about the use of force. Dojo rules repeatedly remind IKA students to "refrain from violent behavior." Soke's message implies that it is unethical to use karate for any purpose other than promoting the cause of justice. According to an old Japanese motto, "True karate begins and ends with blocking."

However, if the need arises, Soke advises readiness with a strong defensive strategy before launching an attack.

Soke also advocates the use of blocking with Gosoku-ryu karate. In the Gosoku-ryu style, all techniques are focused and decisive, with blocking techniques often executed with such power and speed they discourage the assailant from further attack. A single, well-executed karate technique, either defensive or offensive, can be powerful enough to break through a dozen wooden boards, crush a number of concrete tiles, or maim an assailant. Soke teaches how to meet force with force—the hard style of defense—but also emphasizes the soft style, or how to redirect an opponent's energy. Soke also teaches:

"Whenever possible, blocks should tend to deflect, rather than stop, a strike."

The following glossary gives the names and meanings of most of the basic defensive techniques used in karate-do.

Technique	Description Application	to defend
AGE UKE	rising block	head/shoulders
JODAN UKE	upper level block	neck/head/face
CHUDAN UKE	middle level block	midsection/chest/ribs
SOTO UKE	outward block	frontal attack
UCHI UKE	inward block	frontal attack
GEDAN BARAI	lower block/sweep	groin/abdomen
CHUDAN UCHI UKE	middle inward block	midsection/plexus
CHUDAN SOTO UKE	middle outward block	midsection/plexus
SOKUMEN UKE	block to the side	head/ribs/sides
HARAI UKE	side sweeping block	direct thrusts, strikes
YOKO UKE	side block	side hooks
KOSA UKE	cross block	all regions
KAGE UKE	hook block	midsection
KO UKE	wrist block	upper body/face
HIJI UKE	elbow block	head/chest
NAGASHI UKE	sweeping block	abdomen/groin
MOROTE UKE	double hand block	midsection
UDE UKE	forearm block	head/chest
SOTO UDE UKE	outside forearm blocking	midsection/head
UCHI UDE UKE	inside forearm blocking	midsection/head
SHUTO UKE	knifehand block	midsection/head/groin
SHUTO UCHI UKE	knife hand inward block	midsection/head
SHUTO SOTO UKE	knife hand outward block	midsection/head
HAITO UKE	insideridge hand block	midsection/head/groin
UDE BARAI	forearm sweep	midsection/plexus
TSUKAMI UKE	grasping or gripping block	arms or legs
OTOSHI UKE	dropping block	groin/abdomen
TSURE-TE UKE	crane hand block	face/head
KENTSUI UKE	hammer hand block	all levels
HAISHU UKE	back hand block	middle/upper level
KAISHU UKE	open hand block	middle/lower level
JUJI UKE	X block	groin/head

JODAN JUJI UKE	upper X block	head/chest/shoulders
GEDAN JUJI UKE	lower X block	groin/abdomen
KAKIWAKE UKE	wedge block	grasping lapels
KAKUTO UKE	bent wrist block	head/face/chest/neck
TEISHO UKE	palm heel block	mid/lower region
SHOTEI UKE	palm block	mid/lower region
URA UKE	back hand block	head/chest
KURI UKE	circular elbow block	head/chest
HARI UKE	bow and arrow block	head/chest
OSAE UKE	pressing block	abdomen/groin/head
SUKUI UKE	scooping block	against front kick
SOTO SUKUI UKE	outward scooping block	against front kick
UCHI SUKUI UKE	inward scooping block	against front kick
MAWASHI UKE	round house block	body/groin
HIZA UKE	knee block	groin
NAMI ASHI UKE	inside snapping block	abdomen/groin
MIKATSUKI GERI UKE	crescent kick block	knife/punch/block
ASHI UKE	shin block	groin/abdomen
KAJI UKE	thigh block	groin/stomach
KOKEN UKE	back of wrist block	upper/mid-section
TETSUI UKE	hammer fist block	all levels
NAGE UKE	throwing block	pick up opponent
HAIWAN NAGASHI UKE	back arm sweeping block	punch or kick
KAGE SHUTO UKE	hooking knife hand block	mid-section/plexus
TATE SHUTO UKE	vertical knife hand block	head/chest
TEKUBI KAGE UKE	wrist hook block	punch or kick
GOSOKU UKE	hard-fast block	multiple blocking

Contrary to common belief, karate-do is not an aggressive sport. It is a way of replacing aggression with self-control and substituting fear for confidence. Karate-do always begins with a block and ends with a block. Between these two blocks there might exist many effective striking techniques.

The physical quality of body movements depends largely on the ability of the muscles to expand or contract. Two factors govern the quality of a technique: first, the correct execution of the technique,

including the position of the body and limbs in space, and the manner of arriving at that position; second, the amount of speed or power needed to perform the technique. Both of these factors are demonstrated most effectively by a qualified instructor in a dojo environment. The next section describes the names and meanings of some of the most commonly used offensive techniques in empty hand combat.

OFFENSIVE TECHNIQUES: KOGEKI

Philosophy of offense

Soke says, "In offense, the student must be taught to overcome the opponent mentally." He teaches the concept of focusing one's entire being, mind, body, and spirit, on establishing superiority, thereby making the opponent feel completely overwhelmed. Soke advocates self-control at all times. True karateka respect the notion "Karate ni sente nashi," or "There is no first attack in karate." Karateka never deliver a first strike against an unarmed adversary. All offensive techniques usually are preceded by a Uke-waza, or blocking technique. The basic offensive hand techniques listed below are divided into two categories; thrusting techniques, or tsuki-waza, and striking techniques, or Uchi-waza. In general, thrusting techniques are more powerful and tend to crush the target area. Striking techniques are faster and tend to break the target point. A short listing of some of these techniques is presented below.

TE WAZA – Hand Techniques

These techniques involve the use of all large and small and sides of all parts of the arms and hands, including knuckles and shoulders. The hand is the most prominent weapon in the karate arsenal. It also is one of the most vulnerable parts of the body.

Term	Meaning	Application
TSUKI	punch/thrust	striking/blocking
UCHI	strike	striking/blocking
JODAN TSUKI	upper level punch	face/head
CHUDAN TSUKI	middle level punch	chest/abdomen
GEDAN TSUKI	lower level punch	lower body
HIRAKEN TSUKI	foreknuckle punch	upper/middle regions
SEIKEN TSUKI	two knuckle punch	upper/middle regions
KAGE TSUKI	hook punch	upper/middle regions
YAMA TSUKI	U/mountain punch	upper/middle
AWASE TSUKI	two handed punch	upper/middle regions
MOROTE TSUKI	two fisted punch	upper/middle regions
NAGASHI TSUKI	flowing/diverting punch	upper/middle regions
CHUKO TSUKI	straight punch	chest/abdomen
URA TSUKI	reversed fist/ close punch	body/close combat
AGE TSUKI	rising punch	chin/face
REN TSUKI	alternate punches	body/face/head
NUKITE TSUKI	finger thrust	face/body/solar plexus
SHOTEI TSUKI	palm heel thrust	chest/chin/face
FURI TSUKI	circular swing punch	head/ribs
MAWASHI TSUKI	round hook punch	head/ribs
TATE TSUKI	vertical fist punch	abdomen/chest
KIZAMI TSUKI	leading jab punch	face/head
OI TSUKI	lunge punch	head/body
GYAKU TSUKI	reverse punch	head/body
SUN TSUKI	one inch punch	face/solar plexus
HASAMI TSUKI	scissors punch	legs
HEIKO TSUKI	parallel punch	body/chest
OTOSHI TSUKI	descending punch	testicles/groin
SANBON TSUKI	triple punch	body/chest

IPPON KEN TSUKI	one knuckle punch	solar plexus/temples
TEISHO TSUKI	palm heel thrust	face/solar plexus
HIRA NUKITE TSUKI	horizontal finger thrust	body/ribs
EIDO TSUKI	twin round house punches	head/ribs
TEISHO UCHI	palm heel strike	middle level
MOROTE UCHI	double hand strike	head/ribs
KEITO UCHI	joint of thumb strike	temples/ribs/neck
TETTSUI UCHI	bottom fist strike	temples/ribs/neck
HAITO UCHI	ridge hand strike	temples/neck
HAISHU UCHI	back hand strike	temples/ears
SHUTO UCHI	knife hand strike	neck/head
URAKEN UCHI	back knuckle strike	face
KOKEN UCHI	bent wrist strike	chin
KAISHU UCHI	open hand slap	general
EMPI UCHI/ HIJI UCHI	elbow strike	body/face
MAE EMPI UCHI	forward elbow strike	chest/face
AGE EMPI UCHI	rising elbow strike	chest/chin
YOKO EMPI UCHI	sideways elbow strike	ribs/chest/head
USHIRO EMPI UCHI	backward elbow strike	ribs/chest/head
TA TE EMPI UCHI	vertical elbow strike	spine/head
OTOSHI EMPI UCHI	descending elbow strike	spine/head
MAWASH EMPI UCHI	round house elbow strike	face/chest/ribs
GEDAN SHUTO UCHI	lower knife	hands/legs
YOKO SHUTO UCHI	side knife hand strike	head/neck/ribs
JODAN SHUTO UCHI	upper knife hand strike	head/neck/ribs
CHUDAN SHUTO UCHI	middle knife hand strike	head/neck/ribs
FURI SHUTO UCHI	diagonal knife hand strike	general
HOJI OTOSHI	augmented push	body/trunk
KUMADE UCHI	bear hand strike	face/chest
ASHI/GERI WAZA	foot and kicking techniques	

KERI WAZA – Foot Techniques

The best way to learn and become familiar with foot and leg techniques is first to get into shape, i.e., to develop sufficient strength, flexibility and balance, then study some basic standing forms, and then actually perform them repeatedly in the presence of qualified instructors. Some standing forms provide better platforms for certain kicking techniques than others.

Term	Meaning	Basic application
KERI/GERI	kick	offense and defense
MAE GERI	front kick	middle/upper level
MAE GERI KE AGE	front snap kick	abdomen/face
MAE GERI KE KOMI	front thrust kick	abdomen/groin
MAE GERI FUMI KOMI	front stamp thrust	lower regions
USHIRO GERI	back kick	groin/body/head
USHIRO GERI KE AGE	rising back kick	head/chest
USHIRO GERI KE KOMI	thrusting back kick	groin/abdomen
USHIRO GERI FUMI KOMI	stamping back kick	legs/feet
KIN GERI	groin kick with instep	testicles
UCHI MAWASHI GERI	inside roundhouse kick	face/ribs/thighs
SOTO MAWASH GERI	outside roundhouse kick	head/ribs/thighs
USHIRO MAWASHI GERI	backward roundhouse kick	head/back/neck
GYAKU MAWASHI GERI	back roundhouse kick	head/ribs/face
URA MAWASHI GERI	reverse roundhouse kick	head/spine/neck
KANSETSU GERI	stamping joint kick	knee cap
MIKATSUKI GERI	crescent kick	ribs/thighs/head
HIZA GERI/ HITSUI GERI	knee kick	ribs/groin
FURI GERI	swing kick	general
TOBI GERI	jumping kick	head/body
TOBI MAE GERI	jumping front kick	head/body
TOBI YOKO GERI	jumping side kick	head/body
TOBI USHIRO GERI	jumping back kick	head/body
REN GERI	double snap kick front foot first	as applicable

BODY PARTS AS A MEANS OF OFFENSE AND DEFENSE

NIDAN GERI	double snap kick back foot first	as applicable
SOKUTO GERI	knife foot kick/side kick	legs/body head
KAKATO GERI	heel kick	as applicable
TSUME SAKI GERI	toe tip kick	as applicable
YOKO GERI	side kick	legs/body head
YOKO GERI KE AGE	rising side kick	head/neck/chest
YOKO GERI KE KOMI	thrusting side kick	abdomen/groin
YOKO GERI FUMI KOMI	stamping side kick	knee/legs/feet
TAORE GERI	falling/ground kick	defensive kick
KAKATO OTOSHI	heel drop	hard areas
ASHI BARAI	foot sweep/leg sweep	disturbing balance
OKURI ASHI BARAI	two feet sweep	disturbing balance
KESA GERI	diagonal kick	general
USHIRO KAKATO GERI	back of heel kick	groin
SANKAKU TOBI GERI	three way jump kick	
ATAMA WAZA	Head technique	

ATAMA WAZA – Head Techniques

Head techniques are not part of the training program at IKA. They are very difficult techniques to control and use effectively. However, they are demonstrated and discussed from time to time, only by highly experienced instructors, so that the students would not be totally unaware of such techniques. Students are advised to use head techniques only as last resort.

Term	Meaning	Application
TSU TSUKI	forehead attack	face/nose/chest
ATAMA YOKO UCHI	side head strike	face/nose/chest
ATAMA USHIRO UCHI	backward head strike	face/nose/chest
ATAMA UCHI	skull attack	face/nose/chest

In karate there are no short cuts or easy methods. Both the blocking and attacking techniques must be practiced frequently and correctly to develop the reflexes needed to execute them efficiently and effectively.

The list of waza introduced in this section is by no means complete. These waza are the basic skills from which others can be developed. The best way to learn the names of these techniques is to say them out loud while practicing on your own. Learning and mastering karate skills is discussed in Chapter 15.

CHAPTER 11

Karate-Do and Basic Science

Karate-do generally is associated with a large number of interpretations and sentiments, each of which adds value to the beneficial nature of the practice. It is, however, a highly scientific discipline developed to protect society and enrich the lives of its practitioners.

All fundamental concepts of karate-do are based on principles of psychology, physiology, physics, and applied mechanics. The scope of this chapter is confined to a brief discussion of the mechanical aspects of karate practice.

Notions of strength and brute force commonly associated with the ability to displace heavy objects are neither applicable to karate-do nor do they properly define the act of performing work.

The nature of the dynamic forces encountered in karate practice is similar to those observed in the throwing events of track and field. The effort made in delivering a tsuki or throwing a javelin is quite different from the static type of work needed to perform a bench press. In karate, muscular power alone will not accomplish the task. Muscular power must be combined with speed of movement to generate high momentum at impact.

Force and momentum are felt and implied but not seen. Their effects can be seen, felt, and measured. Both momentum and force can be described in terms of their magnitude, direction, and point of application. Karate training, however, can be considered scientific only when it is conducted on the basis of correct physical and physiological principles.

The remarkable physiological and psychological attributes of practical karate-do are demonstrated most effec-

tively by the spectacular act of Tameshiwari. Brittle objects, such as blocks of ice, layers of bricks, concrete tiles, or wood boards are broken into pieces with a single powerful strike. The act of Tameshiwari is an excellent example of the generation of force through speed and the union of mind, body and spirit at the moment of impact. In Tameshiwari, the principles of science and psychology combine to illustrate higher levels of achievement in karate practice.

Trying to understand the mechanics of karate-do can be difficult. There is a multiplicity of unknown factors and precise analysis often is impossible. As in any form of physical activity, the principles of rigid body mechanics can be used with some degree of accuracy to introduce the theoretical features of the art.

The main purpose of this chapter is to draw attention to the scientific aspects of empty hand combat through practical examples and the analysis of a simple combination. The following sections should provide interested students with enough basic information to be of real value to their growing understanding of practical karate-do.

DEFINITIONS OF SCIENTIFIC TERMS

Karate practitioners frequently use such scientific terms as power and speed to communicate and compare the qualities of their techniques. The concepts of force and motion are fundamental to karate practice.

To appreciate the mechanics of karate-do, students must understand the meaning of some of the scientific terms used to qualify and quantify karate action. For this reason, we will define some of the basic terms commonly used in daily training. Two simple examples are provided to explain the meaning of each term: one as the concept might be explained in general, and a second example illustrating how it applies in terms of karate training. Hopefully, these definitions and examples will help students gain insight into the inner workings of basic karate techniques and the scientific aspects of karate-do.

Terms	**Definitions and Examples**
Motion	Displacement of a body in space.

	The flight of a ball in the air.
	Karateka performing kata
Linear Motion	Displacement of an object along a straight line.
	Car traveling along a straight road.
	Chuko-tsuki delivered to a target.
Circular Motion	Displacement of an object along a circular curve.
	Movement of the earth around the sun.
	A Mawashi-Geri delivered to an opponent's head.
Velocity	Distance traveled per unit of time in a certain direction.
	Running 100 meters in 10 seconds or at 22.5 miles per hour going north.
	Velocity of the fist in Oi-tsuki, 30 miles per hour in the direction of the target.
Speed	The measure of velocity or distance traveled per unit of time, regardless of direction.
	The message implied by the speed limit sign.
	Developing hand or body speed in karate.
Acceleration	Rate of change of velocity.
	A car reaching a velocity of 60 miles per hour in six seconds.
	A tsuki starting from rest at zero velocity and reaching its target at maximum velocity over a very short period of time. Also the time needed to develop a certain velocity at impact.
Force	The effect that one body has on changing the shape or position of another. Also, mass of a body times its acceleration in space.
	That which tends to squeeze a spring.
	The force of a tsuki punching a bag.
Inertia	Property of matter by which it remains at rest or in motion, unless acted upon by an external force.
	What a sprinter has to overcome after the finish line to keep from running forever.

	What must be overcome to keep a powerful tsuki from making contact with an opponent. The inertia of the forward moving hand must be reduced to zero to avoid contact with the target.
Reaction	Resistance or opposition to force.
	Tension of the arm muscles experienced in the arms during a bench press because of the force of the arms against the weight raised overhead.
	The horizontal frictional force generated between the underside of the feet and the ground when performing chuko-tsuki on a bag. Also, the sliding backward of a puncher standing on roller blades due to the absence of frictional resistance.
Magnitude	The amount of force.
	The amount of weight lifted overhead.
	The force of a tsuki at impact.
Work	Product of force and distance.
	Lifting a weight overhead.
	Mawashi-Geri to opponent's head. Raising the weight of the foot and leg from rest to a certain height.
Energy	Capacity to perform work.
	The energy needed to climb a mountain.
	The energy needed to perform a kata.
Kinetic Energy	Energy of an object by virtue of its motion.
	The energy of a bullet flying through the air.
	The energy generated in a forward moving snap kick or body punch.
Potential Energy	Capacity or energy by virtue of position or shape.
	Energy stored in a compressed spring.
	Energy stored in a retracted arm before delivering a punch.
Power	Rate at which work is performed.
	Pushing a weight overhead quickly, or raising it slowly.
	A tsuki with higher velocity delivers more power at impact than a slower tsuki.

Center of Gravity	A point within an object that has the property of representing the effects of the total mass of that object.
	The midpoint of a uniform rod.
	The point believed to be located approximately two inches below the navel, within the abdomen of a human being.
Balance	The ability to establish equilibrium at rest or in motion.
	Riding a bicycle or walking a tightrope without falling down.
	Performing kata, without the body wavering.
Pressure	Amount of force per unit area.
	The average body weight sustained by the bottom of the feet for every square inch of contact area.
	The force of a tsuki distributed over the small surface of a knuckle.
Stress	Amount of internal pressure sustained by objects.
	Pressure induced in the bones of the arm when lifting a weight overhead, and developed in the muscles of the arms when lowering or pushing the same weight.
	Tension induced in the muscles of the arm by a retracted arm position. Compression produced in the bones at the impact of a fully extended punch.
Strength	The capacity of materials to resist force.
	The ability of a reinforced concrete column to hold up a freeway bridge despite the force of gravity.
	The ability to remain stationary when one is pushed. The ability of the boards to keep from breaking in Tameshiwari.
Momentum	The quantity of motion possessed by an object; or the product of mass and velocity.
	A marble possessing the same momentum as a cannon ball, given sufficient velocity.

KARATE-DO AND BASIC SCIENCE

	A fist moving twice as fast as a fist that is twice as heavy.
Impulse	The act of motion through sudden force, or a force so applied as to produce motion suddenly.
	The kick against the shoulder generated by a gun when it is fired in the same direction, or the force of the explosion itself.
	A short jab to an opponent's face, or the fast twist of the wrist before a tsuki hits its target.
Resultant	Net effect of forces acting on a body.
	The sum of the forces of six horses pulling in the same direction. The sum of the weights carried by both legs in a front stance.

Karate techniques are meant to achieve maximum results from a given expenditure of energy. Indeed, optimum expenditure of energy will result only when the scientific principles of karate techniques are observed.

To understand energy is to understand life. As life goes on, so does energy. As a basic law of nature, energy can neither be created nor destroyed. It only can be modified from one form to another. Karateka transform the chemical energy stored in their muscles into kinetic energy through movement. Muscles gain energy by absorbing carbohydrates, fats and proteins, which ultimately are plant products and as such depend on energy derived from the sun.

Trajectory type techniques, such as kicking, thrusting, and striking, are analyzed most effectively through the concept of momentum rather than energy.

Karate mainly uses force to change the state of motion of an adversarial target by slowing it down, stopping it, or diverting it. The act of blocking, as in a Gedan-barai, is meeting force with force, and entails absorbing a reaction. The Nagashi-uke tends to divert the momentum of an impending strike through softer contact.

Karateka should realize that all students differ in body height, weight, musculoskeletal characteristics, flexibility, and personal and psychological traits. These factors affect the path of action, as well as the magnitude, speed, and accuracy of their techniques.

While the universal laws of physics are applicable equally to all body forms, the quality of performance can be analyzed only by considering the laws of physics in conjunction with the laws of biology, psychology, and other human attributes.

Undoubtedly, all students would like to improve their techniques and optimize their efforts by applying the principles of science as much as possible. Although a good knowledge of these principles is highly desirable, there is no guarantee that such knowledge alone will enable the student to perform the technique as perfectly as desired. A student's mind may be capable of grasping and visualizing the scientific basis of a perfect karate technique, but the untrained body may not be able to perform it accordingly.

For instance, a student may be aware of the theoretical requirements for performing a Mawashi-geri-jodan, or an upper level round house kick, but his body may not be flexible enough to raise his knee above his waist. For this reason, it is vitally important for students to train their bodies, under the supervision of a qualified instructor, in such a way that the commands of the mind will be obeyed as accurately and powerfully as desired.

A brief account of the process of learning through repeated practice is presented in Chapter 15.

To demonstrate the effects of the mind-body-spirit connection, and the applications of the principles of science to the evolution of karate-do, read the analysis of the simple Oi-tsuki discussed in detail in the next section. Again, the object is not to teach the Oi-tsuki, but rather to complement the student's practical knowledge with the corresponding scientific background.

It has been established experimentally by Professor Yoshio Kato and Grand Master Nakayama that the terminal speed of a straight punch delivered by an expert karateka is about 5.2 meters per second. The terminal speed of a lunge punch delivered by the same karateka is 8.2 meters per second.

The same experiments resulted in the conclusion that both the body and hand speeds of an expert karateka were twice as fast as that of a beginner. This also implies that the force generated by the expert is practically twice as much as that produced by the beginner.

THE ANALYSIS OF A BASIC COMBINATION

The number of combinations of movements in karate-do is so large that it would be impossible to compile an analysis of all conceivable variations in a single volume. However, once students grasp the basic principles needed to analyze a simple combination, they will be able to unlock the mysteries of more complex permutations with relative ease and sufficient accuracy.

To illustrate the important components of a basic combination, we will examine the case of the Oi-tsuki, starting from a left forward front stance. This technique is taught to all beginners during their first few lessons. This important combination, together with the Gyaku-tsuki, is the most popular technique practiced in all dojos and encountered in most katas.

The lunge punch is the most natural fighting tool available to man. In spite of its apparent complexities, it is relatively easy to perform. Whether it is performed effectively and efficiently is something that students might ask after developing an understanding of the information contained in this section.

The methods of analysis presented in this manual are applicable to both the Shotokan and Gosoku-ryu styles practiced at IKA. However, by comparing the katas of Gosoku-ryu karate with those of Shotokan and other well-known styles, it may appear that Gosoku-ryu combinations tend to rely more on the principles of science than other traditional as well as contemporary styles.

Both the Shotokan and Gosoku-ryu styles advocate generation of momentum by sequential production of force rather than by simultaneous creation of the same effect. As its name implies, speed is an essential ingredient of the Gosoku-ryu style.

In all blocking and striking techniques, the result obtained is dependent on the speed of performance. An efficient thrusting waza is one in which the practitioner utilizes the forces of the entire body over the greatest range possible.

The speed of the hand or foot at impact is proportional to the average force exerted through the center of gravity by the fist or foot. All things being equal, the greater the body forces, the greater the speed at impact.

The effective force at impact is the sum of all the components of the body forces acting in that direction. In Oi-tsuki, the horizontal components of all body forces are combined to create maximum horizontal speed at the knuckles of the forefist upon impact.

The chain of events and the important phenomena that compose the Oi-tsuki consists of the following components:

Kokoro That which empowers the mind and spirit with determination, willpower, awareness, confidence, tranquility, and control. The Kokoro, literally the guts, prepares and executes the plan of attack, in this case a right hand Oi-tsuki from a left forward stance, by coordinating the movements of the body and controlling the flow of energy. The Kokoro instructs the neuromuscular system of the body to remain soft and relaxed during all phases of the attack until kime, or the finish, when it becomes hard and tensed at the completion of the last segment of the technique.

Dachi The standing form that provides the ability to launch, drive, and boost the entire body forward with sufficient initial velocity while maintaining control and balance during motion and landing. The ready position is a left side forward Zenkutsu-dachi. The initial charge is accomplished by the forceful thrust of the right foot against the ground and the momentary shifting of the weight of the body over to the front foot.

Hanmi In the Yoi position; in this instance, the left forward Zenkutsu-dachi, the head is front facing and the hands are held high in a defensive posture. Just before the Oi-tsuki is set in motion, if the body is not already half facing, the left non-punching hand is quickly and fully extended to the front in a defensive mode while the shoulders and hips are turned into a half facing, or Hanmi, position. By doing so, the defensive posture is improved and the range and power of the Hikite is increased.

Ashi sabaki The essence of this combination is having the ability to approach a target along a straight line while gaining momentum in a state of balance over a very short period of time. The foot movement used in this case is the traditional Oi-ashi, performed in a smooth but explosive manner. As the right foot moves forward, the left leg tenses up in anticipation of the next leg thrust just before the right hand connects with the target. Greatest force is achieved when both feet are firmly in contact with the ground at impact.

Hikite As the feet are brought together just before completing the step, the striking fist falls to the right hip with palm facing upward. As the foot movement continues, the outstretched hand is retracted with great power, as if pulling the opponent's hand and delivering a back elbow strike, simultaneously rotating the pelvis counterclockwise to increase the speed of the driving action. At the same time as the reactive hand is being pulled back, the right fist begins its motion toward the target with the same power and intensity as the left hand. This maneuver, which is known as the Hikite, gives extra power to the right hand thrust technique that is on its way toward the target.

Waza The hand technique is the basic Choku-tsuki, which is delivered at a much higher speed than is achieved from Hachiji-dachi or Kiba-dachi. The punch is delivered in a straight line to the target with the back of the fist facing down. As the thrust nears full extension, the right hand is rotated strongly into final position with the back of the fist facing up. To this point and just before impact, the body is relaxed and in motion, with no muscle fully extended. The entire body is preparing to become motionless and fully tensed immediately after impact.

Kime This is the act of instantaneous concentration of all forces at the proper time at the proper location, or the finish. The action components described above together generate seven vectors of force, accelerating in the same general direction as the target. In order to maximize the effort, these forces are given their final impetus at impact through focus and split-second concentration. At this moment the powers of mind, body, and spirit unite to direct all neuromuscular energies toward and through the. The act of focusing is accompanied by the shout of the spirit, the kiai, adding yet another component of force to the total effort. The muscles are relaxed immediately after the kime and the body is withdrawn into a state of alert relaxation, ready for the execution of the next movement.

Kiai This is the shout executed by karateka at the moment of impact of a strong strike or block. The kiai, otherwise known as the shout of the spirit, is a unique and intense act of breathing out. Ki means spirit, or energy; ai implies union. Kiai, therefore, means the coming together of all inner power at the same time. It is most effective when performed with kime, as it involves exhaling through the sudden contraction of the abdominal muscles. The tightening of the abdominal muscles is an act of natural defense meant to protect the all-important hara, or stomach and abdomen. The roar of the kiai also is intended to boost the morale of the performer and upset the psychological balance of the opponent.

Target Whether a target, such as the opponent's solar plexus, is at rest or in motion, it represents a mass on a collision course with the approaching fist. At the moment of impact, the momentum of the attacking tsuki (punch or thrust) is converted into destructive power by the instantaneous application of kime. The momentum transferred to the target is absorbed by its mass. By the law of conservation of energy, part of the momentum becomes kinetic energy because of the movement of the target. Some of it becomes strain energy from stress to the material near and around the target. Some energy is absorbed when living tissue is crushed. The remainder is dispersed in shock waves traveling into the body. To maximize the effect of the attack, the actual target point usually is assumed to be a small distance further away from the visual target point, along the line of action of the force and within the body of the opponent.

Jiki Timing is the split-second process of decision making that leads to the selection and execution of a chain of events, such as the Oi-tsuki. This means finding or anticipating an opening and targeting it for attack. The time needed to react to a situation is called quickness, or reaction time. Quickness is a quality of timing and must not be confused with the speed or velocity of a technique. Speed is the time taken to execute the selected technique. Good timing is a state of mind and is governed by the *kokoro*. Quickness should not be confused with timing. One can be quick and still have poor timing, and vice versa. Developing a good sense of timing is of the utmost importance in empty hand combat. Without good timing, the techniques will fail. A technique executed either too late or too early often is useless. A sense of timing is achieved only with training and experience. With experience, it is possible to sense an opening before the target becomes available.

Ma-ai In executing a karate technique, the distance between the target—such as the chudan region—and the attacking body part—such as the right fist—is something that must be judged correctly and monitored and adjusted constantly. When the target is stationary or relatively slow moving, it may be reached through a single Oi-ashi. However, if both the target and the opponent are moving around, then Ma-ai becomes a matter of personal experience. Without a proper sense of distancing, no decisive or effective waza can be executed. It is important for the student to become experienced in the use of ma-ai by experimenting in different situations with different targets. The best way to understand and experience ma-ai is to engage in prearranged and semifree types of sparring.

Balance This refers both to the emotional stability of the mind and the ability of the neuromuscular system to maintain physical equilibrium. Correct balance, mental and physical, at rest and in motion, is the single most important factor in karate practice. Good balance must be preserved under all circumstances. Emotional stability is achieved most effectively by emptying the mind of all concerns, negative thoughts and preconceived ideas. Maintaining physical balance while in motion entails the continuous act of balancing the upsetting effects of body parts with the center of gravity of the body. Maintaining good balance is essential to preserving energy and executing techniques properly. Mental and physical balances are interdependent. When one is lost, the other becomes less effective. The key to developing good balance is practicing kata and random combinations of the basic techniques with emphasis on correct postures and strong stances.

Kokyu Respiration is the process by which oxygen is carried from the air to the organs and muscle systems. The breathing, or kokyu sequence, begins by taking in oxygen as the Oi-tsuki is begun. The lungs then process the oxygen while the body is still in motion. Carbon dioxide, the waste product, is exhaled as the combination is completed. During karate practice, inhaling takes place through the nose, as if smelling the air and pushing it down to the lowest regions of the lungs. Exhaling takes place through the mouth by tightening the abdominal muscles. Breathing is performed fully and from the depths of the body, from the diaphragm rather than the larynx, and it is from deep inside that the kiai emerges. The more air supplied to the lungs, the greater the energy stored in the muscles of the body. All physical exertion is performed when breath is being exhaled. All passive action is carried out when breath is being inhaled. The body should be relaxed but alert during the inhalation phase and tensed during the exhalation phase of the breathing cycle. Regulated breathing is essential to maintaining physical balance and emotional stability.

The Oi-tsuki is most common and the simplest example that could be discussed in this section. The same could also be said for more complex combinations. The reader is encouraged to repeat the analysis for a similar combination, say the Oi-gyaku-tsuki

MECHANICAL COMPONENTS OF THE OI-TSUKI

Each of the major actions described above contains additional components of neuromuscular action. Those descriptions are far beyond the scope of this section. A summary of the ten basic sources of action creating the final force of the Oi-tsuki are, in this order:

- The thrust of the right leg.
- The thrust of the left leg.
- Body rotation due to hanmi.
- Body rotation due to pelvic action.
- Shoulder rotation due to back elbow action.
- Forward movement of the right arm.

- The momentum of the body.
- Twist of the right wrist.
- The boosting effect of the finishing chime.
- The impetus of the kiai.

Motion is generated first by the largest muscles in the body, then intensified by the actions of medium-sized muscles, and eventually maximized through the use of the smallest group of muscles in the hand. It is a well-known fact that larger muscles are more powerful but slower than their smaller counterparts. Smaller muscles are weaker than larger muscles, but faster.

This sequence of events follows a basic principle of science: that a progression of speeds is needed to attain maximum velocity within a given amount time. Otherwise, deceleration would occur and the maximum velocity would not be reached at the desired moment. For this reason, Soke Kubota urges his students:

"Move first and then execute the desired technique."

CHAPTER 12

Kata

Kata literally means pattern, shape, or form. Kata generally consists of prearranged sets of maneuvers that are practiced in many of the Oriental martial arts so students can become proficient in the applications of the corresponding skills.

A karate kata, or formal exercise, is a prearranged and systematic series of karate movements in which the practitioner fights imaginary multiple opponents. A kata is choreographed so that all the important basic techniques are tied together. It is a peaceful ritualization of empty hand combat.

Since ancient times, kata has served as a means of teaching and practicing martial arts. The practice of kata still is the basis of instruction in karate. The performance of a kata to the best of one's ability truly reflects the student's mastery of the essence of karate fundamentals. In showing the challenge of combat without an opponent, the kata draws on grace, skill, coordination, and the power of the body and spirit. Kata is, in a sense, perfection in waiting.

Kata is a medium through which personal fulfillment and spiritual contentment are achieved. Experienced karateka are able to perform kata through meditation. They also can meditate through kata. Katas are unique phenomena that manifest the combined powers of mind, body and spirit in a harmonious display of combative gestures.

Each kata is the story of a battle retold through a series of classical maneuvers. Each part of each movement expresses a message and defines a purpose.

All practitioners adhere strictly to the traditional ways of performing kata. Performance of each kata is a unique personal experience and another step toward spiritual satisfaction each and every time.

Perfect kata is performed unconsciously almost as second nature. It is said that a good kata performer also is a good fighter. The reverse, however, is not necessarily true.

Perfection in kata is achieved only through systematic training, additional study, and hard work. Additional study may include attending special kata classes, understanding and visualizing the applications, viewing pictorial texts and video tapes, observing advanced students performing kata, and reading approved material regarding the history and development of traditional forms. IKA students are urged to complement their dojo training with regular viewing of approved video tapes.

There are two basic methods of teaching and learning kata. The direct method is the most common technique used at IKA and other schools of traditional karate-do. Students attempt to learn the form first; then bunkai, or its application; followed by actual practice. In the indirect, or applied, approach, students attempt to learn the kata from the bunkai. Both methods have their merits and drawbacks and depend on the availability of time, space, and qualified instructors. Most experts, however, believe the indirect approach is more effective even though it is not as time efficient as the direct method of learning, and it certainly is not suited to teaching kata to several students at the same time. For best results, students are encouraged to experiment with each system separately and, if necessary, to use them in conjunction with each other. Whatever method of learning they choose, beginners should complement their studies with systematic and repeated performance of whole, or sections of, kata, always visualizing the bunkai of each movement. When the basics are mastered, students may look forward to perfecting their performance through refinement and further practice. It usually takes the beginner only a few lessons to learn the choreography of a complete kata and a few weeks more to learn to perform it. But it takes students many years to come close to perfecting the performance.

Perhaps the most rewarding and unique aspect of kata as a means of human expression is that it can be performed by anyone regardless of sex or age, anywhere and anytime. One of the most gratifying events observed in IKA dojos is the practice of kata, where men and women of all ages, races, religions, and national origins perform group kata in a great display of individual calm and social harmony. In his famous book, "The Way of Karate," Master Funakoshi refers to kata as:

"The highest expression of karate-do."

A kata is one of the most intricate forms of expression ever developed by mankind. The essence of a kata is intertwined very closely with the nature of man and often becomes an interpretation of life itself.

There are no spoken words in kata, but the message is simple and clear. It conveys the human desire for victory of right over wrong and the triumph of good over evil. In kata, training performers visualize the movements of their opponents through the eyes of the mind and react to them by executing a defensive block followed by an appropriate offensive strike. In spiritual terms, the opponent is a reflection of the confrontation of oneself.

Asian cultures have been familiar with kata for hundreds of years but kata is relatively unknown in the United States and in most Western cultures. According to Soke:

"At the moment, most people who practice a kata have no idea of its real meaning or the benefit it brings. They practice kata and kumite as though they are two different things. Of course, kumite starts with kata and kata starts with kumite."

Therefore, all kata should be practiced with their practical uses in the mind. Each combination, even each individual waza, may have several interpretations and applications.

Rudimentary forms resembling kata are common to all cultures. For instance, the Japanese tea ceremony, classical ballet, pre-arranged chess moves, and standard military maneuvers all are examples of choreographed forms of events. Shadow boxing, strategic exercises in ball games, and methods of using tools through repeated actions are random forms of action, or crude forms of kata— designed to promote certain physical skills.

There is a key difference between karate kata and other forms of skills training. In karate, the contents of the form are more important than the corresponding skills. In kata, the contents of the form define the spiritual aspects of the exercise. This is something often ignored in Western sports and physical training. For this reason, kata performance, like karate itself, has been the subject of many definitions and esoteric interpretations.

Before the introduction of jiyu kumite in 1920, kata and bunkai were considered the most fundamental ways of karate teaching and training in Asia. Originally, most katas were developed as solo exercises, known as tandoku, for the individual karateka. Later the method of *sotai*—or training with one or more partners—was devised to improve the efficiency of the practice. Although the method of sotai is a great method of karate training, it is more difficult to use because it requires the participation of several students of equal rank and a larger space in which to maneuver.

There are two major classifications of kata practice and competition: Kojin-kata for individual performance and Godo-kata for team or group practice. A student's favorite form is called Tokui kata.

Spiritual fulfillment and mental development in karate-do are impossible without correct performance of kata and that requires a true understanding of its bunkai.

BUNKAI

Soke says:

"Comprehending a kata and its bunkai is as important as performing it."

Performing a kata without understanding the inner nature of its actions reduces its value to an exercise in calisthenics. As one aid to understanding, Soke recommends the methods of bunkai for demonstrating the applications and philosophies of kata movements.

Bunkai literally means "breaking into components" or "application" and is explained further in other sections of this book. It is vitally important for practitioners to correctly understand and interpret the physical, psychological and philosophical implications of each movement of each kata.

To appreciate the wealth of information and multitude of components contained in a single kata, the reader is urged to compare the intricacies of the simple Oi-tsuki (analyzed in the preceding section) consisting of only one set of actions to those of a kata, containing as many as 20 or more sets of combinations.

Each movement of each kata may have many simple, complicated, compound and even hidden applications. In general, there are six different levels of bunkai interpretation and analysis:

Omote Bunkai or obvious applications: These include most of the basic thrusting, striking, kicking and blocking techniques encountered in all katas. For example, the first left-hand Gedan-barai of kata Heian Shodan generally is interpreted as a standard lower level block against a front kick. This does not, however, imply that there aren't other interpretations of this basic move, either as a single defensive action or as part of a more complex combination. Omote bunkai are discussed and taught regularly to all mudansha and yudansha at IKA headquarters and affiliated dojos.

Ura Bunkai or alternative applications: A large number of Uchi-waza may be interpreted both as striking and/or blocking actions depending on the circumstances surrounding the set of actions containing the particular technique in question. By the same token, a large number of Morote-waza also may be interpreted as throwing, grappling and restraining applications. Kata Empi and Kata Kanku-Sho both include throwing techniques. The retraction of a striking or blocking hand over the hips, or Hikite, also can be interpreted as an Ushiro-empi uchi.

Okugi Bunkai or secret applications: These concealed, and sometimes illegal, applications are the so-called dangerous techniques taken out of the katas by the old masters to prevent accidental deaths and severe injuries during practice. Strangulation techniques, pressure point applications, joint dislocation and bone crushing methods fall into this category. The Okugi Bunkai are not part of the IKA curriculum.

Kenka Bunkai or evolving applications: These applications were introduced to teach weapons techniques that used agricultural implements, such as the sai, tonfa, bo, and nunchaku mentioned earlier. For example, the basic Sai-jodan-age-uke (upper level block performed with the long section of the sai protecting the outside of the forearm) is an effective defensive technique against a direct attack to the head by someone using a sword or similar object.

Sutemi Bunkai or sacrificing applications: These are highly advanced and complex applications devised to save the lives of samurai during life threatening situations. In essence, these techniques try to make the best of a worst case combat situation. A samurai might sacrifice his arm to prevent a direct hit to his chest. A ninja might be willing to dislocate his joints to escape prison. These are examples of sacrificing techniques that still are used in the training of special forces of certain law enforcement agencies.

Sonota Bunkai or miscellaneous applications: Sonota bunkai are associated with the Sonota kata. These are simple, yet highly effective, training tools that were devised by Soke Takayuki Kubota to facilitate the teaching and comprehension of both basic and advanced karate concepts in the dojo environment. The Sonota kata and bunkai are considered by many to be among the most significant contributions to karate practice in 20 years. The Sonota kata and bunkai are practiced regularly at IKA headquarters and affiliated dojos.

The present volume is concerned only with the most basic or obvious applications of IKA katas described in this chapter.

All students are urged to fully visualize and master the basic bunkai of each movement in each kata and to envision new applications for each situation. The most obvious example of a noncombative bunkai can be seen in the interpretation of the Yoi position assumed at the beginning of all katas. Although the Yoi position implies a condition of neutral readiness, it doesn't give away the next move or the intentions of the performer. The performer may move in any direction into any stance and execute any combination of blocking and/or striking techniques appropriate in that particular situation. On the other hand, a retracted fist over the hip almost always indicates an impending blow.

A simple Gedan-barai may imply a lower-level block against a low-level tsuki, a low-level Mae-geri, a low-level Mawashi-geri or indeed any other low-level attack. In general, the interpretation of defensive moves is much more difficult than the explanation of attacking techniques. The stances and postures assumed by the performer also may indicate both the attacker's and defender's intentions.

Bunkai and kata are inseparable parts of our common karate-do heritage. Bunkai interpretation is a skill learned with many years of dedicated karate training.

The description of IKA katas that follows is preceded by a discussion of karate-do maxims inherent in every kata. The next section is devoted to karate maxims and the relationship between kata training and mental and spiritual development.

KARATE-DO MAXIMS AND KATA

Most katas tend to follow the same overall format and convey the same general message, despite often radical differences in their patterns of movement and philosophies of action. All katas are meant to be performed exactly as intended by their originators, without deviation.

All katas contain and express the same important ideals and social traits central to karate-do: courtesy, courage, nonaggression, perseverance, and perfection. Practicing these principles eventually will lead to improved human values and personal development.

All kata also generate certain feelings and ideas associated with the characteristics of their movements. Performers may perceive different feelings and ideas from each performance depending on their own degree of proficiency and personal sophistication.

Spectators, especially those with a background in martial arts, also perceive the same general ideas inherent in the movements of each kata simply by watching the performance. For instance, the opening sequences of Kata Hangetsu may reflect the idea of developing extreme muscular strength and personal determination. The jumping combinations of Kata Empi may generate a feeling of agility, speed and freedom of action.

The first attempt at understanding kata is a first attempt at learning it. True understanding of kata comes much later. It may take many years before the meaning of a kata is understood fully. Patience, perseverance and determination are fundamental when learning kata.

Systematic performance of kata generates the virtues needed to understand the inner meanings of its actions. Patience is one such virtue.

A helpful step toward understanding the important ideals and maxims of karate-do through kata is becoming familiar with some of the fundamental principles of kata performance.

First Principle of Kata: Courtesy – Rei

Courtesy, the outward display of respect, is the most important aspect of karate practice. "Karate do wa rei ni hajimari rei owaru" ("Karate-do begins and ends with respect").

All kata begin and end with an expression of respect, Kaishurei and Keshurei respectively, with the performer facing front, toward the imaginary opponent. The student performs Rei from Musubi-dachi while saying Osu and looking directly ahead. As the bow is completed, the student assumes the Yoi position while taking a full breath.

The inhalation phase is accomplished by retracting both fists to the hips (as if performing a double hand back elbow strike) in a relaxed, but fast, movement. Exhalation follows by tightening the abdominal muscles and lowering the fists simultaneously while performing a passive and quiet kiai. The beginning and ending bows are actually part of the kata and should not be confused with other instances of expressing respect. The student remains alert but relaxed, waiting for the instructor's command to begin the kata. This also indicates lack of pretense and ego.

The instructor or the kata leader calls out the name of the kata to be performed. Students acknowledge the command by repeating the name of the kata in loud, clear voices and remaining at attention, anticipating the order to commence the kata.

The instructor or the kata leader orders the class to perform the kata in single steps, sets or all the way through. If the latter option is selected, the instructor/kata leader calls out "Hajime!" and students begin to perform the kata.

The first step (described above) is repeated after the instructor/kata leader acknowledges the end of the kata by calling out "Yame!"

Second Principle of Kata: Passiveness or Nonaggression

In karate-do, there is no anger or first strike. There is no aggression or defeat. There is no gain in first attack. "Karate ni sente nashi," or "No first attack in karate," generally is regarded as a call for overall self-control. Grand Master Funakoshi says, "To subdue the enemy without fighting is the highest skill."

As a sign of nonaggression, all katas begin with a defensive block, never a striking technique.

All other sets of combinations also begin with a defensive block.

All multiple opponents are confronted first with a defensive technique.

All moves are smooth and in harmony with each other. There are no abrupt or sudden moves intended to challenge or aggravate the opponent.

Almost all katas begin and end at the same spot, facing the same direction in a state of. Yoi. While no ground is lost, no gain is made either.

All katas end in victory over one's ego and inner conflicts. Peace always prevails at the end.

The famous Japanese phrase, "Go no sen o toru," which means "Defense is equal to offense," further emphasizes passive thought in karate practice.

Third Principle of Kata: Perseverance

In karate-do, there is no emotion, no hesitation. All opponents are subdued as efficiently as possible, each with a single effective strike, or "Ikken hissatsu."

In kata, all techniques are executed confidently, deliberately and decisively with kime–or focus–and determination.

All katas contain at least two kiais associated with the most emphasized techniques of the particular kata.

All katas include many maneuvers involving turning, returning, jumping and side stepping. Performers are required to look first by turning the head. Then they move to face the opponent and execute their technique. The golden rule in kata and kumite is: "Look first, move, and then strike."

All techniques are executed deliberately and without hesitation.

All blocking, thrusting, striking and kicking is performed with full power and range. No techniques are pulled back. Each waza is meant to be a decisive blow. Each opponent is subdued with a single effective combination.

Fourth principle of Kata: Perfection

A student seeks perfection by constantly evaluating and monitoring his actions. This includes physical proficiency as well as emotional stability.

Each kata practice is an attempt at perfection and is assessed by the quality of its performance. The quality of performance is regulated by how well the student adheres to the following principles of technical control.

The degree of perfection and understanding of these principles, reflected in performance, also serves as a basis for the decision criteria in competition.

Criterion	Japanese term
Spiritual preparedness	"KISHIN NO YOI"
Eye control	"METSUKE"

Breath control	"KOKYU" and "KIAI"
Power control	"CHIKARA NO KYOJAKU"
Speed control	"WAZA NO KANKYU"
Body control	"TAI NO SHIN SHUKU"
Stability control	"JUSHIN NO ANTEI"
Beauty of form	"KEITAI NO HOJI"
Display of awareness	"ZAN SHIN"
Harmony and contrast	"INYO"
Line of movement	"EMBUSEN"
Focus of attention	"CHAKUGAN"

These principles govern and regulate the qualities of the action components described in the preceding section.

Each performance should contain its own bunkai, mentally visualizing the movements and techniques of the imaginary opponents. Each kata movement is a predetermined response to an opponent's move.

ULTIMATE AIM OF KATA

Personal Development

Personal development in karate-do is associated with developing the mind, body and spirit in a balanced and harmonious way. Systematic and conscientious practice of kata empowers the mind with information; strengthens the body through physical exercise; and heightens the spirit through meditation in action. Personal achievement in karate-do is attainable only through conscious effort and persistence.

Physical conditioning

Physical prowess in kata does not imply a show of force. Rather, it is the display of the generation of force through graceful movements. The most obvious gain from kata training is physical fitness.

Physical fitness and good health act on, and react with, each other. Good health is both a prerequisite and a function of compatible mental and spiritual development.

The attributes of physical fitness will be explored in greater detail in Chapter 1.

Mental development

Practicing and understanding kata and bunkai empower the mind with a great wealth of information regarding kata and its techniques.

The mind is also stimulated to search for noncombative solutions to potential problems, such as conflict resolution and enhanced control over one's actions.

Practicing kata also enables performers to bring to bear a higher degree of focus and concentration on the task at hand.

Although the mind and spirit are inseparable and all mental and spiritual attributes are interrelated, the systematic practice of kata can instill and improve such important mental virtues and functions as:

- Fortitude and determination.
- Decision making and planning.
- Predicting future moves and situations.
- Coordination and reflexes.
- Quickness of thought.
- Balance and accuracy.
- Control and quality of action.
- Control of emotion (self-control).
- Concentration and focus
- Optimization of energy.
- Assessment and judgment.
- Consequence and responsibility.

These distinguishing qualities are of even greater value karateka in their everyday lives.

Spiritual development

Spiritual training is the cornerstone of traditional karate-do. Many masters consider kata training an exercise in meditation, or, meditation in motion.

In kata, every move displays a unique karate action. Every act reflects different spiritual attributes and states of mind, all depending on the real situation surrounding the karateka.

For instance, the Gedan-barai always expresses a block against a lower level attack but it may be controlled to fend off a strike or release sufficient power to maim an opponent.

The Yoi can symbolize a state of readiness, impassive courage or even alert neutrality, as the case requires.

Systematic repetition of meaningful gestures brings about the spiritual values associated with such acts. Conversely, these spiritual values express and signal their presence through the same gestures.

Repeated performance of kata with an open mind and accepting spirit can inspire and instill sufficient inner strength and belief to create, through imagination, real spiritual values such as courage and confidence.

It is up to the individual performers to open their hearts to positive spiritual virtues and drive away the negative ones. Kata is also the medium and the vehicle through which spiritual awareness and personal fulfillment can be achieved.

In real life, there is no limit to the extent or number of spiritual values- good and evil- associated with human nature. Spiritual/human values may not be exactly the same in different in cultures. However, good-spirited people are empowered with the knowledge to cope conform to new situations.

Some of the most desirable spiritual attributes associated with kata practice and the symbolic acts through which they emerge are listed below.

Spiritual attribute	Supporting act in kata
Patience	Remaining in Yoi
Humility	Performing Rei
Obedience	Responding to Hajime and Yame
Loyalty	Walking in the steps of masters
Awareness	Intuitive knowledge of Kata and Bunkai
Devotion	Act of repeating Kata
Compassion	Avoiding aggression
Tranquility	Lack of excitement
Courage	Act of engaging in Kata
Confidence	The will to perform Kata
Modesty	Reciting Osu
Tolerance	Act of defense first

The combined state of the mind and spirit embracing the mental and spiritual attributes mentioned above is expressed as

"Mizu-no-kokoro," or a "mind-spirit-like water."

The surface of calm, clean water free from dust and disturbance can reflect the image of any object in a passive and nonaggressive way. In human terms, this means being aware without adverse emotional feelings. Calm water is sensitive to the slightest breeze. Unsteady or dirty water can neither reflect images nor sense the wind.

A mature and experienced karateka can enter a state of body awareness in which the right technique or movement happens by itself, effortlessly, without any interference from the conscious will. This is known as the state of Zen and explains the momentary oneness of the practitioner and the practice. The kumite flows by itself; combat is indistinguishable from the combatant; and the kata performs itself. The spectator can't tell the performance from the performer.

"Ken Zen Ichinyo," or "the fist and Zen are one," is the oldest Japanese reference to the strong spiritual relationship that exists between the state of Zen–or intuitive awareness–and the practice of karate-do.

It has been known for centuries that regular, focused practice of kata increases and redirects blood circulation, regulates breathing and facilitates the flow of Ki (Chi in Chinese), or vital energy in the body. This in turn elevates the awareness of the mind and spirit to a much higher level than ordinarily can be expected in normal life. This is the main reason why kata also has been referred to as:

"An expression of Zen meditation in motion."

All human beings are gifted with the potential of possessing the best offerings and positive virtues of life and with the ability to reject all that is evil and wrong. It is up to the student to decide how to develop his or her personality through the practice of karate-do.

IKA KATA

The IKA curriculum gives students the opportunity to learn the katas of two major styles of karate at the same time. These are the katas of the Shotokan style–compiled and rearranged by Grand Master Gichin Funakoshi–and the Gosoku-ryu style developed by Grand Master Soke Takayuki Kubota.

Soke teaches us to treat his contemporary katas as natural evolutions of the traditional katas, without preference for any one style or particular kata. A brief description of IKA katas is presented at the end of this section.

The distinguishing features of different styles of karate are characterized by the specific types of kata adapted to form the basis of that style. The Shotokan and Gosoku-ryu katas are referred to collectively as the IKA karate katas. IKA katas also include a large number of weapons training forms that were developed mainly by Soke Kubota. The discussion of weapons katas is beyond the scope of this book.

The IKA curriculum currently offers approximately 10 Shotokan and 20 Gosoku-ryu katas as part of the qualifying requirements for the black belt test.

To attain the rank of Shodan, IKA students must demonstrate a high degree of proficiency in performing numerous selected katas in each style. They also are expected to demonstrate a solid understanding of the bunkai of these forms.

IKA kata training usually begins with Soke's Kihon forms, which are prerequisites for all other IKA kata. Beginners are required to master the Kihon katas and their applications before moving up to higher forms.

Recognizing the importance of traditional values in karate-do, the classical forms of the Shotokan style, as practiced at IKA, are introduced before the katas of the Gosoku-ryu style.

THE IKA SHOTOKAN KATA

Shotokan is the official style of karate-do practiced by the Japan

Karate-do Association (JKA). It is also the most widespread style of karate in the world. The two main categories of Shotokan katas belong to the traditional Shorin-Ryu and Shorei-Ryu schools and were rearranged and renamed by Master Funakoshi in the early 1900s. Comparing these katas from a purely physical point of view, they have been classified arbitrarily as "light" and "heavy" forms, respectively, with reference to the physical characteristics of the most dominant movements of each kata.

Although improving or maintaining physical fitness is not the prime objective of kata, it generally is agreed that the former class of kata is better suited for developing cardiovascular endurance and rapid reflexes. The latter forms are more appropriate for developing muscular strength and efficient breathing techniques. It is quite natural for students and instructors to favor one or a few katas over others. However, each kata has its own place in the development of a karateka and no kata is superior to others.

All Shotokan katas have been arranged to minimize the space needed for practice. With some minor variations, they are performed along straight lines conforming to parts of the imaginary letters "I," inverted "T," and the simple dash line (—). The lines of movement, or Embu sen, are confined to a small area measuring approximately four shoulder widths by eight shoulder widths. The stem, or length, of the letter "I," measuring approximately eight shoulder widths, signifies the direction of the forward and backward movements. The horizontal arms of the letter "I" indicate the direction of the lateral movements encountered in various kata. All other movements are described with reference to these base lines.

The first two kata of the Heian and Kanku series, Heian Shodan and Jion, are performed along the straight lines of the imaginary letter "I." All Tekki katas are conducted along a short straight line. The line of movement for all other katas conforms to the straight lines forming the imaginary inverted letter "T."

All Shotokan katas start and finish at the same point: that spot where the two base lines of the inverted letter "T" intersect.

The names and meanings of the Shotokan katas practiced by Shotokan stylists are as follows:

Name of kata	Meaning of kata
HEIAN SHODAN	Peaceful mind Number 1
HEIAN NIDAN	Peaceful mind Number 2
HEIAN SANDAN	Peaceful mind Number 3
HEIAN YONDAN	Peaceful mind Number 4
HEIAN GODAN	Peaceful mind Number 5
TEKKI SHODAN	Horse riding Number 1
TEKKI NIDAN	Horse riding Number 2
TEKKI SANDAN	Horse riding Number 3
BASSAI DAI	To penetrate a fortress (The great)
BASSAI SHO	To penetrate a fortress (The small)
KANKU DAI	To look at the sky (The great)
KANKU SHO	To look at the sky (The small)
HANGETSU	Half moon
EMPI (ENPI)	Flying swallow
GANKAKU	Crane on a rock
JUTTE (JITTE)	Ten hands or temple hands
JION	A name identified with Jion Temple.
GIIN or JIIN	The temple grounds
GOJU-SHIHO-SHO	The 54 steps (The small)
GOJU-SHIHO-DAI	The 54 steps (The great)
NIJU-SHIHO-SHO	The 24 steps (The small)
CHINTE	Small hands; also, magic hands
SOCHIN	The grand prize
MEIKYO	The vision of a white heron
WANKAN	Pine tree wind
UNSU	Hands in the clouds

The Heian and Kanku series, Tekki-Shodan, Bassai-Dai and Hangetsu, are the selected Shotokan katas included in the IKA curriculum for the black belt test.

The brief characterizations of individual katas presented in this section have two purposes: to complement the student's dojo training with background material on the essence of each form and to highlight the more significant aspects of each kata. The study of this material without dojo practice is of little use to the student. A complete description of the choreographies of these katas is far beyond the scope of this book.

HEIAN SHODAN

The peaceful mind, first level, is the simplest and most basic form of all Shotokan katas. The pattern of movements is highly symmetrical and conforms to the imaginary letter "I." There are only seven different techniques involved in the entire kata. This fundamental kata is adopted by almost all well-established karate schools and is the first classical form taught to beginners anywhere in the world. However the IKA version of this kata includes minor modifications to make it more compatible with other katas of the same group.

Heian Shodan is performed almost entirely in Zenkutsu-dachi. The emphasis is on correct execution of basic stances and techniques using simple body shifting methods. The defensive techniques used in this kata are, in order: the Gedan-barai, the Tetsui-uchi, the Jodan-age-uke, and the Chudan-shuto-uke. The offensive techniques employed in Heian Shodan are, in order: the Oi-tsuki, the Tetsui-uchi, the Ushiro-empi-uchi, and the Jodan-yonhon-nukite.

Altogether, there are 24 moves in this kata, executed in just under one minute. It should take the beginner one or two full sessions to learn the basic choreography of this kata. Heian Shodan is concerned mainly with correct execution of basic hand techniques, ashi-sabaki and gamae. There are no geri waza in Heian Shodan.

In spite of its simple choreography and apparent ease of performance, Heian Shodan is a very powerful kata and is considered the cornerstone of both the Heian family of forms as well as most other Shotokan kata discussed in this book. This kata is known for its efficiency of movement and for the way it generates power at impact. Students are encouraged to pay specific attention to movements six, seven and eight.

Also of critical importance are the four consecutive actions beginning with a left 90 degree turn, followed by a swinging left-hand Gedan-barai, smoothly retracted into an Ushiro-empi-uchi, and then thrust into a left-hand Jodan-yonhon-nukite with kime. This very fast, continuously flowing combination of movements truly reflects the technical merits of the art of empty hand combat.

Kata Heian Shodan displays great efficiency of movement and speed of action in a uniquely choreographed combination. Another important combination of techniques displayed in Heian Shodan is the consecutive performance of two Oi-tsuki culminating in a burst of power with kime and kiai.

It is instructive to note that these offensive techniques are accelerated through the sequential addition of linear momentum generated in the direction of the target.

While learning Heian Shodan, students should realize that the basis of learning in karate-do is the repeated practice of kata. The beginner should be patient and pay a great deal of attention to the method of learning of this basic kata and its Bunkai. The process of learning should not be rushed.

Breathing control, attention to rhythm, eye and head movement and balance are of the utmost importance in this and all other katas.

When a student has mastered the five Heian katas, he or she should feel confident enough to remain calm and prepared in most adversarial situations. This family of katas is known as the peaceful mind, a name derived from the concepts of self-confidence and the ability to maintain calm. The five Heian katas, previously known as Pinan katas, originally were grouped together and reorganized by Master Itosu Anko in 1905 and were taught in Okinawan high schools and institutions of higher learning. They apparently evolved from the Shorei group of katas that were brought to Okinawa from China at the beginning of the seventeenth century.

HEIAN NIDAN

The peaceful mind, second level, is a graceful and multi-technique form involving about 30 moves and completed in approximately one minute. The pattern of movements is symmetrical in relation to the imaginary base lines and includes the stem and arms of the imaginary capital letter "I."

Heian Nidan contains almost all of the Heian Shodan techniques. It also introduces the concept of Morote-waza or double techniques, used in empty hand combat.

The beginning posture after the Yoi position is the Koshi Gamae or hip stance, where both fists are clenched one on top of the other, touching the right-hand side of the body just over the hip. It is continued by performing a simultaneous left-hand Jodan-soto-ude-uke together with a right-hand (overhead) Haiwan-uke while assuming a left Mahanmi-no Kokutsu-dachi.

Heian Nidan also introduces the important double forearm block, or Morote-uke, as well as the formidable attacking combination of a right Uraken-uchi to the opponent's face, together with a right Sokuto-geri to the groin. The other new techniques introduced in this kata are the Tetsui-yoko-uchi and the Kage-tsuki, both performed as part of the opening set of movements.

The classic combination of the left-hand Chudan-osae-uke, or the press-down (cover) with an open hand, followed by a right-hand vertical spear hand attack, or Chudan-yonhan-nukite, also is introduced for the first time in this kata.

The emphasis in this kata, besides simultaneous use of the limbs, is on the practice of balance in turning to face multiple opponents. Heian Nidan is the first Shotokan kata to introduce the use of foot techniques, or ashi waza i.e., the Mae-geri and Sokuto-geri.

The act of balancing on one foot and kicking with the other is introduced as part of the third set of movements. The rhythm of movement is slightly more complex than the first kata.

Heian Shodan and Heian Nidan together form the basis of many of the advanced kata mentioned in this book. In Heian Nidan, the angular momentum of the body is used effectively to augment defensive techniques every time the performer turns around to face an opponent.

Because of the strong influence of Heian Shodan, students should learn this kata with the same ease as its predecessor

HEIAN SANDAN

The peaceful mind, third level, is a short kata, but more difficult to learn. There are 24 movements in this form that take less than one minute to complete. The lines of movement are symmetrical and conform to the geometry of the inverted imaginary letter "T."

While the basic patterns of Heian Shodan and Heian Nidan are tied to one another and appear to complement each other, the techniques of Heian Sandan differ radically from those of both Heian Shodan and Heian Nidan, as well as the next two katas in the same family of forms. Heian sandan is not a long kata, but beginners tend to spend more time for learning the intricacies of kata than the previous two.

Most of the movements of this kata are technically uncommon to the first time performer. Beginners are advised to understand the applications and meaning of each movement before proceeding with the rest of the form. Heian Sandan introduces a number of new concepts, important techniques, postures and stances.

The exertion of maximum strength in a right-hand Oi-tsuki, preceded by a counterclockwise rotation of the entire body, and the swinging of a left Chudan-yoko-tetsui-uchi, are two important concepts demonstrated in this kata. This series of movements illustrates the importance of coordinating fast and slow movements in offense and defense.

In Heian Sandan, the techniques are accelerated mainly by body rotation in the same general direction as the movement of the techniques themselves.

The new stance introduced in this form is the Kiba-dachi performed from a side-facing posture. The stamping crescent kicks, or Mika-tsuki-geri-fumikomi; the cross block, or Kosa-uke; and the Empi-uke are the new defensive techniques effectively used to block and subdue opponents.

The last two combinations of Heian Sandan are of particular interest in self-defense when the practitioner is grabbed from behind. In these combinations, the effective application of Yoko-yori-ashi, or lateral foot dragging, together with the simultaneous application of Ushiro-empi-uchi to the assailant's abdomen and a Tate-tsuki to his face, are demonstrated clearly. Heian Sandan is an excellent training form for improving concentration, muscular coordination, timing, targeting and balance. Some of its techniques are incorporated in higher katas.

HEIAN YONDAN

Peaceful mind, level four, is a summary of the first three Heian katas described above. The first two forms emphasize the sequential accumulation of linear acceleration The third form demonstrates the use of angular acceleration. Heian Yondan employs both types of acceleration in the same kata.

Heian Yondan introduces a multitude of fundamental techniques, including the Haishu-uke-jodan, the Juji-uke-gedan, the Kakiwaki-uke, the Tate-uraken-uchi-jodan, the Shuto-uchi-jodan, the Heiza-geri, the Yoko-empi-uchi-jodan, and the Morote-kubi-osae, or double-hand head immobilization with pressure. The patterns of movement are symmetrical and conform to the imaginary letter "I."

The importance of leaping to gain distance and add momentum is the central point of this kata. The performer, after executing a mid-level Mae-geri from a stable Zenkutzu-dachi, leaps forward into a Kosa-dachi, adding the entire momentum of the body to that of the downward back fist attack. This combination of leaping and striking is used frequently in higher katas. Three consecutive Moroto-ukes performed on left and right Kokutsu-dachis toward the end of the kata emphasize the importance of hip rotation in karate waza. The concept of Ren-tsuki, or continuous punching, is introduced as an effective method of subduing an opponent. Beginners should make a special effort to learn the variable timing and rhythmic sequences involved in this kata. This graceful kata is an excellent way to practice the basic techniques, both in combination with each other and at different levels of exertion. Heian Yondan contains a total of 27 moves, and takes about one minute to complete.

HEIAN GODAN

The fifth and last kata of the Heian series, Heian Godan, or peaceful mind, level five, introduces jumping as an effective method of body shifting and avoiding leg attack, or leg sweep.

In all Heian katas, as in most others, body movement generally is accomplished by shifting the center of gravity along the same horizontal level. Physically the head should appear to remain at the same height at all times. However, in certain circumstances, an abrupt change of the location of the center of gravity is justified.

The principal point of Heian Godan is the combination, or set, of moves beginning with an upper level (upright) double forearm block, immediately followed by a Koho-tsuki-age, or rising chin attack, as if expanding the body to reach for the sky. This is followed by jumping and raising the feet as high as possible and landing in a squatting Ushiro-neko-ashi-dachi or Kosa-dachi, with the hands in the Juji-uke-gedan position. In this coiled position the body is ready to burst into action with added power and energy. The point of this maneuver is the generation of momentum during an evasive action. Heian godan expands and contracts the body several times. This is known as "Tai-no-shin-shuku," which is naturally of cardinal importance to all kata.

The new posture introduced in the kata is the Manji-gamae, where the performer assumes Kokutsu-dachi while raising the rear hand above the head as if holding a dagger. The front hand is in a Gedan-barai position. This posture is employed twice in the kata and is preceded, each time, by the spectacular combination of an upper level Nagashi-uke, followed by a powerful Gedan-nukite-uchi, conducted in a deep front stance. This kata also emphasizes the use of the powerful cross blocking techniques performed in a forward stance, such as the successive use of both the Gedan-juji-uke and the Jodan-haishu-juji-uke in zenkutsu-dachi. There are 25 movements in Heian Godan, which altogether take about one minute to complete. The pattern of movements is symmetrical with the center line of the imaginary letter "T."

TEKKI SHODAN

Tekki Shodan is the first in a family of three elegant katas that, with some variation, follow the same pattern of actions. Tekki Shodan, or horse riding, refers to their frequent use of the Kiba-dachi and lateral fighting techniques associated with mounted combat. In fact, Tekki katas are performed almost entirely in Kiba-dachi except when the stances change to Kosa-dachi, a sideways crossed feet cat foot stance.

The pattern of movements is symmetrical and is confined to a short straight line extending two shoulder widths on each side of the Yoi position. This kata also can address the challenge faced by a person standing in front of a wall and confronting opponents coming at him from three directions.

The first new defensive hand technique introduced in this kata is the Yoko-haishu-uke-chudan, or the sideways back hand block. This technique is demonstrated as part of the opening set of movements of the kata. Another important defensive technique emphasized in this kata is the inside snapping foot block, or Nami-ashi-uke, returning wave. This technique is used to protect the groin against a frontal attack and also to avoid a foot sweep.

Nami-ashi adds lateral momentum to the body during landing. Ura-tsuki or the reversed fist, is the most emphasized offensive technique demonstrated in all Tekki katas. This technique is particularly effective in close range combat. It is delivered as the Chuko-tsuki, except the wrist is not rotated but drives forward in a straight line to the opponent's face or body. Almost all offensive techniques of this kata are performed in Chudan.

Because of space limitations, upper body twisting and hip rotation are used extensively to improve the effectiveness of the performance. Beginners should pay special attention to these small but sharp twisting actions that tend to accelerate hand techniques.

There are no Geri-waza in Tekki Shodan. Tekki katas demand a great deal of concentration, precision and muscular control. Tekki Shodan is perhaps the fastest and shortest kata in the Shotokan style. It consists of 29 movements and takes less than 50 seconds to complete. It is a relatively difficult kata to learn, but it is also highly educational and rewarding to perform. Soke usually teaches Tekki Shodan by breaking it into three equal parts. Tekki katas are known to promote flexibility, agility and lower body strength. Tekki Shodan is also known by its classical name of Naihanchi. All three Tekki katas are classified as Shorei-Ryu, forms.

BASSAI DAI

The word Bassai, also known as Passai, is interpreted literally as penetrating a fortress. The Bassai family of forms is related historically to the Shorin-Ryu style of traditional kararte-do and consists of two katas: Bassai-Dai and Bassai-Sho. Dai implies greatness.

The name of this kata—the great fortress penetration—connotes the feeling associated with the will to overcome many difficulties or opponents, symbolized by the will to penetrate a fortress. This is demonstrated by repeated execution of similar defensive techniques in different parts of the kata.

The Yoi position at the beginning and end of this kata is an alert defensive posture. The performer assumes Heisoku-dachi with the right fist wrapped in the left hand about two fists in front of the groin. The knees are bent slightly.

The kata begins with a sharp leap forward into a Kosa-dachi to perform a right-hand augmented Chudan-soto-uke, followed by seven consecutive forearm blocking techniques. It is this repeated switching of the blocking arms that suggests the will and fortitude to face an endless number of opponents until the fortress is penetrated. A similar repetition of defensive techniques also is demonstrated by four consecutive executions of Shuto-soto-uke in Kokutsu-dachi, performed with the same degree of confidence and feeling of defiance needed to progress toward one's goals in life.

The line of movement is not symmetrical but includes the stem and arms of the inverted imaginary letter "T." Bassai-Dai is the longest of the first seven katas described in this section and consists of a total of 42 movements, taking just more than one minute to complete.

Bassai-Dai is a very graceful, powerful, technically rich and somewhat difficult kata to learn.

The new techniques encountered in this kata are the Chudan-tsukami-uke, or blocking by seizing an opponent's arm or leg; the Chudan-morote-tetsui-uchi; the Sukui-uke, or scooping block; the Gedan-fumikomi-geri; the Chudan-tate-shuto-uke; and the Yama-tsuki.

Soke usually teaches Bassai-Dai by breaking it into three or four parts, depending on the abilities of the student.

HANGETSU

Originally known as *Seishan*, this kata now is called Hangetsu, or half moon. The new name refers to several distinctive semicircular hand and foot movements incorporated in the choreography of this kata. There are roughly 15 sets of combinations containing a total of 41 movements, most them new. It takes just over one minute to perform this kata. Kata Hangetsu is the best example of the so-called "heavy" types of kata associated with the Shorei-Ryu style of classical karate-do.

Hangetsu introduces for the first time the use of a stance bearing the same name. The first three movements are performed in Hangetsu-dachi. These movements are executed with great muscular tension combined with coordinated Ibuki, or breathing. The main object of the exercise is to control the neuromuscular system through concentration, focus and directed flow of energy.

The ability to tense and relax the muscles at will, specifically those of the abdomen, is of great importance in karate. Muscular control, together with coordinated abdominal breathing, is considered essential to proper performance in kata, kumite, tameshiwari and any physical act that may require use of force with some degree of accuracy and concentration.

This kata's short and powerful movements represent the type of techniques generally advocated by the Shorei-Ryu branch of traditional karate-do.

Training for muscular contraction also enhances the student's ability to reverse the process by completely relaxing the muscles while at the same time remaining alert and ready for action.

The first three sets of movements in Kata Hangetsu are designed specifically to stimulate alternate modes of muscular tension and relaxation. The movements of these sets are slow and smooth, showing maximum muscular control and focus. The remaining sets of movements are explosive, with fast and powerful movements.

Kata Hangetsu is highly instructive but also a demanding form to learn and perform. It is also one of the most powerful and graceful katas in the Shotokan style. Beginners are advised to devote sufficient time to understanding the intricacies of the new movements employed in this kata.

When teaching Hangetsu, Soke emphasizes the importance of tensing the legs and tightening the stomach muscles during the exhalation phase of the breathing cycle, and relaxing them during the inhalation phase.

The half moon kata introduces a number of new postures and techniques including the Yama-gamae, or mountain posture; the Morote-gedan-kaishu-ryowan-gamae, or extended arms-open hands posture; the low semicircular, outward sliding Ashi-barai; the Haito-uke; the Chudan-ippon-ken; and the Morote-teisho-awase-gedan-uke, or the two-handed palm heel block conducted as the last

technique of the kata. The line of movement is confined to the stem and upper arms of the imaginary letter "T."

KANKU DAI

The original Chinese/Okinawan name of this kata is Kwanku. The new name, Kanku-Dai, is associated with its second movement, in which the performer raises the arms and looks up at the sky through an opening formed by the hands. Kanku-Dai, or the great look at the sky, is perhaps the longest kata in the Shotokan style. It consists of about 30 sets of combinations including a total of 65 movements. It usually takes about two minutes to complete.

The line of movement is the imaginary letter "I." Unlike most other katas, the pattern of movement is not symmetrical with respect to the central axis of the Embusen.

The symbolic act of looking at the sky through one's hands is an indirect reference to oneness of life with the universe. The next symbolic act is the lowering of the hands to a protective position in front of the chest with the right hand, or shuto, striking against the inside of the left-hand palm, as if blocking or breaking an assailant's arm. The performer is unarmed and has no intention of alarming the opponent. He is alert and ready to defend himself.

Although most of the basic techniques demonstrated in Kanku-Dai already have been introduced in the five Heian katas and Bassai-Dai, Kanku-Dai is considered the most complex kata of the Shotokan style. Kanku-Dai has the largest number of turns of all the Shotokan katas. Some of these turns introduce rather unusual combinations of karate techniques.

For instance, beginning with the 42nd move, the performer raises the right knee as if preparing for a kick, making nukite with the left hand and a fist with the right hand. The right hand performs a middle-level back fist augmented by the left open palm hitting the right forearm. The hitting sound of the hands is meant to distract and confuse the opponent. The performer makes a sudden turn to face an opponent approaching from behind, keeping the right knee raised with the hands held together in the same middle-level position. The performer stays in this position for a split second to assess the situation; executes an augmented hand chin attack; then lunges into an exaggerated front stance while dropping the body down and landing on the floor with the right foot and the two hands, a technique known as Morote-hiji-tate-fuse, or double elbow vertical drop. It is important to keep the body as low as possible and look to the front during this movement. The idea is to avoid a frontal attack and startle the opponent with an unexpected move. With the right knee bent and both hands firmly resting on the floor, the performer is in a good position to launch an attack, execute a back kick, an inward left foot sweep or move in either direction.

The new defensive technique introduced in this kata is the double Tetsui-otoshi-uke, or downward hammer block, performed during the 60th movement.

The new offensive combination performed toward the end of the kata is the jumping double kick, or Nidan-tobi-geri, followed by grabbing the opponent with the left hand and executing an upper-level back fist strike to the front. The combination is continued by performing a lower-level right-hand outward block before turning to face the opponent approaching from behind.

The Kanku series consist of two katas, Kanku-Dai and Kanku-Sho, both considered "light" forms related to the Shorin-Ryu style of classical karate-do.

It is said that "if you do Kanku-dai well, you should feel the color of your belt change from brown to black."

KANKU SHO

Kanku-Sho is a light and dynamic kata that consists of 52 movements. It takes about one minute to complete the kata. It often is said that the two Kanku katas together contain most of the essential elements of basic karate-do. The line of movement conforms to the imaginary letter "I."

The kata begins with three powerful and consecutive Chudan-morote-ukes performed in Kokutsu-dachi. It ends with two symmetrical sets of Soto-uke, Oi-tsuki combinations. Although there are no new techniques in this kata, Kanku-Sho introduces new methods for use in combination with old methods in new, imaginary situations. An interesting aspect of Kanku-Sho is its adaptation of Bo-waza, or the techniques of using the long staff as a martial arts weapon, in movements 22 through 28. The central point of this kata is a combination containing an augmented hand grabbing block; a right front kick; a right middle-level back fist attack; a right Soto-uke; a Ren-tsuki; and then, quickly turning around to face another opponent approaching from behind, executing a simultaneous left Gedan-barai and right Soto-uke while in Kokutsu-dachi. This combination is repeated three times in the kata.

The highlights of this kata, however, are the two 360 degree jumping movements or tobi waza that require great muscular power and control. Because of these spectacular maneuvers, Kanku-Sho is used frequently in karate demonstrations and tournaments.

EMPI

Formerly known as Hanshu, kata Empi, or the flying swallow, generally is characterized as the most dynamic, lightest and fastest kata of the Shotokan style. It is also a very powerful, highly coordinated and demanding form. The light and fast movements of this kata typify the basic philosophies of the Shorin-Ryu school of classical karate-do.

The name Empi (also pronounced Enpi) refers to the similarity between some of the movements of the kata and the up and down flight of the swallow. Kata Empi is both rewarding to perform and exciting to watch.

There are 37 movements in kata Empi, which take less than one minute to complete. This kata is not symmetrical. The line of movement is the inverted imaginary letter "T." The opening move contains the new stance Haiza-dachi, or one knee kneeling stance.

The swallow-like movements of this kata are seen in its frequent reversals of direction and in the nonlinear motions of the center of gravity of the body.

However, the leaping forward combinations, which describe the rising and dropping of the center of gravity, together with the subsequent 180 degree counterclockwise rotations of the body in association with the turning of the center of gravity, are performed with such timing and muscular control that one feels smooth transition of motion and continued flow of redirected energy.

The choreography of this ancient kata describes a situation of confrontation against two opponents, one approaching from behind and the other launching a frontal attack. The momentum generated to subdue the opponent in front is redirected to defeat the opponent attacking from behind. The rise, fall and twisting of the center of gravity is designed to magnify the effects of the hand techniques utilized in the corresponding sets of combinations. These back and forth body movements, together with their coordinated foot movements and hand techniques, are executed so smoothly that one may feel the confidence to redirect one's flow of energy to confront an endless number of opponents.

The new techniques introduced in this maneuver are emphasized in the combination of a right Jodan-age-tsuki, a right Kami-zukami, a Hiza-geri, a right Nagashi-uke, and a left Otoshi-tsuki. The next set introduces the use of Ushiro-gedan-barai.

In its penultimate move, the performer starts with a Morote-koko-gamae, or grabbing and overhead throwing posture, leaps backward off both feet as high and as far as possible, turning around counterclockwise 360 degrees while in the air and landing in a Hidari Kokutsu-dachi, performing a right Chudan-shuto-uke. The midair rotation of the performer about the vertical axis of the body, combined with the downward momentum at landing, add tremendous angular velocity to the right sword hand block. This combination contains a loud kiai that is supposed to energize the leap and startle the opponent. Other new techniques introduced in this kata are the simple inward Jodan-haishu-uke and the Teisho-cosa-uke, or crossing palm heel block, repeated several times toward the end of the kata.

Because of its classical nature and the multitude of advanced techniques, kata Empi is performed frequently in karate tournaments.

The remaining advanced Shotokan katas, such as Jitte and Gankaku, are considered as Nidan and higher level forms. Their descriptions are beyond the limitations of the present volume.

THE GOSOKU-RYU KATA

Soke Takayuki Kubota alone developed and introduced to the world of martial arts the basic philosophies of Gosoku-ryu karate. Soke developed and perfected Gosoku-ryu katas over the decades through study, research and teaching. These highly practical, modern forms reflect not only Soke's thoughts on empty hand combat but also introduce new trends in karate teaching and practice.

Although all Gosoku-ryu katas are contemporary products of the present century, their origins are rooted deeply in Soke's mastery of Japanese culture and martial arts, such as Judo, Aikido, Kendo and traditional weapons systems.

The emphasis of the advanced Gosoku-ryu katas is mainly on the generation of power through speed, quickness of body shifting and footwork, introduction of circular movements, and efficiency of techniques. Fast turns and returns, fast foot movements – as well as unique combinations of defensive and offensive techniques – are some of the distinctive features of these forms. Gosoku-ryu katas contain many practical combinations that are ideally suited for close quarters fighting.

In general, there is a greater diversity of techniques and movements in Gosoku-ryu katas than in other traditional forms. Soke deliberately designed these forms to make them suitable for the needs of contemporary society. Gosoku-ryu katas display highly functional and optimized forms of self-defense for everyone, especially children and young adults.

The Shotokan and Gosoku-ryu katas are looked upon as complementary means of training and education, rather than repertoires of two different styles of karate-do.

IKA students who reach Shodan and higher degrees readily grasp the affinity and blending of these two families of katas.

Despite the wide historical gap that exists between the Gosoku-ryu and Shotokan styles of karate practice, their katas are referred to simply as the IKA katas. IKA katas are classified only in terms of their content and degree of difficulty.

However, the Gosoku-ryu approach not only introduces many new technical concepts and practical applications. It also provides a modern and efficient means of teaching and learning.

Gosoku-ryu katas embrace the entire spectrum of kata practice starting from basic, through intermediate, to advanced forms of kata. To fully appreciate the essence of Gosuku-Ryu karate, one first should try to understand the bunkai of its forms.

GOSOKU RYU KATA CLASSIFICATION

The present repertoire of Gosoku-ryu karate consists of 34 pre-arranged Yakusoku katas and one floating, or miscellaneous form, the Sonota kata. The first two elementary forms are not considered as part of the main repertoire.

Each one of these forms has been designed with a specific function and purpose in mind. They range from simple educational forms that emphasize the basics, to purely defensive forms, to forms with highly combative action, to meditative katas. These katas are classified under four general categories: elementary, basic, intermediate, and advanced forms.

THE ELEMENTARY FORMS

These three elementary forms were developed recently by Soke Kubota to facilitate the teaching of the ABCs of karate to newcomers in a dojo environment. Once this phase of learning is complete, the student should find the study of the basics both enjoyable and rewarding. Learning the meaning and application of each move is as important as learning the move itself.

DOJO REI & SEIZA	Basic protocol. See Chapter 4.
GERI-KATA	Kicking form.
TACHI-KATA	Stances or standing forms. See Chapter 9.

THE BASIC FORMS

These short and simple katas were specifically designed to incorporate a large number of different basic techniques. They include as many combinations on as many different stances as possible. Their repeated practice over a period of time will prepare the student for learning the intermediate and advanced forms with ease and understanding. They are also excellent forms for cardiovascular and general conditioning.

There are four distinct but related groups of kihon katas. Each group is characterized by its unique purpose, duration, instants of kiai, line of action, number of sets of movements, and the type and number of techniques.

Currently, there are 18 kihon katas. There may be more in the future. They are simple to learn and fun to perform. Instead of learning these katas one by one, which may appear rather time consuming and overwhelming; the students are urged to study and memorize the grammar or the general rules of each group of katas.

These groups or families of kata are numbered arbitrarily from I to V. The grammar of each one of these groups is discussed in the section describing the first kata of that group.

The numbering of kihon katas from 1 to 18 indicates their chronological order of development. It does not imply progressive difficulty and or complexity. Kihon katas are further discussed in the next section

GROUP I

KIHON ICHI-NO KATA	Basic form number 1
KIHON NI-NO KATA	Basic form number 2
KIHON SAN-NO KATA	Basic form number 3
KIHON YON-NO KATA	Basic form number 4

The following groups of kihon katas were devised and officially sanctioned by IKA after many years of research and development in late 2006. Typically, they all start by sliding the right foot back. However, these forms become greater fun and more instructive when they are performed in their mirror image.

GROUP II

KIHON GO-NO KATA	Basic form number 5
KIHON ROKU-NO KATA	Basic form number 6
KHON SICHI-NO KATA	Basic form number 7

GROUP III

KIHON HACHI-NO KATA	Basic form number 8
KIHON KU-NO KATA	Basic form number 9
KIHON JU-NO KATA	Basic form number 10

GROUP IV

KIHON JU-ICHI-NO KATA	Basic form number 11
KIHON JU-NI-NO KATA	Basic form number 12
KIHON JU-SAN-NO KATA	Basic form number 13
KIHON JU-YON-NO KATA	Basic form number 14

GROUP V
KIHON JU-GO-NO KATA	Basic form number 15
KIHON SONOTA KATA	Basic miscellaneous form

THE INTERMEDIATE FORMS
UKE-NO KATA	The defense form
NI-NO KATA	The second form
GOSOKU KATA	The hard-fast form
DEN-KO-GETSU KATA	The lightening moon form
GOSOKU-YODAN KATA	The hard-fast 4th form
KIME-NO KATA	The focus form

THE ADVANCED FORMS
GO-NO KATA (IKA SAN CHIN)	The three battles form
RIKYU KATA	The circle of advantage form
TAMASHI KATA	The soul (spirit) form
GOSOKU-GODAN KATA	The hard-fast 5th form
RAI-DEN KATA	The thunder bolt form
AN-SO-NO KATA	The peace form

The next three advanced katas were introduced in late 2005.

KIME-NO KATA	The focus form
JU-HACHINO DACHI KATA	The eighteen steps form
JIYU NO MICHI KATA	Long life

Except for the advanced forms listed above, the rest are part of IKA's curriculum for the black belt test.

A brief discussion of the highlights of those Gosoku-ryu katas required for the Shodan grade is presented in the next section.

Students are reminded again that written descriptions of kata are beneficial only when put into practice in a dojo under the supervision of a qualified instructor.

THE ESSENCE OF KIHON KATAS

Kihon katas have been designed specifically to make teaching and learning traditional and advanced forms of kata easier. Kihon katas are also some of the best forms to use when practicing basic techniques and combinations. They are the forerunners of all Gosoku-ryu katas. Most importantly they display the essence of the "hard-fast" method.

All important precepts of kata performance are incorporated in the Kihon series. The number of techniques and combinations in each of these forms is kept to a minimum to allow the student to develop an early sense of appreciation for such important features as:

- Etiquette and expression of respect
- The line of movement
- Timing and speed of performance
- Breath control and flow of energy
- Relaxation and rest
- Balance and coordination
- Kiai and kime
- Proper body and foot movement
- Rhythm and pace control
- Correctness of stance and posture
- Bunkai and visualization
- Spiritual and mental focus
- Endurance and deliberation
- Attention to detail.
- Gosoku-ryu concepts
- Expression of force and power

Because of their great training and educational value, Kihon katas must be practiced frequently and with a great deal of attention to the basic features of kata performance identified above. Brief descriptions of the fundamental movements of the Kihon and intermediate Gosoku-ryu katas are presented in the next section.

Full descriptions of the advanced Gosoku-ryu katas are beyond the scope of this book. The interpretation, or meaning, of these or any other kata can never be described satisfactorily with words. However, the contents of this book should help the student develop a better understanding of the physical conditioning and correct mental and spiritual attitude behind the basic karate moves.

Beginners should make a habit of visualizing the actions of their imaginary opponents while performing Kihon and other katas. Students should continue this method of practice until the action and corresponding reaction become second nature. Then it might be possible, in a real situation, such as freestyle sparring, to counter a similar action with an appropriate reaction. The essence of each kata must be felt intuitively by the karateka. Kihon katas, by virtue of their design, offer excellent opportunities for students to attempt to make their first mental and spiritual connection with kata practice. The basic movements of Kihon katas are easy to memorize. They have been designed to become natural reflexes through repeated and frequent practice of the same movements. This will allow the student to feel instinctively the need for improvement through maturity and deeper understanding of each kata. Maturity in this context means developing a sense of proficiency in all 14 features of kata performance described in this section. Gosoku-ryu karate begins with Kihon katas.

KIHON ICHI-NO KATA

Basic Kata Number One, or the Kihon Ichi-No kata, is the first kata of the first group of kihon katas. There are four katas in this group. Kihon ichi-no kata contains the entire grammar of this group of exercises, and as such it is fully described in this section. It is the first kata beginners learn at IKA headquarters and affiliated dojos. This is followed by the Kihon Ni-No, San-No, and Yon-No katas. The line of action of this family of katas is the imaginary letter "I."

They all consist of only 20 movements, which start and end at the same point. There are two kiais, first at the upper, then at the lower end of the line of action. At normal speed, they take less than one minute to complete.

Kihon ichi-no kata is performed entirely on zenkutsu-dachi with repeated applications of gedan-barai and chudan Oi-tsuki techniques. The choreography of this simple kata from the yoi position is as follows:

The performer turns his head to the left to see the approaching opponent. He pauses fractionally, turns 90 degrees to the left, pivots on the ball of the right foot and assumes a left forward stance, or Zenkutsu-dachi, and performs a left Gedan-barai. As the left hand is lowered into the Gedan-barai position (from near the right ear) the right hand is retracted to the right hip as if executing a right-hand back elbow strike. The two hand movements are performed simultaneously. The body now is poised for a right hand Oi-tsuki attack. The performer pauses a split second, then lunges forward to perform a middle-level right Oi-tsuki while in Zenkutsu-dachi. Exhalation continues throughout the entire attacking motion and is completed at impact.

The performer remains in Oi-tsuki for a split second. Sensing an imminent lower-level attack from behind, the performer turns his head first to the right, then his body 180 degrees in a clockwise direction, this time pivoting on the left foot and performing a right-hand Gedan-barai while assuming a right forward Zenkutsu-dachi. After a split second, a left forward Oi-tsuki is performed to subdue the second opponent.

Having completed the second set of movements, the performer turns 90 degrees to the left and delivers a left lower-level block from a left forward stance. He then manages a right-hand Oi-tsuki, then pauses a split second. The performer then executes two consecutive Oi-tsuki along the same straight line. The second Oi-tsuki is augmented by complete exhalation through the mouth with a loud kiai at impact. There is no pause between the two consecutive Oi-tsukis. Up to this point, the performer has faced three opponents, one after another. There are five more to fend off.

The performer senses another attacker approaching from the right and turns around in a counterclockwise direction, pivoting on the front right foot a three quarters of a circle and delivering a left

Gedan-barai followed by a right Oi-tsuki. This is the halfway point of the kata.

The rest of the kata follows as the mirror image of the first half. If performed correctly, the practitioner should find himself back at the kata's starting point after the last movement.

The last movement of the Kihon katas, or the finishing act, is of great technical and educational value. The 20th move, designed to subdue the eighth opponent with a left Oi-tsuki, finishes along the lower right-hand arm of the imaginary letter "I." The right rear foot must now be near the starting point. The performer remains motionless in this position until the instructor calls out, "Yame!" The performer then pivots on the right foot to face front (or starting position) by turning 90 degrees counterclockwise and assuming a Gyaku-hachiji-dachi or uchi-mata-dachi stance with the knees slightly bent. As the body completes the turn, the hands are thrust down into an open palm Gedan-juji-uke and are retracted to the sides immediately with fists clenched over the hips. This combination blocks a lower-level attack to the groin area and executes a Morote-ushiro-empi-uchi, the two hand back elbow strike. A deep abdominal inhalation through the nose takes place during this set of movements. As the fists are lowered down into the Yoi position, the breath is exhaled completely from the depths of the lungs through the mouth using the abdominal muscles to tighten the stomach and push all air out. All kihon katas end the same way after yame.

Kihon Ichi-No kata and all other kihon katas, regardless of their dachi forms are performed entirely on suri-ashi or sliding steps. Students must observe the golden rule when performing this and other katas:

"Look first, move, then deliver the technique."

KIHON NI-NO KATA

Basic Kata Number Two, or Kihon Ni-No kata, is conducted entirely in Kokutsu-dachi, instead of in the forward stance. The purpose of this kata is, obviously, to strengthen and stabilize the performers back stance in kata and kumite.

The grammar of this kata is exactly the same as the previous one. It is practically the same as Kihon Ichi-No kata except the Gedan-barai is replaced with Gedan-shuto-uke, a lower-level knife hand block. The reactive hand, instead of making an upturned fist on the hip, now becomes a horizontal, open hand, palm up, Shuto-uke protecting the solar plexus. All non-turning stance blocks are Chudan-shuto-uke. The line of action, number of movements and time to completion of this and all group-I kihon katas are similar. Kihon Ni-No kata is an ideal form for practicing suri-ashi from kokutsu-dachi to kokutsu-dachi.

KIHON SAN-NO KATA

The line of movement of Basic Kata Number Three, or Kihon San-No kata, is also the imaginary letter "I." The grammar of this kata is the same as that described above. All techniques are performed with power and confidence.

The entire kata consists of 20 consecutive Yoko-gedan-barai or sideways down blocks, all delivered from Kiba-dachi or horse stances. The rhythm and sequence of movements are the same as in the preceding two katas.

As with Kihon Ni-No kata, this kata consists only of defensive moves. Kihon San-No kata is also an excellent form of exercise for correcting posture and strengthening leg muscles.

KIHOH YON-NO KATA

Kihon Yon-no kata is the fourth basic form and the last kata of its group. The grammar of this kata is the same as that described for basic kata number one except for a slight modification at the end. It introduces thee new techniques: the upper block, the outside and inside blocks. It is a completely defensive kata. It takes less than sixty seconds to complete this kata.

The chain of events is as follows: Yoi. Left turn with left gedan-barai into left front stance, right oi-ashi with right gedan-barai into right front stance. This completes the first set.

Turn 180 degrees clockwise and repeat the set. Turn 90 degrees counterclockwise with a left gedan-barai into a left front stance. This completes the third set. Right oi-ashi into right front stance with right jodan-age-uke or upper block, followed by two consecutive oi-zenkutsu-ashi dachis with upper blocks. Kiai and pause on the last technique. Turn right 90 degrees on right zenkutsu-dachi with right soto-uke, step forward into left front stance with left soto-uke. Turn 180 degrees counterclockwise into left front stance with left soto-uke, step forward into right front stance with right soto-uke.Turn left 90 degrees into a front stance with left gedan-barai. Right oi-ashi into right front stance with right inside block(uchi uke). Continue with two consecutive oi-zenkutsu-ashi dachis with inside blocks. Kiai and kime on the last technique. Turn left 90 degrees into a kokutsu-dachi with left soto-shuto-uke. Slide rear foot next to front foot into a heisoku-dachi. Slide the right foot into a kiba-dachi in the direction of the stem of letter "I" with a right yoko-gedan-barai. Turn 180 degrees clockwise into another kokutsu-dachi with a right soto-shuto-oi-uke. Slide the rear foot to the front right foot into a heisohu-dachi. Slide the left foot into a kiba-dachi in the direction of the stem of letter "I" with a left yoko-gedan-barai. Yame. Perform the standard end set and wait for the command to assume musubi-dachi and rey. End of kata.

KIHON GO-NO KATA

Kihon Go-no kata is the first kata of the second family of the kihon forms. There are only three kata in this group. The line of action of this family of kata is a straight line with short perpendicular branches on each side; however they start and end at the same point. Each kata contains exactly 12 moves, 11 steps, 10 sets of movements, and two kiai.

The first eleven moves all are front hand defensive blocks. The last combination ends with a reverse thrusting strike. There are three kiai in this group of basic forms. The first kiai is associated with the first hand technique of the first set of movements. The last two kias are associated with the eighth and the last hand techniques of these kata. The eighth move is performed without pause after the seventh move. The combination of the seventh and eighth moves is considered a single set.

Each kata is performed on a single dachi from start to end. At normal speed it takes less than half a minute to complete each kata. The timing of the sets is the same for all three katas of this group. The emphasis of the forms is on the correct execution of stances, timing, techniques, hanmi, kime and kiai.

The very last technique is a strong reverse hand strike. It projects the notion that while karate is essentially a defensive method of self-protection, a single strike can end the argument in favor of the defender.

Kihon go-no kata is entirely carried on zenkutsu-dachi. The head is always turned in the direction of the move before turning the body. The choreography of kihon go-no kata is as follows: From yoi, the performer steps back with the right foot and delivers a left-hand gedan-barai. The down block is accompanied with a loud kiai. This completes the first set of moves. He then steps forward with the same foot and delivers a right-hand gedan-barai. Next he pivots on the left foot, turns right 90 degrees and delivers another right gedan-barai. The next move is a 180 degree counterclockwise turn with a left-hand gedan-barai. Pivoting on the ball of the left foot, the performer turns 270 degrees clockwise and down blocks with the left hand. Next, a single forward oi-gedan-barai (step and down block) is performed. A momentary pause is observed. The kata is continued with two consecutive oi-gedan-barai in the same direction with a loud kiai on the last down block. The performer now steps back three times with a front hand down block on each step.

The last down block is followed by a right hand gyaku-zuki or reverse punch accompanied with a decisive kime and loud kiai. Yame, the performer slides the front foot back next to the rear foot into shizen-dachi. Next, musubi-achi and rey.

The general format of group II katas also is the basis of group IV forms described in this section.

KIHON ROKU-NO KATA

Kihon roku-no kata or basic form number six is carried on entirely kokutsu-dachis. The format of this kata is exactly the same as the previous one, with the exception that all gedan-barais are replaced with chudan soto-shuto-uke or mid-level outward knife hand blocks, and that the last combination is replaced with a left hand osae-uke together with a right spear-hand attack. Yame, standard finishing act. Return to shizen-cachi, then musubi-dachi and rey.

KIHON SICHI-NO KATA

Kihon sichi-no or basic form number seven is the third and last kata of the second group. It is performed entirely on kiba-dachi or horse stance.

The general format of this kata is the same as kihon go-no kata. The difference is that the zenkutzu-dachi are replaced with kiba-dachi. The gedan-barai are unaltered. After performing the last left-hand down block, the performer changes the last stance from kiba-dachi to zenkutzu-dachi by pivoting on the heel of the rear right foot and sliding the left foot to the right.

The last act, i.e., the change of stance, is accompanied with a strong right hand gyaku-tsuki and kiai. Yame, followed by the finishing ritual.

KIHON HACHI-NO KATA

Kihon hachi-no kata is the first kata of the third family of forms. Currently there are three katas in this group. Each kata is composed of 12 simple techniques and eight sets of movements. There is only one type of blocking and one type of thrusting strike in each kata. There is only one kiai accompanied with the last hand technique of the last set of moves.

The first move after yoi is stepping back with the right foot into either a zenkutsu-dachi, kokutsu-dachi or kiba dachi, with the left hand performing a simple front block. The last typical block is followed by a strong reverse-hand thrusting technique with a loud kiai. Each kata is carried on a single but different stance from start to finish. The line of action of this group of katas is highly irregular, and is of little educational value at this stage.

These katas are very stimulating and easy to learn. The first and last moves are accompanied with kiai and kime. At normal speed, it takes less than 30 seconds to finish each kata. The timing is the same for all three forms.

The significant concept introduced in these forms is the left and right "half-turns" that take place consecutively three times at the end of the kata.

Kihon hachi-no kata is performed entirely on zenkutsu dachis. The defensive technique is the gedan-barai.

After yoi, the performer steps back with the right foot and delivers a left hand down block with kiai, then pauses and performs a forward right hand Oi-tsuki chudan. Next, he turns 180 degrees clockwise, delivers a right hand down block, followed by a left hand Oi-tsuki chudan. He then turns back 180 degrees counterclockwise and performs a left hand down block, followed by a right hand Oi-tsuki chudan.

Again, he turns around 180 degrees clockwise, delivers a right hand gedan-barai, followed by the last left hand io-tsuki chudan. At this time, he pivots 180 degrees on the ball of the left foot, i.e., makes a "half-right turn," and delivers a right hand down block. He then makes a "half-left turn" followed by a "half-right" turn accompanied with a strong gyaku-tsuki and kiai. End of kata. The performer returns to shizen–dachi.

KIHON KU-NO KATA

Kihon ku-no kata follows the same grammar is its predecessor, the kihon hachi-no kata. It is carried on 11 consecutive kokutsu-dachis together with 11 soto-shuto-ukes. After completing the last outward knife edge block on back stance, the performer quickly changes the last dachi into a front stance by shifting his front foot to the left. Simultaneously, he performs a left hand osae-uke (an open hand press down) together with a right hand gyaku-tsuki. The tsuki is delivered with strong chime and kiai. Yame, standard finishing act, shizen-dachi.

KIHON JU-NO KATA

Kihon ju-no kata or the tenth basic form, is the last kata of the third group. Once again, the general format of this kata is exactly the same as that described for kihon-hachino kata. It is carried on 11 consecutive kiba-dachi together with 11 front hand sideway down blocks, (yoko gedan-barai). The first 10 sets of movements consist of consecutive down blocks on horse stance.

All sets involve either a right or a left turn except the fourth and last sets. In the fourth set, the performer's body is parallel with the beginning shizen-dachi position. The head is turned right and the right hand is in right side down block.

The transition from the fourth to fifth set takes place by sliding the entire body from right to left into the next kiba-dachi, simultaneously performing a left hand yoko gedan-barai. In the last set, the performer quickly changes the last kiba-dachi into a front stance by pivoting counterclockwise on the ball of the back foot and shifting the front foot to the left. At the same time delivers a strong right hand gyaku-tsuki while retracting the left fist over the left hip. The tsuki is of course performed with kime and kiai. Yame, standard finish and shizen-dachi.

KIHON JU-ICHI-NO KATA.

Kihon ju-ichi-no kata, or the eleventh basic form is the first kata of the fourth group. There are four katas in this group. The general format is exactly the same as that described for group II forms. In fact it is considered a natural extension and development of the latter group of kata. It consists of 17 consecutive hand techniques, 11 steps, 10 sets of movement and 2 kiai, all carried on the same stance.

They are all purely defensive forms, except the very last technique, which is a right hand thrusting attack. A reminder that the defender, the "Uke" is not defenseless, is confident, and can end the conflict with a single strike after patiently but deliberately blocking the offender's attacks several times.

The highlight of these forms, besides demonstrating Gosoku-ryu's quick turns, returns and side stepping maneuvers is the introduction of a simple but very effective defensive combination. This combination encourages the use of the palm down "Yonhon-nukite" or the extended arm spear hand technique at eye level. It is the best and the quickest first line of defense before resorting to any other technique.

Another important idea reiterated here is the retreating step combined with a defensive technique.

The chorography of the eleventh basic form after yoi is as follows;

The performer steps back with the right foot and simultaneously performs a right side, eye level, spear hand technique, in an attempt to either defuse or slow down the opponents attack. He then performs a left-hand jodan-age-uke. This completes the first set of moves. He then steps forward with the same foot and delivers a left side spear hand attack followed by a right-hand jodan-age-uke. Next he pivots on the left foot, turns right 90 degrees and delivers another combination of left yonhon-nukite and right jodan-age-uke.

The next move is a 180-degree counterclockwise turn with a right hand yonhon-nukite followed by a left-hand jodan-age-uke. Pivoting on the ball of the left foot, the performer turns 270 degrees clockwise while thrusting a right hand yonhon-nukite forward followed by a left hand jodan-age uke. This completes the last combination of two hand techniques on the same dachi. Next a single forward oi-jodan-age-ukei (step and down up) is performed. A momentary pause is observed.

The kata is continued with two consecutive oi-jodan-age-uke in the same direction with a loud kiai on the last up block. The performer now steps back three times with a front hand up block on each step. The last up block is followed by a right hand gyaku-zuki or reverse punch accompanied with a decisive kime and loud kiai. Yame, the performer returns to shizen-dachi.

Once the student understands the general format of this kata, the next three katas will become very easy to learn. The fourth kata does not fully belong to this family of forms, but its general format is the same for all intents and purposes.

KIHON JU-NI-NO KATA

Kihon ju-ni-no kata, the twelfth basic form is an exact replica of its predecessor, with the difference that all jodan-age-uke, the upper blocks, are replaced with corresponding soto-ude-uke-chudan, or mid-level forearm outward blocks.

KIHON JU-SAN-NO KATA

Kihon ju-san-no kata, is the third kata of the fourth group. Once again it follows the same exact format as kihon ju-ichi-no kata, i.e, the same number of sets of movements, the same rhythm, the same timing, kiais, etc., except that all upper blocks are replaced with uche-ude-uke chudan, or mid-level inward forearm blocks.

KIHON JU-YON NO KATA

Kihon juyon-no kata is the last form of the fourth group of katas. The general format of this kata is the same as that described for its predecessors, with one exception: there are no spear-hand blocks. The statistical numbers are the same.

The kata is performed entirely on front stance, except the last act where he performs a front hand down block, kneels on the rear right knee, and delivers a right gyaku-tsuki. The gyaku-tsuki is accompanied with a loud kiai.

The new ideas introduced in this form are the use of the double hand blocks and the "hiza-dachi." The first eight sets are composed of simultaneous two-handed basic blocks: a left hand outward mid-level block and a right hand down block.

All "migi-chudan-soto-ukes typically start from the opposite hip, as if drawing a sword, and stop just below the chin. All "gedan-barai"s start from behind the opposite ear and stop in front of the groin.

The ninth through eleventh sets of movements portray retreating steps on consecutive zenkutsu-dachis with augmented outward blocks or "morote-ukes."

KIHON JU-GO-NO KATA

Kihon ju-go-no kata is the fifteenth and last basic form. Others may be introduced in the future. Presently there is only one kata in this group. It is an invigorating kata to perform and esthetically pleasing to watch. Its degree of difficulty is slightly higher than the last ten basic forms. There are 14 consecutive sets of movements in this form. There is only one kiai associated with the last hand technique of the kata.

This kata introduced several new stances and techniques. A few of the sets display rather advanced combinations of blocks and strikes.

The new dachis introduced in this forms in order of occurrence are: Kosa-dachi, shiko-dachi, ippon-dachi, re-no-dachi, neko-ashi-dachi, sanchin-dachi, and uhci-mata-dachi. The new techniques, also in order of occurrence are: yoko-tate-shuto-uke, haito-uchi, gosoku-uke, teisho-uke, and ippon-nukite.

From yoi, the performer steps forward with the right foot into a kosa-dachi or crossed foot stance while turning his body 90 degrees counterclockwise and delivers a left hand down block, with the right hand retracted to his right hip. This completes the first set of movements. Then he pivots 180 degrees counterclockwise on the ball of the right foot and assumes a shiko-dachi stance with both hands splayed straight at the sides, and palms facing front. Next he pivots 90 degrees counterclockwise on the ball of the left foot into an ippon- dachi, with the supporting left leg slightly bent to assure momentary equilibrium. The arms are extended horizontally on each side of the body with both hands open and held vertically, tate-shuto-uke, as if pushing things away from the performer. This completes the third set of actions.

Next, the performer drops the right foot forward into a reno-dachi and delivers a left hand shuto-gedan-uke with the other hand shuto protecting the solar plexus, then he performs two consecutive shuto-gedan ukes both in reno-dachi. This brings the performer to the end of line of kata. He pauses momentarily and retreats backward on three consecutive neko-ashi-dachi while blocking the opponents advance by front hand shuto-gedan-ukes on each step. He stops going back, instead pivots 90 degrees counterclockwise on the front foot, steps into a sanchin-dachi and performs a lower level juji-uke. Next, he pivots on the left foot, 90 degrees clockwise into an uchi-mata-dachi, and strikes the opponent with morote-haito uchi at the neck and retracts the fists over the hips, as if delivering a two handed elbow attack. The double handed neck attack is accompanied with a strong kiai.

For the last combination, the performer slides his right foot forward into a neko-ashi-dachi, performs a two handed gosoku-uke, followed by ippon-nukite attack. Next, he performs a double handed press up or morote-age-teisho-uke, as if volleying a large ball upwards with both palms up, followed by a similar press down.Yame.

KIHON SONOTA KATA

The concept of the Sonota kata, or basic miscellaneous form, is a reflection of Soke's genius as an expert in the field of martial arts education.

Kihon Sonota kata is one of the most effective methods of self-training available to all karateka, especially beginners and intermediate level students.

Kihon Sonota is a generic kata with no prearranged combinations or stances. It can be executed using any combination or mix of basic techniques. For instance, instead of performing consecutive Gedan-barais followed by Oi-tsuki, as in Kihon Ichi-No kata, the performer or instructor may elect to replace the Oi-tsuki with Mae-geri. In this case, the kata will be called Kihon Mae-Geri-No kata, or the basic front kick form.

The basic rules for the Sonota kata are these: the embusen or the line of movement is the imaginary letter "I"; there are exactly 20 movements, and the eighth and sixteenth movements are accompanied with kiais.

The student is free to select the dachi-kata, the ashi-sabaki, and the tai-sabaki. Kihon Sonota kata provides excellent opportunities for being creative and innovative

While exploring new ideas, the student should visualize the actions of imaginary opponents throughout the kata. This kata can be used to improve any particular technique, combination of techniques or combative skills that the instructor may wish to select for a student.

Kihon Sonota kata is an ideal method of practice for techniques such as the Mawashi-geri, the Ushiro-geri, the Ura-mawashi-geri, and other waza that are not encountered very often in the classical forms.

INTERMEDIATE KATAS

The next six forms are called intermediate katas as they involve a higher degree of difficulty and are required for passing the black belt test.

UKE NO KATA

Among its many applications, this kata demonstrates the first functional uses of Gosoku-ryu karate. Uke No kata consists of 30 basic movements and takes about one minute to complete, depending on the proficiency of the student.

Although the name of this intermediate level kata means "blocking or defense form," it includes a number of offensive techniques performed with great speed and power before and after quickly executed Gedan-barai.

All turns are performed quickly to add angular momentum to the Gedan-barai that follow. All Gedan-barai start with the fist of the blocking hand near the opposite ear for maximum distance, acceleration and power.

The kata begins with a 90-degree left turn accompanied by a left Gedan-barai. This is followed by a right Oi-tsuki and a counterclockwise Mawate into Zenkutsu-dachi, accompanied by another left Gedan-barai. The stance is almost normal length. The next Zenkutsu-dachi is somewhat shorter, allowing a rapid counterclockwise pivot of 90 degrees into the third Zenkutsu-dachi of the first set of movements. The first three moves are performed rapidly one after the other. A very short pause takes place after the completion of this set.

The next set of three movements consists of a right Oi-tsuki, a left Oi-gedan-barai, and a 90-degree left turn accompanied by another left Gedan-barai. The second set of movements also is performed in a quick and brisk manner. A second short pause takes place, followed by a right Oi-jodan-age-uke. Another split second pause takes place.

The next set of movements along the stem of the letter "I" consists of a nonstop left Oi-jodan-age-uke followed by a right Oi-tsuki. The Oi-tsuki is augmented by a loud kiai. The kata continues after a split second pause, the performer making a half circle counterclockwise turn from a near normal length Zenkutsu-dachi and delivering a left-hand Gedan-barai. The Gedan-barai is followed by a right Oi-tsuki and a rapid 180 degree counterclockwise Mawate into Zenkutsu-dachi with a left Gedan-barai.

The next set of three movements is an exact copy of the second set of movements. The performer is looking now straight back at the starting point of the kata. The performer then executes two consecutive Oi-soto-ude-uke, starting with the right arm, followed by a right Chudan-oi-kwntsui-uchi augmented by the second kiai of the kata. The performer is now back at the starting point but facing in the opposite direction.

The next move is a half circle counterclockwise turn with a powerful left Gedan-barai. After a split second pause, two consecutive Oi-tsuki, starting with the right hand, are performed, followed by a clockwise Mawate and a right hand Gedan-barai. This is the first clockwise turn of the entire kata. Two consecutive Oi-tsuki followed by a counterclockwise Mawate with a left gedan-barai are executed to bring the performer back to the starting point with both shoulders in line with the stem of the imaginary letter "I." The performer then pivots on the ball of the front left foot, turns the body 90 degrees clockwise, assumes a normal left forward Zenkutsu-dachi, while performing a right Gedan-barai; a left Jodan-yonhon-nukite, or spear hand eye attack; and a right hand Chudan-gyaku-tsuki. The Gyaku-tsuki is performed with full force and kiai.

After a split second pause, the right hand is retracted slowly to the hips as if delivering a slow motion Ushiro-empi-uchi. The left hand performs a slow motion middle-level punch. The performer then assumes Gyaku-hachiji-dachi at the starting line and brings both fists to the sides of the rib cage, as if performing double backward elbow strikes.

Immediately, the performer bends the knees, lowers the body quickly and executes a lower-level open hand Juji-uke. He/she then slightly straightens the knees and raises the hands up to the chest level, while holding the crossed hands block. The fists are clenched and squeezed. Both hands are lowered slowly to the sides, as if performing Yoko-gedan-barais. The fists still are clenched. They are squeezed one more time, and then released into open hand forms. After "yame" the performer automatically assumes musubi-dachi for the final rey.

NI-NO KATA

This very elegant and highly educational kata displays many basic ideas unique to Gosoku-ryu karate, notably several fast turns and returns, foot shuffling, half steps, close quarters fighting techniques, and generation of power through speed and abdominal breathing. Ni-No kata, literally *The Second Form*, has a more challenging choreography than the preceding Gosoku-ryu forms.

The line of motion, with some variations, conforms generally to the imaginary Letter "I." The kata contains a total of 42 movements conducted from a variety of stances. At normal speed this kata takes about one minute to complete.

The first movement of the kata, starting from the Yoi position, resembles an open hands Juji-uke-gedan, accompanied by a strong kiai. This is followed by a powerful two hand back elbow strike, or Morote-ushiro-empi-uchi, also with a kiai. While performing the Juji-uke, the knees are bent slightly and the toes turned inward into a Gyaku-hachiji-dachi stance. The double elbow strike is augmented by the slight straightening of the knees and tightening of the abdominal muscles by exhaling through the mouth.

This dynamic movement is followed by a slow motion lowering of the fists back to the Yoi position. The hands are lowered simultaneously with a complete exhalation through the mouth. From Gyaku-hachiji-dachi, the performer slowly moves the left foot forward in a counterclockwise suri-ashi arc into a left foot forward Zenkutsu-dachi while keeping the tensed hands at the sides as if blocking lower-level strikes to the thighs. The body still is facing front.

The performer then executes a very slow double outward forearm block, or Morote-ude-soto-uke, followed by the slow return of the hands to their original side blocking position. While still in Zenkutsu-dachi, the performer begins to execute a slow left outward forearm block and retracts the right fist over the right hip, shifting to Fudo-dachi during the block, in preparation for a reverse punch. This slow motion combination is completed with a slow but powerful right Gyaku-tsuki with the reactive hand pulled back over the left hip while shifting into Zenkutsu-dachi. The stomach muscles are tightened and exhalation is completed when the punch is concluded. These seven movements complete the opening set of the kata. The rest of the movements are performed at normal speed.

The next set consists of a simultaneous right step and left reverse middle-level punch, followed immediately by a right middle-level Oi-tsuki. A left Oi-gedan-barai is performed next. The performer then delivers a right Chudan-oi-yama-tsuki, in a right Ren-dachi, continued into a right Jodan-Oi-tsuki while extending the half step (the Ren-dachi) into a full right forward stance. This combination is completed with a left Gyaku-tsuki-chudan with kime and kiai. The last three sets of combinations are performed rapidly with very brief pauses between the sets.

At this point, there is a split second pause, the performer proceeds with the next set of movements that starts with a counterclockwise half circle turn, pivoting on the right foot and performing a left outward middle-level forearm block in a left forward stance. This is followed by a right Chudan-oi-soto-ude-uke and a left Mawate in conjunction with a powerful Chudan-soto-ude-uke. The three forearm blocks are executed rapidly and smoothly one after the other.

The next set of three movements in the same direction consists of a right half step Oi-jodan-age-uke, a half step Oi-mawashi-empi-uchi-jodan, and extension of the left half step into a full left forward stance with delivery of a right middle-level reverse punch with kiai. After a split second pause, the performer turns 90 degrees left, pivoting on the ball of the right foot and assuming a left forward stance. This left turn is accompanied by a sweeping Haito-uke-gedan delivered with speed and accuracy to counter a Mae-geri attack. This defensive move is followed without interruption by a right Oi-kentsui-uchi-gedan. The next movement is a left inward Oi-ashi-barai becoming a left forward Zenkutsu-dachi, executed simultaneously with a middle-level breaking technique.

The next two sets of movements describe typical Gosoku-ryu combinations. The first set consists of stepping forward with the right foot into a Kiba-dachi. Both feet are perpendicular to the forward line of movement and the line of vision remains fixed at the starting point of the kata. The practitioner delivers a strong right-hand Yoko-gedan-barai. At the completion of the Gedan-barai the head is turned quickly back in a counterclockwise direction to face an opponent approaching from behind. Consequently, the body is shifted to a left forward Kokutsu-dachi and facing the opposite direction, and performs a left hand Gedan-shuto-uke.

Next, the body turns half a circle in a clockwise direction, pivoting on the left foot into a left forward Kokutsu-dachi, performing a left hand Chudan-shuto-uchi-uke.

The last two sets are performed quickly without any delays between them. After a split second pause, the kata is continued by executing a Gyaku-mae-geri-chudan followed by a right Yoko-tsuki-chudan at the same time the kicking foot is brought down into a Kiba-dachi stance with the head again facing toward the starting point of the kata. This anticipates further action from the opponent, who has just been subdued. Shifting the weight of the body to the rear left foot, the right foot is retracted into a Reno-dachi followed by a right Gedan-barai protecting the groin area.

The next two combinations also display methods of close quarter fighting. From the Reno-dachi, facing toward the starting point of the kata, the performer turns a half circle counterclockwise, pivoting on the front foot into a left forward Kokutsu-dachi while executing a left chudan-shuto-uchi-uke. A split second later the performer steps into a Kiba-dachi in the plane of the body with the left foot remaining fixed in its place. As the Kiba-dachi is being completed, the left hand executes a Chudan-ude-uchi-uke while the right hand delivers a Gedan-barai. The right hand is retracted to deliver a back fist attack to the opponent's face while the left hand simultaneously blocks a Chudan-tsuki.

The performer next conducts a clockwise Mawate and repeats the last three techniques in the same order. The next move is a brisk 90 degree left turn into a Reno-dachi with the left hand performing a lower-level knife hand block. The performer steps back with the left foot into a Fudo-dachi and performs a right Jodan-age-uke. The stance is shifted into a Zenkutsu-dachi while performing a left Gyaku-tsuki.

The next set, which represents typical Gosoku-ryu action, consists of a fast shuffling of the feet from a right foot forward Zenkutsu-dachi to a left foot forward Kokutsu-dachi. This is followed by a left Chudan-shuto-uke and a double spear hand neck attack in Gyaku-hachiji-dachi. The performer then executes a Morote-ushiro-empi in the same stance.

The last set of movements in this kata demonstrates the use of the Ippon-ken together with a double hand press-down block. These two techniques are conducted through a breathing sequence that is designed to enhance the performance and calm the spirit.

KIME NO KATA

Kime No Kata or the focus form is the latest intermediate Gosoku Ryu form created by Soke Takayuki Kubota. This kata was introduced to IKA students in early 2001. It is a beautiful, relatively short and highly educational kata that emphasizes: in-depth concentration, generation of power through twisting and changing of stances, localized fighting and breathing control.

It consists of 40 consecutive techniques performed with a variety of postures and stances. At normal speed it takes less than 50 seconds to perform the kata. The embusen does not confirm to any familiar line of action such as the "I", "T" or straight line configurations. The line of action is highly irregular but realistic and revolves about the "Yoi" position as if the performer is surrounded by many opponents attacking from all four sides. The kata begins and ends at the same position. One or both feet are always on or near the "Yoi" position, reflecting the performer's determination to hold ground during the entire encounter.

The new techniques introduced in this kata are: the upper level open hand palm attack or the face and temple slap, the twisting side punch and an arm breaking technique. The basic choreography of the kata is as follows where the word "pause" indicates the beginning and/or start of a set of actions.

From Yoi, right leg back, zenkutsu-dachi, left gedan-barai with kiai, pause. Right chudan-oi-tsuki. Pause, look right, pivot 90 degrees right on left foot, assume right foot front stance with right down block, and pause. Perform left oi-tsuki chudan, pause. Look left, pivot 125 degrees counterclockwise on the right foot, assume left foot front stance with left hand down bock, and pause. The next five techniques are all conducted on front stance consecutively without stopping. These are: straight right oi-tsuki, mawate counterclockwise left down block, right oi-tsuki, 125 degrees counterclockwise rotation on the ball of the front foot, facing front, right gedan-barai followed by left gyaku-tsuki with kiai, pause. The next three moves are also conducted consecutively without stopping. Pivot 90 degrees clockwise on the ball of the front foot, step into kiba-dachi, left yoko-gedan-barai, look right, mawate right into ren-dachi, right gedan-shuto-uke, mawate left into neko-ashi-dachi, gosou-uke, pause. Look right, step into shiko-dachi at 45 degrees to Yoi position, both hands lowered to the sides with palms facing front and in the same plane as the shoulders, pause. Next pivot 90 degrees clockwise on the ball of the left foot and assume hangetsu-dachi as the hands move forward in symmetric circular motions, crossing each other and coming to rest at the hips as if delivering a double backward elbow attack, inhale, slow juji-uke gedan, exhale, pause. The next three moves constitute a set and are executed without stopping. Pivot counterclockwise 315 degrees on the left foot, assume left zenkutsu-dachi facing front and deliver a right open hand face attack or temple slap, withdraw the left foot half a step into a left ren-dachi, left jodan-age-uke, drop into a left front stance and deliver a right hand reverse punch with kiai, pause. Step forward into a right foot front kokutsu-dachi simultaneously performing a soto-shuto-uke chudan, pause. Mawate counterclockwise into a left foot forward kokutsu-dachi with an accompanying left hand soto-shuto-uke-chudan, pause. Right oi-tsuki-chudan, pause. Mawate counterclockwise into a left front foot neko-ashi-dachi with the hands forming a cosa-ude-uke or cross armed block where the right hand executes a gedan-barai and the left a soto-ude-chudan, pause. Place the back foot in front of the front foot and assume a right foot front kosa-dachi with the left hand performing a gedan-barai and the right fist being retracted over the right hip as if performing an ushiro-empi-uchi, both knees remain bent, pause. The next set of moves is conducted seamlessly without stopping. First the body is twisted counterclockwise by straightening the knees and assuming a right foot front ren-dachi as the right hand delivers a face punch, then the left foot takes two consecutive half steps forward, the first accompanied with a short ura-tsuki-chudan which continues to become a straight face punch at the completion of the second half step, the performer remains in this left foot front zenkutsu-dachi and delivers a right gyaku-tsuki, pause. Pivot 180 degrees clockwise on the ball of the front foot, place right foot next to left foot and assume heisoku-dachi with both knees slightly bent, at the same time swing the right hand to perform a gedan-nagashi-uke and continue to become a stiff jodan-age-uke, the knees remain bent, with the right foot fixed to the ground the left foot moves forward into a front stance accompanied with a left tsuki-chudan. Now, with the left foot fixed to the ground perform a counterclockwise mawate into a right leg back front stance, the hands them move upwards and downwards in a circular motion to come to rest at the sides forming yoko-haiwan-gedan-uke or lower level sideways forearm blocks, pause. Both arms are forcefully moved to form a middle level double outward block, pause. Look left, shift left leg 90 degrees left into a left foot front stance with the left hand performing a soto-ude-uke as if trapping a straight right punch, while the right hand performs a hammer fist attack on the trapped hand in order to break it, pause. Right oi-tsuki, pause. Look right, pivot 90 degrees clockwise on the ball of the left foot bring the front foot next to the left foot into a momentary heisoku-dachi with both knees bent, perform a seamless circular 3 block technique by swinging the right hand first into a gedan-barai continued to form a jodan-age-uke and another gedan-barai, with the right foot fixed in position the body drops into a left forward front stance while performing a left hand jogan-age-uke followed by a right gyaku-tsuki, pause. Pivot 90 degrees counterclockwise on the heel of the front foot and shift the right foot forward into a low kiba-dachi with the right hand forming a yoko-gedan-barai, pause. Look left, bring the left hand under the right armpit with palm facing down, slowly move the same hand in an outward circular horizontal motion to the other side of the body and turn it into an outward back hand or haishu-uke, pivot 180 degrees counterclockwise on the left foot as if performing a mawate into a kiba-dachi, but before the right foot hits the ground it performs a knee level ashi-barai and throws the opponent on the floor, next the performer assumes a heiko-dachi and straightens the knees in order to distance his/her face from a low level attack, meanwhile the left hand performs a gedan-teisho-uke to protect the groin area, pause, yame, end of kata.

GOSOKU KATA

This kata bears the name of the style it represents, the hard-fast method. It provides a clear and meaningful demonstration of the fundamental aspects of Gosoku-ryu karate as intended by Soke Takayuki Kubota.

Like most intermediate and advanced Gosoku-ryu kata, this form is not perfectly symmetrical. This is a hint that real combat situations do not follow set patterns. It contains approximately 74 movements and takes about 75 seconds to complete. The line of movement resembles the stem of the imaginary letter "I" and is traversed back and forth four times along the same line.

Gosoku kata contains and introduces a number of new ideas, techniques and combinations that are unique to the Gosoku-ryu style. The idea of generation of power through speed is inherent in most of the moves of this form.

The free flowing (hand and foot, defensive and offensive) succession of rapid movements encountered in this form exemplifies some of the sparring tactics favored by Soke.

The highlights of the Gosoku kata are as follows:

The opening moves and sets of techniques begin with an exhibition of power and speed that amply introduce the meaning of hard and fast, both to the viewer and the first time performer. This kata also is characterized by the introduction of the important Gosoku-ryu combination block, which consists of five rapid circular motions of the two hands.

The first application of the Gosoku block utilizes a left Jodan-tsuru-te-uke, or upper-level crane hand block, as the fourth component of the block. The Tsuru-te is preceded by an exaggerated right-hand Gedan-soto-nagashi-uke, or lower- level outward sweep, which is performed on ren-dachi in order to counter a low level attack from the right. Having completed the gedan-soto-nagashi-uke, which is the first component of the block, the right hand travels along a large inward circle to protect the face. This is the second part of the Gosoku uke and represents a Jodan-uchi-teisho-uke or a Jodan-uchi-shotei-uke. The same hand is then lowered down into the third part of the block, a Gedan-teisho-uke or Gedan-shotei-uke, whichever is appropriate.

The fifth and last part of the block consists of a right hand Chudan-teisho-uke, which is performed immediately after the

Tsuru-uke. Although these five different techniques are conducted in rapid succession, they appear to be occurring simultaneously. This combination is demonstrated gracefully on two occasions in the kata. The next spectacular exhibition of Gosoku-ryu action is a unique hand shuffling combination, which consists of a rapid succession of hand techniques (moves 13 through 16).

Starting from a left middle-level outward block, move 13 becomes a short upper cut chin attack. Move 14, starting from a Gedan-barai, becomes a rising strike, or Jodan-age-tsuki. Move 13 continues the same circular motion to form move 15, which is another upper cut. Move 14 is retracted along a horizontal line and turned into a direct straight upper level punch. All four hand movements are executed smoothly and continuously one after the other during the same breath without interruption.

Another important concept emphasized in this kata is the use of the same hand for delivering two consecutive but different strikes to the same opponent. For example, the execution of a Jodan-uraken-soto-uchi is followed by a Chudan-tetsui-soto-uchi, performed by the same hand. This combination is demonstrated on four different occasions in the kata. This effective combination always is followed by an opposite hand strike or thrust. The advantages of adjusting posture and stance to enhance offense and defense are demonstrated clearly in this and most other Gosoku-ryu katas. For instance, the 48th move begins from a left foot forward stance, with a right hand inward lower-level Nagashi that rises to become an Ushiro-empi-uchi. As the Nagashi is being performed, the left foot is retracted half a step back into a Reno-dachi. The left hand performs a Jodan-age-uke. The performer then moves the left foot forward into a Zenkutsu-dachi while the right hand delivers a powerful Gyaku-tsuki.

The added momentum of the body enhances the power of the reverse punch to its maximum. This subtle, yet powerful, combination is but one of many creative techniques that are unique to Gosoku-ryu karate. The last combination of the kata presents a brilliant demonstration of power, balance and muscular control.

CHAPTER 13

KUMITE

Kumite is the only means of sharing true combat experiences with real sparring partners. It is different from the shadow training used in waza and kata, which is the fundamental method of karate practice against imaginary opponents.

Literally translated, kumite means "an encounter with the hands" or "the meeting of the hands." It simply means "sparring." It was devised in the late 1920s as a complementary and more realistic means of karate practice.

Kumite provides karateka with an opportunity to refine their basic skills by putting them to use in a combat-like situation. It also aids development of certain other skills, such as instinctive blocking, body shifting and footwork, which kata and shadow practice alone cannot do.

Originally, kumite training amounted to limited Bunkai practice, when two equal ranking karateka would practice certain techniques of known kata repeatedly while trying to simulate real combat applications. This rather rigid method of training was replaced later with Kihon Yakusoku Kumite, or basic prearranged sparring, where the selected techniques did not necessarily come from a kata, and the sparring partners were not necessarily equal in ranking or grade.

In karate, sparring implies simulating true combat situations through mock fighting with a fellow karateka. Although kumite appears to be more in line with what most people imagine karate to be, it is neither all-out combat nor freestyle fighting. The moral and philosophical aspects of kumite extend far beyond the physical interpretations of sparring. Kumite is considered the ultimate learning experience in karate-do. Because of this, karateka do not engage in kumite with nonkarateka, or untrained individuals. Gaining mutual experience is the most beneficial aspect of kumite practice. Like kata, it is conducted most effectively with a free mind, devoid of emotions or preconceived ideas. Correct kumite practice is an excellent way to develop instinctive fighting and self-defense capabilities.

The ability to receive and deliver effective strikes is very much a function of proper timing, distancing, targeting, anticipation and confidence, which all are spontaneous reactions guided by the mind and the spirit.

True kumite involves the free exchange of effective techniques without thought as to whether you hit your opponent or get hit yourself. Kumite is neither a game nor a way of establishing physical superiority. It certainly is not a way of settling differences.

There are no losers or winners in kumite practice. Students learn through experience and enrich their way of life. Scoring, gaining points, determining a winner and loser are completely irrelevant. Competition training, however, is an entirely different concept that has little to do with regular kumite practice. Many regular fighting techniques, such as spinning back fist strikes are barred in tournament sparring.

There are three main types of kumite training: prearranged sparring, or Yakusoku kumite; semi-free single step sparring, or Ju Ippon kumite; and freestyle sparring, or Jiyu kumite. Each type serves a certain educational purpose and is performed in accordance with its own strict rules of conduct.

PRE-ARRANGED SPARRING

Yakusoku kumite is the most fundamental and valuable method of developing basic karate skills. The strict rules and conventions of engagement are devised to eliminate all nonapplicable activities, both mental and physical, and to concentrate all effort on the particular action being practiced. The goal is the gradual preparation of the students for semi-free and eventually freestyle engagements.

Although Yakusoku kumite appears to be simplistic and nonexciting in nature, it is one of the most important methods of basic karate training because it is relatively safe, practical and highly effective. Prearranged sparring is the most popular method of karate training, especially for higher ranking karateka who wish to share new ideas with their fellow students. The purpose of prearranged sparring is threefold.

First, prearranged sparring instills the moral values of karate-do, specifically courage, composure, courtesy, restraint, obedience, patience, focus, concentration, nonaggression, and the development of proper mental and spiritual attitudes. Rules of conduct prohibit the use of any technique that actually strikes a vital point on the partner, reflecting the need for the highest degree of mutual trust and respect between partners.

Second, and equally important, prearranged sparring develops certain strategic and tactical skills, such as prediction, anticipation, timing, distancing, targeting, quickness, responsiveness, and control of power.

Finally, it encourages the development of particular motor skills in both defender and attacker, as the same techniques can be deployed in self-defense and freestyle kumite. It has been designed to maximize benefits while reducing the chances of serious injuries.

Prearranged kumite is divided into three categories:

One-Step Sparring	or	Kihon Ippon Kumite
Two-Step Sparring	or	Kihon Nihon Kumite
Three-Step Sparring	or	Kihon Sanbon Kumite

There are other multi-step sparring exercises, like the Five-step or Gohan kumite, but they all are simple variations of the three-step sparring practice.

All three types of prearranged kumite are designed to imprint the applications of the essential techniques into the subconscious. Each technique or combination should be practiced over and over by partners, the attacker, also known as Tori or Semeite, and the defender or blocker, Uke or Ukete. All exercises should be repeated from both the right and left sides. All techniques should be performed as accurately as possible without variation.

In all types of prearranged kumite, partners face each other, adjust their distance or "awasete' roughly three feet apart, assume Musubi-dachi and bow to each other before and after practicing a given waza. It is customary for students to form two straight lines along the length of the dojo, with the instructor and the highest ranking student facing each other at the start of the lines near the Shomen. The rest of the class lines up in descending order of rank or grade, the highest near the Shomen and the lowest farthest from it. It also is customary for the highest ranking karateka to call out, "Seiza!" This command tells the class it is time to kneel down and pay attention to the instructions of the teacher.

The type of attack and block, the target area, and the speed of action always are demonstrated by the instructor. Often, he will specify the required number of repetitions as well. Beginners are advised to rehearse their techniques in slow motion before practicing with increasing force and speed.

All techniques must be performed with full power, control, and a commitment to make the practice effective. Partners should keep their eyes on each other during the entire sequence, as well as during resting and bowing. Students should keep their eyes fixed on the eyes, neck, chest, and shoulders of their partner to become familiar with the body language that signals an impending thrust or strike. Punches and kicks are not pulled back, but must fall short of contact or barely touch the opponent. Because of this, protective equipment usually is not used during prearranged sparring. The mind is not allowed to wander aimlessly and the limbs are not allowed to move needlessly.

Prearranged sparring is not limited to basic hand and foot techniques. Any other karate waza–such as throwing, holding, or pinning–may be practiced as long as they can be executed safely as demonstrated by an experienced instructor.

Finally, students should remember that karate is primarily a method of self-defense. Therefore, it is a mistake for students to practice the attacker's role all or most of the time. The role of attacker should be shared equally by both partners.

Basic One-Step Sparring

Kihon ippon kumite, or the fundamental single movement set drill, consists of the following steps:

While students are in seiza, the instructor describes the new lesson. For example, the new lesson may consist of practicing the offensive technique of a right upper-level lunge punch, as well as the defensive technique of a left-upper level block followed by a right reverse punch.

If the students understand the lesson, they yell out, "Osu!" Otherwise, they may request further clarification from the instructor.

The partners then face each other, assuming Musubi-dachi, and bow upon the orders of the instructor. After bowing, both sides assume Hachiji-dachi and wait for further instructions. In this stance, the karateka remain relaxed while maintaining an air of quiet alertness.

The instructor then calls out the first instruction, in this case: "Attacking side, right leg back, Gedan-barai." Both partners remain in Hachiji-dachi anticipating the next order. After a split second pause, the instructor yells out, "Yoi." The attacking side immediately responds by moving the right foot back into a left foot forward Zenkutsu-dachi, performing a left-hand Gedan-barai and drawing the right fist over the right hip with kiai and kime. The attacker now is ready to lunge forward, but waits for the instructor's command. The defender is still in Hachiji-dachi, relaxed but focused. The absolutely resolute defender already knows how to deflect the expected face punch and counter with an equally decisive but controlled middle-level reverse punch.

Next, after making certain that both the attacking and defending sides are ready for action, the instructor commands, "Hajime!" or "Ichi, ni." The attacking side lunges forward with full force and power, performing a correct Jodan-oi-tsuki with kiai and kime. The defending side steps back into a left foot forward Zenkutsu-dachi while performing a left Jodan-age-uke. This is followed by a right Gyaku-tsuki with kiai and kime. Both partners remain still, checking and correcting their forms until the instructor tells them to step back to their original positions. Both karateka then smoothly withdraw to the starting position. The command used in this instant is "Yame!" The exercise is repeated several times until the instructor calls for Yasume, or rest. He also may ask the partners to change sides or explain the next practice item to them.

In a more advanced and creative type of Ippon kumite, the attacker announces the name of the techniques and the selected target area, such as Mae-geri-gedan. The defender is free to be equally creative and select an appropriate block and counterattack, such as a Gedan-barai followed by a Gyaku-tsuki. This somewhat less restricted type of basic one-step sparring sometimes is referred to as Ippon kumite, distinguishing it from the more rigid Kihon Ippon kumite. Ippon kumite also provides an excellent opportunity for partners to practice and regulate the breathing sequences associated with this type of training. Both partners breathe normally before engaging in Ippon kumite. The attacker starts inhaling through the nose after receiving the order to attack and exhales forcefully through the mouth on completion of the punch. The defender inhales through the nose during the blocking phase and exhales forcefully at completion of the counterattack. Both sides should tighten their stomach muscles during kiai. Sparring partners should create the patterns and sequences that best meet their individual needs.

Basic Two-Step Sparring

Kihon Nihon kumite is the intermediate fixed technique sparring method between the Kihon Ippon and Kihon Sanbon methods of practice. The text of the next section describing the mechanics of basic three-step sparring also is applicable to basic two-step sparring.

Basic Three-Step Sparring

Kihon Sanbon kumite is similar to basic one-step sparring, except that it consists of three sets of movements instead of one. The line of movement is a straight line. The partners move back and forth along this line without deviating from it.

In its most basic form, Sanbon kumite incorporates three sets of consecutive matching offensive and defensive movements. These usually are three different techniques aimed at three different areas of attack, such as Jodan, Chudan, and Gedan.

For instance, at the count of ichi, ni, and san, the attacking side advances, perhaps in Zenkutsu-dachi, delivering straight tsuki to the upper, middle and lower levels in the order requested by the instructor. The defending side will step back, perhaps in Zenkutsu-dachi, practicing blocks such as Jodan-age-uke, Chudan-soto-uke and Gedan-barai. The third block always is followed by a decisive counterattack, in this case perhaps a Chudan-gyaku-tsuki. Kihon Sanbon kumite is practiced in this way in a series of three alternating movements, starting with the right side. Partners then change roles and the practice continues.

As partners become more competent, their actions may become swifter and stronger. For instance, the same three thrusting techniques may be used by the attacker, one after the other, in a series of fast and powerful movements without pausing for the count. The attacker tries to overwhelm the defender by acting as forcefully and swiftly as possible. The defender, as resolute as before, responds with forceful blocks and steps back confidently, preparing for the counterattack immediately following the last block. This type of less restricted sparring also is known as Sanbon kumite, or triple engagement, as opposed to the more controlled Kihon Sanbon kumite.

Triple sparring is an excellent way of exercising creativity and experimenting with different combinations of offensive and defensive techniques. In a more advanced and demanding type of triple engagement, the attacker and the defender change roles three consecutive times in accordance with a previously agreed upon pattern. Each strike is blocked and countered. The starting side executes three attacking and two defending techniques. The other partner performs three attacking and three blocking techniques. This type of sparring usually is conducted in hand practice with the partners standing closer to each other.

Semi-free One-Step Sparring

Jiyu Ippon kumite is the intermediate stage between prearranged and completely free sparring. This exercise develops defensive and counterattacking techniques under more realistic conditions. All beginners must become thoroughly familiar with the elements of semi-freestyle kumite before engaging in freestyle sparring. Because of the possibility of bodily contact, protective mouthpieces and other safety devices commonly are used during semi-free and freestyle kumite practice. This type of sparring is similar to Kihon Ippon kumite, except that both partners are free to move about the dojo in any appropriate stance. The attacker initiates the attack whenever he/she finds an opening in his/her partner's defense. The defending partner either evades and guards his/her vital points or blocks and instantly counters with an appropriate thrust or strike.

Initially, the attacking side holds the final position at completion of his/her attack to allow the partner practice in blocking the blow and driving home the counterattack. In the next stage, the attacker instantly assumes a defensive position and attempts to block or evade the counterattack. Once the exchange is over, each partner acknowledges the efforts of the other by saying Osu and repeating the sequence as many times as agreed on. As in Kihon Ippon kumite, partners should change roles and sides for each selected set of movements.

In more advanced Jiyu Ippon kumite, only the attacker and defender are predetermined. The attacker is free to deliver a single controlled technique as soon as the opportunity presents itself. By the same token, the defender is free to block and counter at will. Partners must ensure that all attacks and counters are completed with kiai and kime, or the practice will not be as effective.

Trust, honor, and respect are integral parts of kumite practice. Both partners must ensure that semifree sparring does not degenerate into freestyle fighting. The restraint exercised during the engagement and after completion of the sequence of movements is itself part of the training. Semifree sparring should be practiced with as many different partners as possible so that students are not limited by experiencing the sparring habits of only one person.

Soke has devised an interesting form of limited free sparring. Only the number of techniques and roles of the partners are predetermined. Everything else is left to the imagination and creativity of the two individuals. The initiating side is free to use any combination of hand and foot techniques up to the predetermined number. The defending partner is free to evade and/or block assaults at will and counters with a single blow after the last block. The object of this exercise, in limiting the partner's role, is to activate their reflexes and tactical skills. Students should have total confidence in themselves, and should respect each other, but should not think about scoring or getting hit. They should concentrate their thoughts on the development of proper sparring strategies, such as footwork, body shifting, timing, distancing and targeting.

Freestyle Sparring

Semifree sparring, if conducted properly over a long period of time, will bring about the physical skills, spiritual values and emotional qualities needed to instill responsible action in free sparring practice.

Jiyu, or Ju kumite, is the ultimate in karate practice, but not karate-do. In the physical sense, freestyle sparring is the same as empty hand combat or actual fighting except that partners do not make forceful contact or aim at hurting each other. Through Ju kumite, as in kata, students reaffirm the idea that the ultimate aim of karate-do is empowering the spirit rather than developing combative skills. True karateka never engage in fighting unless forced to do so by a life threatening situation. Self-control is the most repeated personal virtue in karate maxims. Students should know how to restrain themselves while attacking before engaging in free sparring. It is all too easy to injure or maim a partner inadvertently.

The level of proficiency in Jiyu kumite is measured by effectiveness of fighting techniques and ability to pull back in time to avoid contact with a vital point. It can appear that Ju kumite involves only physical action. In fact, it is a battle of the minds. To the untrained eye, it may resemble kick-boxing. In reality, it is closer to the game of chess, with parts of the body taking on the roles of the chess pieces. As in chess, all unnecessary actions in freestyle sparring are avoided. An unwarranted move can create an opening and invite an attack by the opponent. The movements of Ju kumite should be confined to lessons learned from waza, kata and prearranged sparring. It is quite common for karateka to detect their own technical deficiencies during sparring practice. Only then will they begin to appreciate the importance of the basics.

Waza, kata, and kumite constitute the triad of karate practice. Having experienced Jiyu kumite, the need to excel in waza becomes more real. Kata becomes more meaningful. As karateka begin to discover and correct their individual and personal deficiencies, they become more aware of the world around them. Kumite, like kata, helps students search for self-recognition through their sparring attitudes. Very soon, every sparring karateka grasps the meaning of humility and feels the need for improvement. Such is the benevolent nature of kumite practice.

Tournament style sparring

Tournament style sparring is a very restricted, competitive and highly regulated version of the jiyu kumite described in the preceding section. Still being refined, it originally was devised specifically to test the fighting skills of karate students in relatively safe, combat-like encounters. The rules and regulations of sport karate vary from country to country and sometimes from dojo to dojo within the same country.

The main premise of sport karate, winning at tournaments, is contrary to the spirit of traditional martial arts. However, most experts believe that sport karate can be included in the wider spectrum of traditional karate practice, given the correct frame of mind. Winning the fight is not the ultimate goal of the art. A karate contest never is regarded as a combat situation. A brief account of the history of tournament style sparring, or sport karate, and a summary of the rules and regulations generally adopted by IKA and other traditional schools, is presented in Chapter 14.

Basic sparring principles

The more the student practices techniques, either individually in kata or in prearranged kumite, the closer he/she will come to perfection in actual self-defense or sparring practice. Although a great deal can be said about freestyle sparring, the best way to succeed is to spar with as many partners, and as frequently, as possible. For a safe, injury-free and fulfilling sparring practice, karateka should observe the following basic principles:

Be courteous – Your partner is as worthy an individual as you are. Always bow to your partner before and after an engagement. Observe all rules of conduct at all times. If you hit a vital point or inadvertently hurt your partner, stop the fight immediately, apologize, and bow to your partner. Ask if he/she wishes to continue with the practice session. Remember, karate begins and ends with courtesy.

Be kind – Never abuse your karate skills. Never spar with an untrained person. When sparring with a less experienced partner, do not pursue the attack further than needed. Always leave enough room for your partner to maneuver and retreat. Let your partner learn from you. Try to share the sparring experience with your partner.

Be safe – Be safety-minded at all times. Be careful not to hurt yourself or your partner. When attacking a vital point, always control your blows and pull back your techniques. Make sure your gloves, and your partner's, are well-padded. Make sure you both are wearing protective equipment, especially mouth guards and cups. Keep your guard up and protect your face and solar plexus at all times.

Be confident – Be positive about your abilities and be true to yourself. If you do not feel right, either physically, mentally or spiritually- do not engage in serious sparring. Do not be intimidated by your opponent's ranking, size, or reputation.

Be clear minded – Empty your mind of all concern, negative thought, preconceived ideas and aggression. Prepare yourself for a fulfilling experience. Do not think of winning or losing match points during a sparring practice. Never think of the outcome of the sparring experience.

Be fit – Kumite is a physically demanding practice. Warm up and stretch properly before an engagement. Always maintain a proper level of physical fitness. If you are tired, do not engage in serious sparring.

Be tactful – Use what you have learned. Know what you are doing. Do not move around aimlessly. Do not move your head, body, hands and feet needlessly. Move around and change postures tactfully. Avoid offering a target. Avoid direct hits by blocking, backing up and body shifting. Try to read your opponent's thoughts through their body language before they have a chance to formulate an attack.

Be focused – Do not think of anything else. Focus on the job. Concentrate and let your instincts take over. Fight your own fight regardless of the identity of your partner. Try to remain composed and retain the initiative. Keep your distance and remain focused at all times. Do not let anything divert your attention from the task at hand.

Be alert – Keep your eyes on your opponent at all times. Try to decode his/her every move instinctively but do not fall victim to a false signal. Be aware of the space around you. Do not allow unfamiliar acts or noises to attract your attention.

Relax – Do not let your mind wander. Do not tense your muscles. Stay loose but alert. Being tense will decrease your efficiency and drain you of vital energy. Your body must be in harmony with each situation.

Be resourceful – Use a variety of techniques and avoid developing a set pattern of movements. Otherwise, your opponent very quickly will decode your game plan, thereby creating an opening for attack. Advance and retreat with the proper form when the opportunity presents itself.

Be comfortable – Always retain comfortable, but stable, stances. Keep your back and head straight, always facing your opponent throughout the sparring practice. Do not remain in the same stance for longer than necessary.

Be decisive – Always block and counter decisively. All effective blocks, counters and blows must be accompanied with kiai and kime. Never allow your emotions to take over your instincts. Let your opponent feel that you are capable of defending yourself.

Breathe normally – Develop the breathing rhythm that is most natural to you. Conserve your energy and avoid unnecessary moves. If you and/or your opponent are out of breath and liable to make mistakes, stop the kumite; bow to your opponent; and take a break.

Be creative – Feigning, otherwise known as a false attack or Sorashi, is a very important skill to the karateka. It deceives the opponent into believing you intend to do one thing when, in fact, you intend something else entirely. Practice your feigning combinations as you practice other techniques.

Be responsible – Always be prepared to assist an injured person. Familiarize yourself with the principles of basic first aid. Despite all precautions, accidents do happen. If you are involved in a training accident, it is your duty to do what you can to help the injured party. Even if you are not directly involved in the accident, if you are capable of helping others, you must do your best to help with the situation at hand. See also Appendix A1.

CHAPTER 14

Teaching and Instruction

Teaching class and assisting instructors during training sessions are customary requirements in all karate and martial arts schools. In fact, being involved in the daily chores of the dojo is an important part of martial arts training. Teaching solidifies and enhances the student's knowledge of the art at all levels. Soke says:

"Teaching is part of learning."

All students, from brown belt upwards, are required to be involved in teaching and teaching assistance. Any student in the dojo may be asked by a higher ranking student to handle a task or to introduce the elements of karate practice to a group of new comers.

Teaching is the most important part of karate training. It is perhaps one of the best ways of self assessment. It is a reflection of a student's character and abilities. Teaching could be both very challenging and frustrating as well as fun and rewarding. If a student can not impart his/her knowledge to others the same way or better than it was passed on to him/her, then the student must humbly accept the fact that he/she needs further work towards his/her development as a martial artist. Not all students succeed; true martial artists never fail or give up.

Teaching regular classes at any level is an honor and a privilege that not many individuals can attain.

Karate teachers are empowered with a sense of self-recognition, but they should also develop a sense of assessment of the abilities of groups or individuals, as the case may require, of new students. One way to avoid pitfalls is to realize that not all people are equally gifted nor blessed with fortune. Not all people are blessed with all gifts of life. There are not many people who could claim extreme health, wealth, education, physical prowess and spiritually fulfilling lives. On the other hand the majority of people, the average folks, are more than happy to lead normal lives without extremes. Almost all IKA members, the karate folks, belong to the latter group of the society.

Many karate greats and international champions were trained by unknown but well informed, highly devoted teachers, who never competed in any tournaments or carried impressive titles. The reverse also is true. Not many world class athletes can claim coaching any one person to half their own capabilities. In teaching karate-do, the knowledge of the technique, together with the ability to communicate it, is as important, and some may argue even more important, than the perfect execution of the technique.

There are many facets to becoming a good instructor in karate practice. As in teaching anything else on regular or part-time basis, practice, patience, experience, etc., all are indispensable factors that can and will improve a teacher's skills in time. Given the diversity of the IKA students worldwide, an instructor can be asked to teach a six-year-old novice, a sixty-year-old war veteran, a teenage overweight couch potato, and an accomplished young ballerina all as fresh students. The challenge, of course, is formidable. The instructor is, above all, a martial artist and is prepared to meet the challenge, even though martial arts teaching has little or no financial rewards.

The teaching staff at the IKA Headquarters center consists of a large number of high-ranking students with many years of hands on experience, whose work is directly assigned and supervised by Soke. The list contains an impressive number of former world champions, university and college professors, doctors, engineers, actors and other established professionals. There are at least 10 shihans and the same number of shihan-dais and senseis on active duty at the Hombu. There are always long lines of talented, high ranking volunteers waiting for the opportunity to become IKA instructors.

The journey toward becoming a good sensei begins as an apprentice at the first brown belt level. A good sensei may work his/her way up after many years of challenging contribution to become an expert teacher, a master, or a shihan after serving many more years as fifth-degree black belt.

IKA karate teaching and training can be divided into two major categories: technical or physical and nontechnical or theoretical.

The technical part, consisting of two distinct sections, includes all physical training as well as corresponding studies and literature reviews.

The nontechnical part also is divided into two related but different sections, both dealing with historical, moral, holistic, and administrative aspects of karate practice. These two parts discuss general and IKA specific subjects.

A simple chart showing these subdivisions is presented in Appendix A4.

DO's AND DON'Ts OF TEACHING

The following tips and guidelines are provided to help future and first time teachers with their common challenges.

- If your new students are visiting the dojo for the first time, make them feel good about themselves as well as the dojo. The sight of all those handsome black belts battering each other amidst their kiais and groans is both overwhelming and intimidating, as well as distracting. Show them the ropes as much as you can, but send them home with the feeling that one day they all can become great samurai.
- If the student cannot perform a technique as perfectly as you wish, first break the technique into its constituent parts, then figure out if the deficiency is due to joint stiffness, muscular weakness, lack of grasp by the student, language barrier, or a combination of all. Encourage your students to work on their weaknesses both outside and inside the dojo.
- Always try to verbalize all actions and their components at the same time by demonstrating them as slowly, clearly, and as many times as possible. It is almost impossible for a new student to mimic a high ranking student's near-perfect techniques. An instructor's superb performance may be a source of inspiration for some of the students but also loss of confidence for others. The student should feel that the instructor is on his side rather than a future competitor.
- Feel free to talk to your students or their parents on a one to one basis about how karate training could be improved by supplementary exercises outside the dojo, e.g., improving cardiovascular capacity, weight loss, temperament control, personal matters, etc. Remember the student also is a member of your family, the IKA family.
- Dojo hours are limited. Teaching time is precious. The effective learning time, after time taken by warm up, soji, opening, and closing ceremonies is too short to address any one student's problems while keeping the rest of the class sitting idle in seiza. Students should learn to benefit continuously from a teacher's presence every single minute during a scheduled session.
- Karate teachers can enhance their work by complementing their knowledge of the arts through reviewing relevant literature in sports psychology, human development, and physical education. All instructors should be somewhat familiar with scientific aspects of stretching, physical coordination, strength, and cardiovascular training as well as basic first aid.

- To respect Soke's wishes, all instructors and their assistants should glance at this and similar books on the subject. They also should require their students to familiarize themselves with the material presented in this and similar books.
- Provide your students with as much reading material as possible. Do not shy away from preparing your own handouts and looseleaf information sheets. Encourage your students to make comments about their progress and training.
- Take preventive action by demonstrating common errors in performing the basics. Remind your students that bad habits are difficult to correct.
- Devise a system of gauging your own progress as a teacher, an instructor, or a coach over a given period of time. It always is beneficial to keep logs of student and/or class progress on a weekly basis. Any written form of planning and recording is helpful. Passing a ranking test always is a good indication of a student's progress, thereby illustrating the teacher's success. But ranking should never be construed as a goal in a teacher-student relationship.
- Always emphasize the noncombative aspects of karate practice. Let your personality reflect all those wonderful traits that karate-do can offer. Remember, when you are teaching, you are the focus of the dojo; all eyes are on you. Not only your students but everyone else present in the dojo is looking at you. Never lose your temper. Never overteach, i.e., do not get ahead of your class simply to make a point or to make an impression. Feel free to update and polish your karate-related Japanese terminology. Children and younger adults, especially those attending school or college, tend to learn the basic vocabulary faster then everyone else. Teachers should be better at this than their students. Do not limit counting to ichi-ni repeatedly unless it is absolutely necessary. Pronounce all Japanese words as completely and as clearly possible.
- Teach Kime and Kiai correctly from day one. Kiai is a shout, a unique exhalation initiated from the diaphragm, whereby the tightening of the muscles results in a sound starting with a vowel and finishing with a vowel. A kiai can not be started and maintained with a consonant. Do not let any of your students recite the word "kiai," a sound from the chest, instead of the actual yell, which may sound as "Aiii," "Hiii," etc. The finishing kime is the act of instantaneous concentration of forces at the proper time and the proper location. At finishing kime, all muscles, especially the lower abdominals, should be tight enough to absorb the force of, say, a front kick or a reverse punch. Most lower-ranking students either fake the kime or simply don't know how to achieve it. Do your best to explain

the importance of these phenomena to your students.

❖ Do not allow theatrical and unorthodox behavior in your class. Do not allow whistling sounds as opposed to breathing sounds during practice. Discourage the occasional student from hitting himself on the chest or the hips with the reacting hand to mimic the snapping sound of the gi at kime. Discourage other students from stomping or hitting the floor with their bare feet during kata or waza practice. While hitting the wooden floor generates impressive sounds and attracts attention toward the performer, the floor hits back at the soles of the performer with the same force and sends shock waves throughout his body to his brain. This is contrary to logic and modesty, as well as technical requirements.

❖ All students, particularly newcomers, tend to pose challenging questions, mainly in connection with more esoteric aspects of karate practice. They may ask you about zen in combat. They may be interested in the mind-body-spirit connection in the context of karate-do. If you have a convincing answer, by all means furnish it; otherwise, refer them to existing literature on the subject. It is always instructive to ask them to contemplate about the "dojo kun." However, if you feel the student in question is either to young or not yet ready for the somewhat philosophical answer, then be honest, and respond that this is something he/she should find out by continuing the way of karate for many more years to come.

❖ A preferred method of assessing a student's general knowledge in relation to IKA karate is to ask him/her questions posed in chapter 16 of this book. These are typical interview questions frequently asked during scheduled testing by Soke and other examiners.

❖ Last but not least, be an example and a role model for your students. Be patient and courteous, so that they will learn the same from you. Be that which you wish others to become. Mentally review your last teaching session; appraise the effectiveness of your work with respect to learning capacities of a particular student or group of students. If you are not satisfied, try to find the root of the problem and then improve the situation.

CHAPTER 15

Fitness, Learning and Physical Conditioning

Fitness is a relative term and implies different levels of physical ability to different people. According to the President's Council on Physical Fitness, fitness is defined as:

"The ability to carry out daily tasks with vigor and alertness, without undue fatigue, and with ample energy to enjoy leisure time pursuits and to meet unforeseen emergencies."

What this really means is that a person is healthy if that person is fit enough to do what he or she needs or wants to do. Simply stated, physical fitness should match personal needs and ways of life.

While there are many physical activities that fulfill most of the requirements of this statement, karate-do offers a way of life that not only satisfies the criteria for fitness, but also stimulates the mind and soothes the spirit.

According to this statement, there are four levels of fitness. The first level is minimum fitness or a state of being just barely fit, in which people experience degeneration of function and structure. This minimum maintenance level requires the incorporation of just a few healthy habits in everyday life.

The second is a general level of fitness that provides people with a safe margin of adaptation for changes, including some emergencies, and enables them to get through the day without an undue amount of fatigue. This level, known as general fitness, requires a daily, mild, physical workout of 10 – 15 minutes performed in the comfort of one's home or workplace.

The third level is preparation for fairly strenuous or occupational activity. Karate-do falls within this category and requires specific conditioning, including *pre* and *post* training workouts.

The fourth level is preparation for short-term but extremely strenuous activity. Championship games, certain special forces missions, and professional fights fall within this group and require highly specialized conditioning, including tactical workouts and regular assessment of results.

There are four basic elements of physical fitness: cardiovascular endurance, muscular strength, flexibility, and muscular stamina, each of which are stimulated and improved through karate practice.

As in all martial arts, karate offers a physically demanding and mentally enriching way of life. It is as demanding as it is rewarding. The concept of reward in karate-do is associated with the feeling of accomplishment achieved through progress in the art. It is a goal-oriented activity that requires a strong desire for personal achievement and a solid will for hard work, or practice through repetition.

Although athletic prowess is a desirable attribute, there are no fitness requirements for those who wish to become students of karate-do. IKA caters to all people, including those who are unfit, those who have disabilities, and world class athletes. The only prerequisite is the willingness to change and improve one's way of life through karate-do.

Karate itself is a means of achieving good health through meditation and physical training. If practiced frequently and properly over a sufficient period of time, it will develop the basic athletic abilities needed to succeed in the art.

In karate-do, physical conditioning is as important as technical training. Good health and physical conditioning, in fact, are the essential ingredients of meaningful karate practice.

However, because dojo time is limited, students should not overlook the benefits of technical training in favor of physical conditioning. In this context, physical conditioning is the additional preparation needed to maintain a certain level of effort over a given period of time. Ideally, karate drills always should be conducted at close to maximum effort.

For best results, IKA experience has shown that, in general, students should try to maintain and improve their fitness level in accordance with the following approximate guidelines.

- Beginners, fresh students from 10th through 5th kyu: 50 percent for 30 minutes or 100 percent of maximum effort for 10 minutes.
- Intermediate level students from 4th through 2nd kyu: 60 percent for 40 minutes or 100 percent of maximum effort for 15 minutes.
- Advanced level students from 1st kyu and higher: 75 percent for 50 minutes or 100 percent of maximum effort for 20 minutes

A physician should be consulted prior to training, however, as the physical activities described in this book may be too strenuous for beginners to engage in safely. To appreciate the importance of physical fitness and supplementary conditioning in karate-do, students should try to understand the basic physiological concepts involved in learning karate skills. The interrelationship between karate skills and physical fitness is sufficiently important to warrant a brief introduction to the mechanics of learning and acquiring these skills.

LEARNING AND PRACTICE

Learning karate is a voluntary process that requires a great deal of conscious effort. Ideal performance, on the other hand, is an instinctive response that does not necessarily involve the conscious mind. Learning a new technique or combination of techniques demands a modification of existing movement patterns to confront new situations and challenges. Such modifications do not represent the addition of new motor abilities but are the reorganization of whole patterns of existing skills.

Karateka, like all other athletes learn their skills through their kinesthetic sensations or sensory experiences with the movements of the whole body, i.e., is by mimicking, remembering, comparing, adjusting and repeating.

Karate training is a three-phase process that consists of perpetual cycles of learning, application, adjusting and readjusting.

Introductory phase: During this first phase, students make a conscious effort to learn the skill as demonstrated by the instructor. The effort consists of acquiring a mental image of the skill; understanding the mechanics of the movement; and duplicating it as accurately and effectively as possible. In this context, learning implies the deliberate memorization of signals relayed by the senses, as when learning kata from a video or the dojo-kun from an instructor.

How quickly a student learns depends on the amount of information he/she can absorb in a given period of time. A gifted student may learn an entire kata at once. An average student may need to break it up into several parts.

The correct execution of a karate technique depends on two things: the ability of the student to grasp mentally the image of the technique and whether the student has the necessary physical abilities to reproduce the component motions of that technique. Naturally, athletically inclined and intelligent students will be more apt to develop such skills than other individuals. Almost all students easily grasp and visualize the components of karate techniques as demonstrated by the instructors.

However, not all students, whether beginners or so-called old-timers, are capable of duplicating the same movements effectively and efficiently. In fact, most karateka feel the need at one time or another to improve their physical conditioning in order to make learning easier and to increase the stamina necessary to endure the demands of sustained karate drills. In other words, students should be sufficiently fit to allow for sustained mind-body interaction during practice sessions.

Refinement phase: In the second stage of the training process, students work to improve their newly acquired skills by adjusting them in accordance with the recommendations of the instructor or a given set of preconceived images. Every adjustment is a new lesson that needs to be tried out and readjusted again. This cycle of events is repeated over and over until the correct form of the technique is acquired. At this stage, the processes of learning and responding still depend upon one another, as well as on the conscious mind.

Since the phenomenon of learning is associated with the deliberate memorization of various signals, the muscular response—or application of skills—also is construed as the action resulting from intentionally recalling the same signals, as in performing kata or reciting the dojo-kun.

The mind and body interact almost instantaneously. The mind does not command the body to do something. In effect, they are one and the same. However, to avoid complex scientific arguments, it is instructive to assume that the muscles actually do obey the commands of the mind.

For example, if the student is trying a new hand technique, the mind receives sensory feedback from that movement in about two hundredths of a second. The technique is tracked visually in space and is directed in accordance with a preconceived pattern as to how it should be performed. As the movement progresses, an instant by instant mind-body interaction takes place. There is a mental image showing where the hand should be in space at any given time. The image corrects the difference between the intended and actual positions of the hand in space.

In other words, karate skills are acquired and improved through the repetition of specific movements over long periods of time. The approach in the first two phases involves the student's analytical process of thought. In scientific terms, this type of stimulus and response is known as voluntary reaction. Once again, endurance and fitness are the key ingredients needed to support the strenuous physical activities involved in this stage of the training process.

Automatic or semivoluntary phase: The effort involved in the third phase of the training process is directed toward imprinting these skills on the memory in such a way as to make the student respond instinctively to any action with an appropriate reaction; in other words, to act without resorting to the conscious mind.

The student learns to respond consciously in the correct way, to make any technical adjustments that may be necessary, and eventually to reach the stage where the difference between thought and response is diminished completely.

Once the performer knows what the hand is doing, mental tracking becomes unnecessary. There is a kinesthetic sense of its position and function in space and the performer does not need to think about it. The movement has become automatic. This completes the ideal cycle of motor learning.

The efficiency of the entire training process depends largely on the type and quality of the drills used and how the corresponding skills are memorized. The quality of karate drills, or sets of pre-arranged movements, is determined by the purpose of the drills, the accuracy of the techniques, the number or repetitions, and the magnitude of momentum generated at completion of each drill.

The relative merits of performing different types of drills—such as waza, kata, and ippon-kumite—are commensurate with the learning abilities of the performers, as well as their relationship with the way the drills are memorized. To understand this relationship, students need to learn about the two basic ways of memorizing karate skills.

The first method is the indirect mode. This involves constant repetition of the same signal, or series of signals, that eventually imprint themselves on the cortex of the brain and are memorized for a certain period of time. For example, repeating Gedan-barai hundreds of times will instill the skill in the memory in such a way that the command bearing the same name will prompt a down block without there being an actual front kick or real stimulus.

Similarly, IKA's telephone number may be repeated many times until it is memorized. It then may be remembered or recalled without the need for dialing (no real stimulus). In this mode, the acts of remembering the phone number or performing the Gedan-barai are voluntary responses that are associated only with the names IKA and Gedan-barai, respectively. There is no actual physical need for either action. Regular waza practice without a partner is associated with this voluntary type of reaction.

The direct mode, however, involves memorization in response to real action, as opposed to memorization in association with an imaginary situation. Jiyu ippon kumite, with mild contact, is perhaps the best example describing the relationship between the type of practice and the direct mode of memorization.

Consider one such practice with the attacker performing right Mae-geri and the defender responding with a left Gedan-barai. If the first round of practice results in a direct stomach hit, the defender's memory will associate all future approaching Mae-geri with pain in the stomach. When this happens again, the image of the kick is recognized, the association (kick and pain) is made, and the message

is sent to the motor cortex. This immediately activates the response to move aside or block the kick before it reaches the target. The signals generated by the impact of the defender's hand and the attacker's foot register new information in the memories of both parties. The defender's memory associates proper blocking with no pain in the stomach but tolerable sensation in the hand. It also registers all other pertinent information with respect to the attacker's Mae-geri, such as the opponent's body language, footwork, and speed. By the same token, the attacker's memory associates the pain of being blocked with bad timing and lack of speed. It also registers all other pertinent information with respect to the defender's body language and mode of defense.

Jiyu ippon kumite is the type of practice that promotes semivoluntary or automatic responses and is an excellent way of acquiring karate skills.

Experience has shown that reflexes instilled through the direct method of memorization can be several times faster than those acquired through the indirect mode. Information memorized in this manner also is retained in the memory longer than facts learned in other ways. According to Aristotle:

"For things we have to learn before we can do them, we learn by doing them."

The goal therefore is to train and condition the body to the extent that it will automatically respond to any signal from the mind. The path to this goal is through determination and physical exertion. Finally, to achieve progress in technical proficiency, there often will be more to gain by exertion, as techniques so often depend on strength and stamina.

The next section discusses the type of supplementary conditioning that is needed to achieve the goals set in karate training.

SUPPLEMENTARY CONDITIONING

Supplementary conditioning methods, or Hojo-Undo, are systems of physical exercises designed to promote good health and enhance karate training and performance. Weight training, rope jumping, jogging, and striking the makiwara are but a few examples of hojo-undo. IKA's curriculum recognizes good health, physical conditioning, and karate practice as complementary functions. The will power and confidence gained through karate practice help students push their limits to the utmost.

Supplementary exercises help with strength and stamina, both of which improve skill quality and the training program overall. Hojo-undo programs can be designed to address a wide range of needs for any student or group of students practicing karate and other martial arts. Hojo-undo also can be designed to address the specific needs of any karateka, such as flexibility, toughness, cardiovascular capacity, and muscular strength.

Luckily, most students are familiar with basic methods of physical education and the use of standard equipment available in many training halls. It is relatively simple for karate students to assess their own special training needs.

Once the specific goals of a physical conditioning program are established, its details can be worked out easily with the help of an experienced instructor or qualified trainer. Ideally, a well-balanced combination of karate and supplementary exercises can help develop most of the essential physical attributes needed for meaningful karate practice.

The present section is aimed at the general needs of those students who want to achieve IKA Shodan through normally scheduled karate classes while at the same time maintaining a high level of physical fitness.

It is assumed that the average student can attend the dojo two or three times a week and that he/she can devote the same number of hours to supplementary conditioning.

Supplementary exercises, depending on their objectives, are grouped into three categories: preparatory, short-term and long-term conditioning programs.

Preparatory conditioning consists of special programs including meditation, stretching and warm up periods preceding each karate training session.

Long-term conditioning consists of carefully planned supplementary workouts specifically designed to enhance karate skills and training processes. These programs include the use of common methods of cross training, such as running and weight lifting, as well as the use of special tools and equipment specifically intended for karate practice.

Obviously not all students can commit themselves totally to such programs. They should no be discouraged or disappointed. Rather, they should seek alternative systems of workouts that might better serve their physical abilities, lifestyles and schedules.

PREPARATORY CONDITIONING

Preparatory conditioning or Junbi-Undo (literally warming up) consists of complementary activities that enable the body to make necessary physiological adjustments prior to strenuous exercise. Sudden heavy, exhausting workouts can tax the muscles, heart, lungs, arteries, and joints, causing damage. The same applies to a sudden cessation of movements after very vigorous activities.

A large percentage of karate related injuries are self-inflicted. They are direct results of being physically unprepared or unfit. To prevent such mishaps, muscles must be strengthened and stretched to levels above the normal requirements of the sport. It is excessive pulls that cause injuries

Preparatory conditioning is the key to successful martial arts practice. IKA practice sessions always are preceded by pretraining preparation and followed by post-training cool down. Such preliminaries are designed to prepare the mind and body for the highly demanding and strenuous activities that follow. The purpose here is to lessen or erase completely all mental, nervous and muscular tensions and replace them with a feeling of lightness and positive anticipation. Without proper preparation, students are likely to forego the full benefits of the training session, thereby increasing their chance of injury.

When conducted properly, preparatory conditioning is beneficial for many reasons. It will help clear the mind, alleviate anxiety and soothe the nerves through meditation and mental preparation. It will loosen up ligaments, joints and muscles in addition to increasing coordination and suppleness through stretching drills. Warming up also will increase energy, endurance, speed and mobility.

Preparatory conditioning usually consists of meditation, warming up and stretching.

For best results, students should coordinate their regular karate training with the following schedule of preparatory conditioning:

- Meditation   1–2 minutes
- Warming up   7–10 minutes
- Stretching   10–15 minutes
- Resting   2–3 minutes

This means that 20 to 30 minutes should be allocated to preparatory exercises before scheduled sessions.

Besides physical variations among people, there are emotional and physiological differences as well. One student, for example, may need to spend more time warming up but less on stretching. Another student may be just the opposite. Adults and experienced students should be able to design their own preparatory programs depending on personal and environmental conditions.

A well-designed combination of warming up and stretching drills will result in light perspiration toward the end of the preparatory period. The next three sections provide background information on basic concepts involved in preparatory conditioning.

MEDITATION AND MENTAL PREPARATION

Increased anxiety and degenerative processes are natural byproducts of civilized living and have prompted many individuals to change their habits and seek a more wholesome way of life through karate-do and martial arts. Karate-do maintains and improves motor ability as well as the balance of motor and sensory enervation essential to good health.

The efficiency of our nervous tissue improves with increased use. Muscular activities requiring great concentration improve the brain-nerve-muscle interaction. Use of muscles gives the brain command over the muscular system. Muscles become the servants of the mind. Muscle contraction is induced by nerve impulses. A nerve impulse is controlled by the mind. A tired or damaged nerve cannot transmit a clear signal. By the same token, a tired or overworked muscle will not respond to the signals from the cortex ordering it to contract or relax. A tired or anxious mind can't decode the nerve's signals or dispatch correct commands to the muscles.

Each component of this complex network must be as relaxed and healthy as possible for the brain-nerve-muscle network to function properly. Meditation is an effective way of relaxing the mind and getting rid of bodily tensions.

The integration of the mind, body and spirit through karate-do is a unique phenomenon that helps the mind become clear and allows the person to become totally aware of his/her surroundings. This is achieved by Mokuto, a short meditation at the start of each training session. Through makoto, students relax, breathe calmly and try to maintain a clear mind, thus freeing themselves from all tensions. The ability to clear the mind of all thoughts is known as no-mindedness, or the state of Mu-Shin.

Meditation is an excellent way of calming the spirit, regulating breathing, and stabilizing the mind-body interaction at any place and time. However, as with other aspects of karate, the act of meditation should be practiced on a regular basis. With practice, students can learn to clear the mind and focus thoughts and mental energies. The ability to control state of mind is useful in life and in practice.

There are several simple methods of meditation. The method of Kubokido, created by Soke Takayuki Kubota and available on tape, may be the most appropriate choice for IKA students.

To calm the mind and soothe the spirit, Soke intones the chant, "Gon mizu no kokoro," repeated in a slow, counterpoint rhythm to the pulse of the Shogun bell. This chant echoes a feeling of peace, or Gon, through the power of the mizu-no-kokoro, or mind like water, which students may repeat as an active meditation.

WARMING UP

Physical activity elevates the metabolism, gradually increasing the heart rate and blood flow, raising the temperature of muscles and connective tissue, and improving motor function. Muscles and blood become warmer until the body feels the need to dissipate the excess heat through perspiration. If physiological changes produce a rise in body temperature during increased physical activity, the reverse process also should be true.

Elevating the body temperature should bring about the necessary physiological conditions compatible with strenuous physical work. Stated simply, working out and warming up are physiologically interactive processes. Therefore, any workout involving increased physical activity should be preceded by warming up.

Karate is an activity in which the muscles, tendons, ligaments, and joints need to be introduced gradually to top performance. One of the leading causes of injury in karate practice is pushing body parts beyond their capacity too quickly. Preventing injuries and muscular cramps is not the only function of warming up.

There are many other ways in which warming up improves karate performance. Most importantly warming up helps improve the following factors:

- Extends the joints' range of motion.
- Increases the blood flow and the speed of nerve impulses.
- Increases the speed and strength of muscular contractions.
- Increases the speed and rate of muscular relaxation.
- Increases the rate at which oxygen is delivered to and utilized by active muscles.
- Motivates the student for more strenuous activity.
- Reduces and conserves the rate of expenditure of energy.
- Expands muscle volume through heating and blood flow.
- Makes tendons and other tissues more pliable through heating and expansion.
- Lubricates the joints and prevents excessive wear and tear.
- Reduces viscosity and friction all over the body.
- It tends to reduce stress due to daily activities.

There are two types of warming up procedures:

- Passive, or indirect, procedures include raising the body temperature by sauna, hot baths and showers, diathermy and warm blood transfusion. These procedures are generally impractical and have gained few followers among karateka.
- Active, or direct, methods of warming up are known to all athletes. They involve mobilization of the body through various exercises. Active procedures are subdivided into two groups: general, or generic; and related, or specific.

Generic exercises—such as rope jumping, jogging, running in place, and stationary cycling—are full body warm-ups not necessarily related to karate but providing the desired physiological changes. Because they employ the large muscle groups, general warm-ups are most effective for raising deep muscle temperature. Karate students are urged to start with a general warm-up before stretching and proceeding with specific warm-ups.

Specific warm-ups are slightly less vigorous repetitions of the skills and exercises performed later in the training session and in competition. Specific warm-ups are particularly useful because they rehearse the nervous system that controls movement. Students therefore should pay more attention to those muscles used more frequently during karate practice.

Specific warm-ups may include basic waza, combinations of techniques or kata. Ideally, such drills should start with a slow pace and small range, gradually increasing to 60–75 percent of maximum effort and full range to achieve a warm up condition. However, if a warm-up is too intensive, body temperature will rise too quickly and endurance will be diminished.

Warming up methods are beneficial particularly when combined with compatible sets of stretching exercises. Research has shown that a rise in muscle temperature of two degrees can speed muscular action by up to 20 percent and facilitate joint extension by 15 percent. A later section of this chapter will be devoted to the development of a generic program of specific warming up and stretching exercises.

STRETCHING

Stretching is the technical term used to describe extensions of the fascia, or connective tissues surrounding muscle fibers and tendons, which connect the muscles to the bones. The process of muscular revitalization and growth takes place through microscopic tearing and healing of the individual tissue. Strenuous exercises always cause microscopic wear and tear in the fibers of the active muscles.

When fibers heal, they become slightly shorter than they were before. The sum total of fiber contractions results in a general shortening of the entire muscle. Stretching reverses this process. The aim, therefore, is to stretch the appropriate connective tissue, thereby increasing overall pliability and range of movement in the joints of the body.

A flexible body requires less energy and moves and stretches farther. Stretching exercises tend to reduce adhesions and elongate tissues. Stretching generally should be preceded by a proper warm-up because over-stretching actually can injure cold muscles and tissues.

Like warming up, stretching also fills the muscles and connective tissues with blood and makes them more pliable. Proper stretching on a regular basis can benefit karate students in many ways, including:

- Mental and physical preparation of the karateka through mental relaxation and tuning of the body in anticipation of more strenuous action.

- Reduction in muscular sprains and strains through added pliability.
- Eliminating or reducing stress due to daily activities.
- Reduction in muscular tension and making the body feel more relaxed.
- Promotion of motor function by allowing easier movement.
- Promotion of muscular speed and range through relaxation.
- Improvement in coordination and balance through increased articulation of the joints.
- Improvement in metabolism, circulation and breathing.

There are two types of stretching exercises: dynamic, or phasic; and static, or very slow. Dynamic stretching is difficult to control and may cause more harm than good by exceeding the limits intended by the student. This type of stretching should be tried only by experienced practitioners who know their stretching needs and have control of their body movements. Static methods, on the other hand, are easy to control and provide ample warning before an injury can take place.

Muscle physiology is such that slow and deliberate extensions are more beneficial because they inhibit contraction in the fibers being stretched. Jerky motions cause the reflexes to react by shortening the muscles.

The natural tendency of muscles and tendons is to generate motion by contracting. Muscles become taut and shorter when performing work. They elongate and relax while at rest. Research shows that proper warm-up and stretching can increase range and flexibility up to 20 percent.

The following suggestions should help students maximize the benefits of stretching exercises.

- Plan the entire stretching and warm-up program for the available amount of time. This should include the type, sequence, duration, intensity, range and number of repetitions of each exercise.
- Avoid phasic stretching as much as possible. If such movements must be included, they should follow the static versions of the same movements.
- Push each joint extension just beyond its normal range and hold the stretch position for at least 60 seconds, retracting slowly when completed. Do not overstretch.
- Mentally visualize the extensions of the muscles and tendons being stretched. Visualize the rotations and widening of the corresponding joints.
- After completing a stretching exercise, pause a few seconds and shake the muscle group 5 to 10 seconds.

In general all muscle groups should be stretched. However if time is short only stretch muscles and joints that will be used during practice.

A GENERIC PROGRAM FOR PREPARATORY CONDITIONING

There are as many preliminary conditioning systems as there are dojos and instructors. Traditionally, most instructors use their own method of preliminary exercises. These may or may not meet the warming up and stretching needs of the individuals present in the class. For this reason, students are urged to complete their own preliminary workouts prior to joining class.

The purpose of this section is to develop a generic system of preparatory exercises that could apply, with some variation, to most students in all climatic conditions.

The idea is to warm up and stretch properly all the body parts involved in karate exercises in a relatively short period of time. Five different types of drills are recommended. They are:

- Hybrid or mixed movements designed to raise the body temperature and stretch the muscles at the same time.
- General warm-up drills involving the entire body, particularly the larger muscle groups.
- General stretching exercises involving the major joints of the body.
- Specific warm-up exercises aimed at warming up muscle groups involved in karate training.
- Specific stretching drills aimed at stretching those joints and tendons that undergo large rotations and strains during kicking, punching, striking, blocking, and similar movements.

The type, speed, duration, range, and number of repetitions of each one of these drills are selected to fulfill the needs of the average student with average athletic abilities. However, each student should be able to adjust the proposed program in accordance with his/her particular need.

Ideally, these exercises should be preceded by a short period of meditation. Students begin by exercising the neck muscles and working down to the ankles, while concentrating on improving the mobility of the hips. There should be no rest as students progress through the program.

It must be emphasized that these exercises are designed to stretch and loosen, not strengthen or harden. Breathing should be normal and the body should remain relaxed throughout the preliminary workout.

For balanced, symmetrical results, all exercises should be repeated equally for both left and right limbs and left and right sides of the body.

The calisthenics of the nonspecific drills of the proposed program, their description, the approximate time required for each exercise, and the corresponding number of repetitions, all are presented in Table 4.

The program begins with a series of hybrid exercises followed by general warm up and stretching. The body should be sufficiently warm, loose and relaxed before proceeding with the specific warming-up and stretching exercises selected by the student.

LONG-TERM CONDITIONING

Long-term conditioning improves and maintains the functions of the basic elements of physical fitness as related to karate practice.

Cardiovascular endurance or stamina, which refers to the functions of the lungs and heart in providing increased levels of life energy during sustained physical activity. Example: a student performing nonstop kata at normal speed over an extended period of time without feeling tired.

Muscular endurance that refers to the ability of a group of muscles to perform repeated contractions in a given period of time. Example: a student executing 20 full sit-ups in 60 seconds without enduring muscular fatigue or pain in the legs.

Muscular strength that defines the ability of a group of muscles to produce force. Example: a student performing a reverse punch or a front kick.

Flexibility that refers to the ability of the joints and connecting tissues to move through their full range of motion. Example: a student who executes thigh splits or side squat stretches.

Strength of character and toughness, both of which have distinct but related meanings in karate-do. The first is a personal trait characterized by uncompromising determination to endure hardship and control aggression. The second is a measure of partial desensitization of the nerves and indifference to pain, such as toughening the knuckles or shins by working on the makiwara.

Naturally, each of these elements can be improved with regular exercise. Because most of a student's time is spent practicing techniques, a long-term conditioning program must have specific goals to achieve meaningful results. This means that each student must decide which elements of fitness require greater attention and select the appropriate combination of exercises.

All things considered, the most effective plan for karate students may be a combination of conditioning exercises aimed at strengthening the musculature and prolonging the endurance of the body.

However, experience has shown that engaging in a variety of supplementary and targeted exercises, along with routine karate training, can be more effective than martial arts practice alone. This is true of all sports and regimented activities in which only certain groups of muscles and joints are exercised regularly.

The supplementary workouts proposed in this section are aimed at improving martial arts performance and overall physical fitness for adult students. Long-term conditioning drills are not beneficial for children and young adults who are active in school physical education programs.

The remainder of this chapter is devoted to discussion of the physiological aspects of the basic elements of physical fitness; how to become stronger, more fit and, as a result, a better karateka.

Cardiovascular Endurance and Stamina

Cardiovascular endurance, or circulo-respiratory capacity, is defined as the sustained ability of the lungs, heart and blood vessels to supply oxygen and nutrients to the cells, convert oxygen into energy, and remove waste products. In simpler terms, it is called stamina, or aerobic power, and determines the ability of the body to maintain a vigorous level of physical activity for an extended period of time. Lack of stamina generally is associated with muscle fatigue, shortness of breath, a pounding heart and mental distraction.

Cardiovascular endurance is the most important element of being fit. Every cell in the body needs oxygen and nutrients to function. Under normal conditions, the cardiovascular system provides enough oxygen to allow the body to perform daily tasks without undue fatigue. Increased physical activity demands greater cell function and an increased need for oxygen supply.

Muscles may perform their functions either aerobically or anaerobically, depending on the type and duration of physical exertion. Anaerobic action is a type of short-term effort that does not depend on a continuous supply of oxygen. During anaerobic, or without air-exercises, such as a dozen push-ups, the muscles draw on existing but limited sources of energy within their own cells. This energy is obtained without an additional supply of oxygen. Anaerobic capacity, therefore, is the point at which no fresh supply of energy is needed to sustain the functions of the muscles.

When the level of physical exertion exceeds the ability of the maximally efficient aerobic (with air) pathways to supply the necessary energy, the body resorts to anaerobic pathways, which are less efficient and lead to fatigue caused by the buildup of lactic acid in the muscles.

High endurance athletes, such as marathon runners, are able to exercise at very high levels for long periods of time because they have a very high aerobic capacity and do not need to employ the fatigue-inducing anaerobic system.

Aerobic capacity is defined as the rate at which the cardiovascular system can supply vital energy during a sustained physical activity. A good aerobic capacity is the basis for meaningful karate practice. Obviously, the longer muscles can work under aerobic conditions, the less the fatigue-inducing anaerobic system will be needed.

Table 4:
A GENERIC PREPARATORY CONDITIONING PROGRAM

	I-MIXED EXERCISES	
Head and Neck	Keep body upright and relaxed, hands on the hips.	Count
Up and down	Move head up and down gently and slowly.	6 each way
Face turns	Move face left and right gently and slowly.	6 each way
Head flexions	Turn head left and right in the plane of the body.	6 each way
Head circles	Rotate head around in small circles.	6 each way
Arms and Shoulders	Keep body upright and relaxed, feet shoulder width apart.	
Arm rotations	Extend both arms out, elbows straight, rotate hands back to front in large circles. Repeat same front to back.	10 each way
Horizontal abduction	Extend hands out horizontally, elbows straight, palms open, move hands back and forth horizontally.	8 reps.
Shoulder shrugs	Rotate both shoulders back to front and reverse.	8 each way
Elbow circles	Extend hands to the front, keep elbows fixed in position, swing forearms inward and then outward.	8 each way
Rotator cuffs	Interlace fingers above head, palms upward, elbows slightly bent, rotate arms together clockwise, then counterclockwise.	10 each way
Hips and Trunk	Feet one and one half shoulders width apart, hold elbows with opposite hands over the head, legs straight.	
Trunk twisting	Keep body axis vertical, twist upper body left and right.	10 each way
Hip circles	Keep shoulders fixed, rotate the hips around horizontally in large circles clockwise and then counterclockwise.	8 each way
Hip and waist	Hold hips in line with feet, move trunk side to side.	6 each way
Hip and back	Bend up and down alternately touching toes of both feet.	6 reps
Back and waist	Clasp hands straight out over head, rotate upper body and hands clockwise, touch the floor, and complete the circle.	8 each way
Hands and Fingers	Relax chest, arms and shoulders.	Time
Finger presses	Press the fingers of the two hands against each other, touch palms and repeat.	10 reps
Thumb flexion	Flex thumb backwards and hold. Repeat for both hands.	10 secs.
Hand circles	Rotate hands about wrists in both directions.	6 each way
Wrist flexion	Flex wrists inward and outward.	6 each way
Knees and Legs	Keep head and trunk upright.	Count
Legs, knees and hips	Assume front stance, bring trailing foot to front knee and back in a clockwise, circular motion. Repeat counterclockwise. Repeat same for other leg.	8 each way
Knee circles	Feet together, bend knees slightly, circle both knees together clockwise and counterclockwise.	8 each way
Ankles and Toes	Hold trunk and head vertical, assume cat stance.	
Ankles	Rotate front foot ankle about the toes, point toes downward.	10 each way
Toes	Flex front foot toes inward against floor, lower knees to half squatting position and back. Repeat same for other foot.	10 each way

I-MIXED EXERCISES (Continued)		
Groin, Hips, Abs and Back	Assume Heisoku-dachi, supporting foot flat on the floor.	
Front leg swing	Swing leg up as high as possible to the front.	10 each leg
Side leg swing	Swing leg up as high as possible to the sides.	10 each leg
Back leg swing	Swing leg up as high as possible to the rear.	10 each leg

II-GENERAL WARM-UP		
Basic Exercises	Select any combination for a total of eight minutes minimum	Time
Jogging and / or	Jog outdoors or indoors at a moderate pace.	8 min.
Running in place or	Run in place on toes, move hands as if jogging.	8 min.
Rope jumping or	Use the pepper rhythm, knees slightly bent	8 min.
Jumping jacks or	Avoid impact by working on toes, knees slightly bent	8 min.
Shadow fighting	Stay on your toes and move around continuously.	8 min.

II-GENERAL WARM-UP		
Body Parts	Keep body as relaxed as possible and breathe normally.	Time
Arms and shoulders	Interlace fingers above head, palms facing away, arms straight, feet together, stretch, and reach for the sky.	20 secs.
Arms and sides	Hold right elbow with left hand above the head, knees slightly bent, pull elbow behind head and bend from hip to the left and hold. Repeat for other side.	20 secs. each way
Quads and knees	Stand on the left leg, hold the top of right foot with right hand and pull toward buttocks and hold. Repeat for other foot.	20 secs.
Hips, legs and trunk	Feet wide apart, legs straight, clasp hands behind head. Bend backward as much as possible and hold.	20 secs.
Hamstrings and spine	Feet slightly apart, legs straight, bend forward, touch toes, and hold.	30 secs.
Inner thighs	Trunk upright, feet as far apart as possible and hold. Bend down at waist, hands on the floor, push feet farther apart, and hold.	20 secs. each move
Hips, hamstrings, thighs	Assume Shiko-dachi, hands clasped behind the neck, keep trunk vertical, lower the hips slightly below knees, and hold.	30 secs.
Hips, legs and toes	Assume exaggerated front stance, chest and front knee above front ankle, stretch rear leg as far back as possible, rear knee resting on the floor, rear toes pointing forward, heels upright.	30 secs. each way
Quadriceps and calves	Squat on left leg, left sole flat on the floor, extend other leg straight out to the right side, push right knee down, keep right toes vertical, and hold. Repeat for other side.	30 secs. each way
Hips and inner thighs	Assume exaggerated Kokutsu-dachi, bend the left knee, right leg straight, hands on hips, lower the body, and let the right knee rotate about the inner edge of right foot until right knee touches floor. Repeat for other side.	30 secs. each way
Groin, Achilles' tendons	Assume Hachiji-dachi, squat down with feet flat on the floor, knees above big toes, grab toes with hands, and push knees out with the elbows.	30 secs.

The more efficient the aerobic system, the more quickly used anaerobic capacity can be restored when the effort has ended.

Two types of aerobic training are appropriate for karate practice. They are classified as general and specific. General aerobic activities that work the large muscle groups of the body are sustained running, aerobic dancing, cross-country skiing and cycling. Specific aerobic exercises duplicate karate skills exactly and include sustained shadow fighting, repeated waza, or combinations, continuous kata performance, at normal speed, and nonstop controlled sparring.

With the regular aerobic exercises suggested in this section, the cardiovascular system eventually will be able to supply more oxygen with greater efficiency. The muscles also will develop a greater capacity to utilize the added supply of energy.

However, aerobic training does not have the same effect on all muscles. Only muscles constantly worked to their aerobic capacity will benefit from this type of training. Therefore, the student must work the whole body with aerobic exercise. This can be achieved by specific aerobic exercises conducted at 60-85 percent of the maximum heart rate at the appropriate age-related level 20-30 minutes a day, three to five times a week.

The simplest way to figure out the age-related maximum heart rate is to subtract the age of the individual in question from 220. Therefore, the 80 percent training heart rate for a 30-year-old karateka would be computed as $(220 - 30) \times 0.8 = 152$ beats per minute. A similar effect may be achieved by combining running, punching, jumping, hurdling and kicking.

Because of vast physiological differences, no single aerobic program will be equally beneficial for all people. In fact, too much of it may be harmful for older students or people who suffer from certain medical conditions. Students therefore are advised to design aerobic programs that best suit their physical conditions and practice schedules. All aerobic programs are characterized by three basic factors, each with a specific lower and upper limit. These factors are:

Frequency of training Three to five sessions per week.
Intensity of training: 60–85 percent of the age-related heart rate.
Duration of training: 20–60 minutes per session.

The more varied the aerobic activity, the greater the benefit. Exercise based on aerobic principles is a progressive process. As stamina improves, so does the degree of endurance of which the muscle groups are capable.

Muscular endurance

Muscular endurance is the quality that determines the ability of localized muscle groups to function over an extended period of time. Muscular endurance and strength are closely interrelated but distinctly different phenomena. The maximum strength of a muscle or muscle group is defined by the effort generated in a one time, high-speed contraction, such as breaking several boards with a single blow. By definition, this type of effort cannot be repeated immediately. Some rest is required. Punching a training bag with 60 percent maximum strength for 20 minutes also would require considerable muscular endurance and general stamina.

The maximum capacity of the body to deliver oxygen to the muscles is limited by genetic makeup and varies substantially from person to person. Even though there is a genetic limit, anyone can–with proper training–get close to that limit and sustain it for a long period of time.

The rules for developing muscular endurance are similar to those for building up general stamina. Similar factors and recommended ranges for training apply. They are:

- Frequency of training   Three to four times per week.
- Intensity of training   60-85 percent of maximum effort.
- Number of repetitions   Three to five sets of 30–100 repetitions.

Here, the rule of progression also applies. For example, if the initial goal is to develop endurance for punching–as in the Gyaku-Tsuki technique, in which developing the arm muscles is the objective–the student should start with an intensity and number of repetitions that can be performed comfortably without a great deal of strain and fatigue. The practice should be repeated until the intensity or number of repetitions can be increased. This may include performing 40–60 reverse punches per minute for two minutes, resting 30–60 seconds, then repeating the same sequence three to four times each session. This will trigger the chemical and structural changes necessary to give the muscle cells the endurance they need for prolonged Tsuki practice.

Once the initial goal is met, students may wish to introduce an element of muscular resistance into the training program. The student concentrates on developing muscle fibers by pumping motions of the muscles against resistance. Continuing the exercise over a period of time, it gradually becomes easier to overcome the same resistance. This also will provide a good basis for developing muscular strength in a particular group of muscles.

If developing muscles in the shoulders, chest and arms is the objective, the student may use expansion pushaways–or push-ups against a wall, table, bench, or floor–to develop gradual muscle buildup and stamina at the same time. The starting inclination of the body with respect to the vertical should be such that after 15–20 pushaways the exercises begin to feel difficult. The degree of difficulty is increased by increasing the number of repetitions and/or increasing the inclination of the body as the physical condition improves. Eventually the student should be able to perform 15–20 push-ups on the floor with only mild exertion.

The way to build further local endurance is through increasing repetition and/or resistance of the muscles. Similar exercises can be devised to increase the endurance of the leg, abdominal and other important muscle groups.

Muscles can perform only what they have been trained to do. Muscles trained to bear light strain and make weak contractions cannot withstand heavy strains or powerful contractions. They will be equal to such tasks only after they have been strengthened gradually.

It is not possible to build up great strength with light exercise. Light exercises cannot develop great strength no matter how often they are repeated. Repetition will increase capacity and stamina, but not strength. On the other hand, exercises that exhaust muscles merely break them down instead of building them up. The fatigue produced by the use of heavy resistance is comparatively mild and muscles recover quickly.

Once a satisfactory level of muscular endurance is reached, students should find ways of maintaining this greater level of endurance while increasing the strength of the muscle group. Muscular strength is increased by exercising with a maximum amount of resistance with some exertion in a few repetitions.

Muscular strength

Muscular strength is the maximum force a muscle–or group of muscles–can generate in a single effort, or contraction. Muscle strength also is reflected in the rapidity of the muscle's contraction. The force of a contraction is more important than frequency when developing strength in a muscle.

When a muscle has been strengthened, it is capable of more intense effort. Intensity of effort manifests itself in two ways: in the ability to overcome more resistance–as in lifting more weight–and in the ability to do equal work in less time. This means that a trained muscle is not only stronger. It is faster, too. Consequently, resistance training is extremely important for karateka trying to maximize their performance by improving speed, dexterity and coordination.

A karateka may spend endless hours in a dojo performing waza. However, waza techniques are performed against fixed resistance, or self-weight, so the increase in muscle strength is limited. Students can increase their muscular strength considerably if they train with weights. Each technique gradually will become easier, extending the ability of the body to perform the particular technique for a longer period of time.

The amount of force generated by a muscle depends primarily on how fast the muscle fibers contract. Effective karate techniques depend greatly on a muscle's ability to contract with great speed and control. The more relaxed and toned the muscles in the initial stages of a movement, the faster the snap of the technique and the greater the power generated.

The focus of the technique is dependent on the forceful contraction of all the muscles of the body involved in the execution of the technique. For this reason, it is important to tone and strengthen the muscles of the entire body uniformly. The most efficient way to gain and maintain muscular strength and overall toning is by weight training.

This section includes a number of basic weight training exercises for the benefit of the average karateka who is sound organically and wants to develop better than average strength in his/her search toward better health and martial arts proficiency. However, if the objective of the training program is to improve specific skills, the best strengthening exercises are those that duplicate karate skills exactly.

The following guidelines and tips are provided to protect students from injury and make weight training as beneficial and enjoyable as possible.

Sample Weight Training Program

Select a weight training hall that has the right training atmosphere, including qualified and well-informed instructors, safety standards, and a large variety of machines and free weights. The hall should be ventilated properly, lit well, clean, and not too crowded or noisy.

Training with a partner

A training partner can give you emotional support by helping prevent accidents, spot movements, and sharing suggestions on timing, form and posture.

Define your goals and schedule your long-term weight training program accordingly. Consult with a qualified trainer and your karate instructor.

Weight training is not to be confused with body building. Cultivating the body for its own sake is contrary to the spirit of karate-do.

Consider obtaining the right clothing, shoes, weight training belts, straps, gloves and a training diary.

The muscles need to be warmed up completely, stretched well and relatively fresh in order to perform exercises requiring powerful contractions. In addition to general warming up and stretching drills, perform specific warming-up and stretching exercises that correspond to the particular muscle groups targeted in your weight training program.

Start with moderate weights and gradually work your way up.

Whenever possible, use your muscles against resistance in the same way you use them in karate.

Try to limit each exercise to three or four sets per session, with 8–12 repetitions per set. Limit resting time between sets and exercises to less than four minutes. Do not allow your body to cool down during a training session.

Allow ample recuperation time between two consecutive training sessions. Never exercise the same muscle groups two days in a row.

If you feel something is wrong, stop the training and consult an expert. Do not overstrain.

Always stretch and cool down at the end of each weight training session.

Include the following muscle groups in your weight training exercises: chest, shoulders, arms, legs, abdominals and back.

A short list of some of the basic weight training exercises for each of these muscle groups is presented bellow.

Weight Training Exercises

These exercises may be too strenuous for some students. They should not despair; rather they should consult a physician and select a milder program.

Muscle Group	Type of Training
Chest	Horizontal barbell bench presses
	Inclined barbell bench presses
	Declined barbell bench presses
	Horizontal dumbbell flies
	Horizontal dumbbell pullovers
Shoulders	Behind the neck military barbell presses
	Dumbbell lateral raises
	Dumbbell shoulder shrugs
	Barbell upright rows
Arms	Barbell curls
	Barbell concentration curls
	Cable triceps pushdowns
	Barbell triceps presses
	Barbell wrist curls
	Dumbbell reverse wrist curls
Legs	Seated or standing calf raises
	Squats or leg presses
	Lunges
	Hack squats
	Leg extensions
	Leg curls
Abdominals	Inclined board sit-ups
	Twisting sit-ups
	Crunches, machine or floor
	Floor sit-ups
	Inclined board leg raises
	Inclined board bent knee raises
	Flat bench leg raises
	Flat bench knee raises

	Hanging leg raises
	Hanging knee raises
Back	Chin-ups
	Rear leg scissors, lying on stomach
	Bench kick backs
	Standing backward leg raises

Flexibility

Flexible joints and pliable muscles are vital to success in karate. Increasing range of motion is a key objective in martial arts practice. A flexible body requires less energy and can move to extreme limits. Even if the student is well-versed in kata and kumite, his/her techniques will be weak if joints are not flexible enough. For this reason, constant training is necessary to maintain and improve the flexibility of the body.

Flexibility, or suppleness, is defined as the combined abilities of joints to rotate through their full range of motion and muscles to stretch through their full limit of linear movement.

Flexibility differs from person to person. As a general rule, children are more flexible than adults. Among adults, women generally are more flexible than men. Most people can improve their flexibility by stretching and long-term planning.

The proper execution of many karate techniques depends largely on two factors: the ability of the joints to articulate through appropriate angles of rotation and the pliability of the connecting muscles in achieving compatible extensions without suffering sprains and tears.

Most upper-level kicks, such as Mae-geri-jodan, Mawashi-jodan, Sokuto-jodan, and Ushiro-geri-jodan, can be performed only with a large degree of hip rotation, hamstring, and inner thigh extension. Flexibility in the hips is of paramount importance in karate. Most effective waza derive their strength from smooth and strong hip rotation.

Performing a full range of stretching exercises at the beginning and end of every training session is the best way to achieve a high degree of joint rotation and muscular suppleness.

However, if the sole purpose of a workout is to increase flexibility, the student should warm up for about 20 minutes, allowing the body to store heat and increase temperature, before proceeding with stretching exercises.

Strength of Character and Toughness

Karate-do is a great source of personal inspiration. It also is a proven means of developing courage, toughness and confidence. Karate practitioners often exert themselves beyond their personal limits, during practice and in real life.

The hardships encountered in martial arts training help develop the determination and will power that are needed to endure stren-

uous situations in karate and arduous tasks in daily life. Enduring many years of psychological and physical exertion gives students a high degree of confidence in their own abilities.

Training solely in waza, kata and kumite confronts the practitioner with his/her own image. Techniques aimed at the air will bring about the benefits of pure karate practice. Supplementary training, on the other hand, will contribute other valuable components and will enhance the benefits of traditional training.

The vigor and alertness associated with long-term conditioning are the basis of the subliminal processes that promote self-esteem, confidence and strength of character.

Weight training, long-distance running, and specific stretching are physically beneficial activities that also instill spiritual strength, self-reliance and courage. These indirect means of confrontation help students become much more capable of dealing with the demands of karate training and daily tasks.

Both direct and indirect toughening exercises eventually lead to more courage and the ability to control aggression.

Direct toughening exercises are those that incorporate special equipment to duplicate karate movements exactly, such as exercises involving sandbags, the makiwara and tameshiwari or breaking brittle objects.

The Makiwara

The makiwara or the striking board is the oriental equivalent of the punching bag. It is an implement unique to karate practice, and is part of the standard equipment in all dojos. Both the punching bag and the makiwara are designed to displace and absorb energy at impact. Unyielding objects return shock waves into striking limbs and cause painful injuries.

The makiwara resembles a short, tapering, branchless tree, sticking out of the ground with a straw padded rope wrapped upper end. It ranges in height from four to five feet, depending on the logistics of the dojo.

Practicing on striking boards with bare hands and feet is the best way to experience and feel the sensations of karate skills applied to an actual tough target. It improves all components of karate strikes, starting from standing correctly, employing proper body movement to finishing strongly with focus and accuracy. It is one of the best practical ways to instill courage and confidence in newly advancing students.

Depending on the training program, which is never part of a regular training session, all striking parts of the arms and hands, as well as legs and feet can be used to hit the makiwara. Makiwara is practiced without any hand or foot padding or protective gear.

For good reason, and for their own protection, children and low-ranking students are barred from using it without permission and proper coaching from their instructors.

First-time users of the makiwara are warned that its use could be painful and may result in bruises and injuries. The straw or cushioned head of the makiwara should be firm in position, clean, dry, smooth, and free from debris. The stem should be straight, sturdy, properly fixed in the ground, and free from cracks and other defects. Its adequacy for use should be checked every time before and after practice. Soke suggests the following regimen for beginners:

- Start with ten push-ups on the two big knuckles of both hands, back straight.
- Strike the makiwara ten times with the two large knuckles. Train both hands.
- Add five push-ups and five strikes at each level of progress until the score is 100.
- Repeat the program using other parts of the hands.

The concept of toughness in karate-do should not be related completely to the partial desensitization of the skin. Rather, it is the knowledge that the skin of the hands and feet has become tough as a result of many years of target practice. The calluses appearing on the hands and feet of advanced students are the by-products of vigorous training against relatively unyielding and hard objects. Working with special implements such as the makiwara, the sandbag, and the punching ball not only improves the student's technical abilities but also introduces the feeling of resistance from a real object. Regular training with these implements adds new and empowering dimensions to the student's experience, something striking at empty air cannot supply. Practicing on the makiwara also prepares the students both physically and mentally to try their skills on breakable objects.

Tameshiwari, or breaking techniques, are alternative methods of sharpening coordination, accuracy, focus and toughness.

Tameshiwari

The makiwara is an unbreakable, stationary training tool. Tameshiwari is the art of breaking brittle objects, with a single strike, at any position within the reach of the performer. These objects include selected pieces of wood, tiles, concrete and clay bricks, stone and ice blocks, baseball bats and cast iron bars. Depending on the skill and strength of the performer, these objects are broken as single pieces or stacked next to or on top of each other.

There are as yet no standards for the general characteristics of these objects and their materials. One thing is clear, no nonbreakable materials, i.e., those possessing any degree of ductility or pliability, ever are used for this purpose. Their overall sizes, thicknesses, and inherent strengths seldom ever are the same, and this is what makes tameshiwari more interesting and challenging.

The practice of tameshiwari serves many purposes, the least of which is shattering objects. First of all, it is an excellent way of assessing a student's advancement in katate practice, where the performer has to make contact and overcome the strength of an unknown entity using enough force with correct form and mind set. Second, it is a spectacular feat that generates a feeling of self-worth in the performer and a sense of admiration for the art by the viewers.

Usually, the most experienced performer, or the person most familiar with strengths and responses of these materials, makes the first selection of the first tameshiwari session with a view to a specific performer's abilities. This often is done with ample reasoning and explanation to prevent injuries to novices. If the selection of the piece or pieces and their manner of fixing in place is not compatible with the performers' abilities, then the outcome of the action could be reversed in favor of the object.

How to avoid such punishment is perhaps the most important lesson of tameshiwari. Before attempting tameshiwari, the student is advised to examine each piece very carefully, so as to understand the strengths and weaknesses of the piece and how to arrange it best for the encounter. The best case scenario is when the piece offers the least amount of resistance to the striking force.

Let's look at the selection process for a breakable piece out of a bunch of square wood boards measuring three-quarters of an inch

thick and 12-inch sides, and all looking apparently the same. At closer examination, certain anomalies and differences are observed. First, it is noted that the grains of all pieces run in one direction, indicating that these pieces would be much stronger in the direction of the grain.

The performer knows that the selected board is to be supported on all four corners and the breaking technique is the vertical knife-hand (shuto-uchi) strike. Instinctively or otherwise, he chooses to strike the boards with his shuto running parallel with the direction of the grains. He obviously has made the right decision, since the boards are much weaker in the opposite direction.

On further examination, he notices that there is a small knot in the middle of one of the pieces. He recognizes the knot by observing two concentric circles with slightly differing diameters on the two faces of the board. He realizes that there is a defect in this particular piece that might offer less resistance than others. He has two choices: support the board on four corners with the smaller circle on top, or otherwise. Which one is in his favor and why?

The moral of the story is that karateka always should gauge the situation at hand before committing to action, and evaluate the opponents' abilities as closely as possible each and every time before engagement. The best course of action is the one that travels through the path of least resistance.

The path of least resistance is detectable only through knowledge, training, willingness, and experience.

CHAPTER 16

Testing and Certification

Testing and certification in martial arts are as important as exams and diplomas in schools and colleges. However, testing and certification alone do not constitute final goals in martial arts. Promotion to a higher rank usually is verified by an official certificate and signified by the ranking of a belt. This ranking may reflect the result of a test but a test never is taken solely to rise to a higher rank.

Although testing and certification are inseparable parts of karate practice, training solely for the sake of promotion is contrary to the spirit of martial arts. Testing is only a means of relating the ranking system to the requirements of the curriculum.

In karate-do, each successful test marks the end of one preparatory stage and the beginning of another, with all stages leading toward personal fulfillment and martial arts proficiency.

While academic examinations demonstrate competency for a specific task or position, testing in karate-do is mainly self-assessment and assurance that one can proceed to a higher level of commitment and hard work. Promotions in rank are awarded according to an individual's degree of development toward the goal of perfection.

Because of the great physical and emotional differences that exist among karate students, individual strengths and weaknesses must be assessed regularly so that both individual progress and group instruction can be organized properly and efficiently. For this reason, IKA encourages its students to take their scheduled tests as soon as they satisfy their attendance and proficiency requirements.

Although there are no other pre-qualifying requirements for testing, students are expected to train diligently in order to qualify for testing. It is customary for all students to seek permission from Soke and their instructors before registering for scheduled testing. The information presented in Table 5 is aimed at familiarizing IKA students with the minimum pre-testing attendance and other requirements.

It is considered impolite to ask to be tested before a scheduled testing announcement. Even then, it is more appropriate for the instructor to encourage the student to take the test, rather than the student insisting to take the test. Higher ranking belts never ask to be tested.

Official testing sessions for Kyu ranks and Dan grades generally are held at IKA headquarters on a quarterly and yearly basis, respectively. Soke, as president and general instructor of IKA, can promote any student at any time to any rank without testing.

Soke directs the entire testing process and presides over the examiners' panel, which consists of four or more high-ranking instructors. Students who have been given permission to test must complete their registration forms one day before the scheduled date.

Candidates are advised to meditate and warm up on their own, beginning at least one hour before the test.

Depending on the number of candidates and their ranks, an individual test may last from 15 minutes to several hours. When testing is in progress, everyone must leave the testing area and refrain from any kind of activity that might distract the students or the examin-

Table 5:
IKA APPROXIMATE MINIMUM ATTENDANCE REQUIREMENTS

Progress Level	Minimum No. of Sessions	Approx. Time No. of month	Cumulative Time No. of month
From 10th Kyu to 9th Kyu	25	2 1/4	2 1/4
From 9th Kyu to 8th Kyu	25	2 1/4	4 1/2
From 8th Kyu to 7th Kyu	30	2 1/2	7
From 7th Kyu to 6th Kyu	35	3	10
From 6th Kyu to 5th Kyu	40	3 1/4	13 1/4
From 5th Kyu to 4th Kyu	55	4 3/4	18
From 4th Kyu to 3rd Kyu	70	6	24
From 3rd Kyu to 2nd Kyu	75	6	30
From 2nd Kyu to 1st Kyu	100	9	39
From 1st Kyu to Shodan	100	9	48

ers. Depending on the circumstances, candidates may be tested either individually or in groups. In either case, the candidate should remain calm, relaxed and confident about what he/she has set out to accomplish.

Depending on the student's ranking, he/she may be asked to perform waza, kata, engage in kumite, demonstrate self-defense techniques and answer questions about karate and related subjects. Although a large number of students pass their tests the first time, there are also those who are asked to try again at the next scheduled test.

Shodan and higher-grade certificates are awarded to successful candidates who are at least 16 years old. Although many talented and hard-working teenagers fulfill the requirements of IKA Shodan and are allowed to wear the Kuro-obi, their diplomas usually are not awarded until they are 16 years old.

To partially fulfill the requirements for any rank or grade, students must demonstrate a high degree of responsibility regarding the social and administrative needs of the IKA. This includes paying fees and meeting other financial obligations in a timely manner and upholding the moral and ethical standards of the school at all times.

All karateka are expected to participate in soji, or physical maintenance and upkeep of the dojo. All students are encouraged and expected to promote the goals of the school and Gosoku-ryu karate by participating in as many social and sporting events as possible. In addition, higher ranking brown belts must help with orientation and training of new students at officially scheduled beginner classes.

According to IKA statistics, one out of every 20 karateka attains Sho-dan; one out of three Sho-dans reaches Ni-dan; one out of three Ni-dans reaches San-dan; and one out of four San-dans attains Yon-dan. Unfortunately, the trend slows down considerably after Yon-dan.

Each test is a great lesson in self-assessment and an excellent opportunity for discovering strengths and weaknesses before moving on to a higher level of responsibility, commitment and expectation.

The information compiled in Table 6 is provided to familiarize potential candidates with the type of minimum ranking requirements that can be expected in a scheduled test.

Examples of interview questions, or Shitsumon

Shitsumon is an important part of testing for all ranks and grades. It has been designed to encourage students to develop a better understanding of the nontechnical aspects of karate practice. The following are some of the typical questions asked in past interviews:

1. What is the difference between KARATE and KARATE-DO?
2. What is a DOJO?
3. What is the meaning of REI?
4. What is KIAI?
5. What is SOKE's full name and background?
6. What kind of karate are you learning?
7. What is the meaning of GOSOKU-RYU?
8. What has karate done for you?
9. What is SOJI?
10. What would you tell new students is the most important aspect of learning karate? How would you teach that?
11. What are the five Dojo Rules?
12. Why is it important to avoid a fight?
13. What would you do if someone challenges you?
14. How would you handle a challenger at the dojo?
15. What is KATA? Why do we practice kata? Why do we repeat the same kata over and over?
16. What is KUMITE? Why do we practice kumite?
17. What is WAZA?
18. What is the difference between IPPON KUMITE and IPPON WAZA?
19. Why do we bow? How do we bow?
20. What are the four important bases for forming correct stances?
21. How is strength or stability established in ZENKUTSU-DACHI?
22. Name all the important elements for performing ZENKUTSU-DACHI correctly?
23. Why do we turn our fist as we strike?
24. What is the meaning of KIME?
25. What are the seven basic ways of using a hand? Name them.
26. What four parts of the foot do we use for kicks?
27. What is the focus point of a fist strike? Why?
28. What are eight major body groupings?
29. What are four basic types of kicks? Name them. Any others?
30. What is one important thing common to all kicks?
31. What are two ways of punching while in Zenkutsu dachi?
32. Name four traditional Japanese martial arts.
33. Why do we meditate and how? What is KUBOKIDO?
34. Why do we recite DOJO RULES and DOJO KUN at every session?
35. What do you know about IKA and its history?
36. What is the importance of ranking? What is meant by GODAN?
37. What are the philosophical meanings of rank and grade in martial arts?
38. What is the definition of a martial art? What is a martial way?
39. Name two traditional schools of Japanese karate.
40. What is meant by SOKE, SHIHAN, SHIHAN-DAI, and SENSEI?
41. Who is the founder of modern karate-do?
42. Talk about the history and the historic importance of karate-do.
43. What are the scientific aspects of karate-do?
44. Name four important spiritual attributes related to karate practice.
45. Name four important mental attributes related to karate practice.
46. Name four important physical attributes related to karate practice.
47. What is a MAKIWARA and what is it used for?
48. What are age and sex limitations for karate practice; why do we have them?
49. Why do we warm up and stretch before a workout?
50. What is meant by aerobic exercises? Name a few aerobic exercises.
51. What are the advantages of weight training?
52. What is the meaning of GAMAE?
53. What is meant by ASHI SABAKI? Give examples.
54. What is meant by TAI SABAKI? Give examples.
55. What is meant by KIHON?
56. Why do we practice the basics over and over again?
57. What is meant by BUNKAI?
58. Talk about the importance of the SONOTA KATA.
59. Which is your favorite kata? Why?
60. What is meant by KOKUSAI KARATE DO KIOKAI?
61. What is meant by SOKE KUNJI?
62. How would you say 23 in Japanese?

63. What are the meanings of the following words: HIDARI, TANDEN, NAGASHI, USHIRO?
64. What are some of the important features of GOSOKU-RYU karate?
65. What is the difference between muscular strength and muscular endurance?
66. What are the similarities between the SHOTOKAN and GOSOKU-RYU styles of karate?
67. How do karate techniques benefit from hip rotation?
68. What is the history of GOSOKU-RYU karate?
69. What is the difference between KARATE-JUTSU and KARATE-DO?
70. What is the difference between a martial art and a martial way?
71. Is karate an art, a science, a sport, a way of life, or a method of self-defense?
72. What is meant by "a way of life"?
73. How would you say, "Thank you very much", in Japanese?
74. What is meant by KARATE NI SENTE NISHI?
75. What is meant by MIZU NO KOKORO?
76. What is the relationship between martial arts and creative arts?
77. What is meant by ATEMI-WAZA, NAGE-WAZA?
78. What is meant by supplementary conditioning?
79. What is the message contained in the IKA insignia?
80. What is meant by AI-UCHI and CHUI?
81. What is IKAT?
82. What is meant by "no first attack in karate"?
83. What is meant by KUBOJUTSU?
84. Name two good books on karate-do.
85. Name two martial arts magazines.
86. What should you do if an injury is bleeding?
87. What should you do if someone loses consciousness?
88. What is the difference between free and tournament-style sparring?
89. What is meant by TAMESHIWARI?
90. What is the difference between MAKOTO and MOKUSO?
91. What is the single most important message contained in this book?
92. What is meant by dynamic stretching?
93. What is the difference between muscular strength and muscular endurance?
94. Name four exercises for strengthening abdominal muscles.
95. Name two basic exercises for improving hip rotation.
96. Name four basic sparring principles.
97. What is the main purpose of testing and ranking in karate-do?
98. What are the similarities between the GOSOKU-RYU and SHOTOKAN styles of karate?
99. What is meant by GOSHIN-JUTSU?
100. What is meant by tournament-style sparring?
101. What is meant by SHU-DO?
102. What is the difference between a WAZA-ARI and an IPPON?
103. Where is Okinawa?
104. Who is GICHIN FUNAKOSHI?
105. How old is KARATE? How old is KARATE-DO?
106. What is meant by SANBON-SHOBU?
107. What is a HANSOKU?
108. What is the difference between MUBOBI and ATENAI-YONI?
109. What is the difference between a KANZA and a SHIMPAN
110. Name two of Soke's books.
111. What is HOJO-UNDU?
112. Name your favorite book on karate practice.
113. What do you do if someone gets injured in the dojo?
114. What does RICE stand for?
115. How do you stop bleeding?
116. Name the nearest hospital to the dojo.
117. What is the first thing you teach a new student?
118. What are the components of KIHON?
119. Name two common COMPONENTS for all kicking waza.
120. Is KIAI common to all martial arts?
121. What is meant by KIHON KATA?
122. Name five KIHON katas.
123. How do you say BLACK BELT in Japanese?
124. What is meant by EMOTIONAL CONTROL?
125. How do you show your respect to the dojo?
126. What are four basic types of hand blocks?
127. How many Kihon katas do you know?

Table 6:
INTERNATIONAL KARATE ASSOCIATION GENERAL RANKING REQUIREMENTS

	Requirements	BELT										
		Wt	Ye	Or	Bl	Pu	Gr	Gr	Br	Br	Br	Bk
		10	9	8	7	6	5	4	3	2	1	
1	Mae geri	●	●	●	●	●	●	●				
2	Yoko geri	●	●	●	●	●	●	●	●	●	●	
3	Mawashi geri	●	●	●	●	●	●	●	●	●	●	
4	Ushiro geri	●	●	●	●	●	●	●	●	●	●	
5	Mika tsuki geri						●	●				
6	Mae fumikomi geri							●				
7	Yoko fumikomi geri							●				
8	Ushiro fumikomi geri								●			
9	Ura mawashi geri								●	●	●	
10	Soto mawashi geri								●	●	●	
11	Uchi mawashi geri								●	●	●	
12	Ushiro mawashi geri										●	●
13	Sonota geri								●	●	●	●
14	Jodan age uke	●	●	●	●	●	●	●				
15	Chudan uchi uke	●	●	●	●	●	●	●				
16	Chudan soto uke	●	●	●	●	●	●	●				
17	Gedan barai	●	●	●	●	●	●	●				
18	Oi tsuki	●	●	●	●	●	●	●	●	●	●	
19	Gyaku tsuki				●	●	●	●	●	●	●	
20	Sonota tsuki										●	●
21	Sonota uchi										●	●
22	Mawashi uchi									●	●	
23	Empi uchi								●	●	●	
24	Zu tsuki uchi											●
25	Haiza uchi										●	●
26	Nage waza											●
27	Ukemi waza										●	●
28	Yama tsuki										●	
29	Kokutsu dachi	●	●	●	●	●	●	●	●	●	●	
30	Zenkutsu dachi	●	●	●	●	●	●	●	●	●	●	
31	Kiba dachi	●	●	●	●	●	●	●	●	●	●	
32	Heisoku dachi	●	●	●	●							
33	Musubu dachi	●	●	●	●							

KARATE-DO: A WAY OF LIFE

#	Requirements	Wt	Ye	Or	Bl	Pu	Gr	Gr	Br	Br	Br	Bk
		10	9	8	7	6	5	4	3	2	1	
34	Neko ashi dachi								●	●	●	
35	Uchi mata dachi								●	●	●	
36	Ren dachi								●	●	●	
37	Kihon ichi no kata			●	●	●	●	●				●
38	Kihon ni no kata			●	●	●	●	●				●
39	Kihon san no kata			●	●	●	●	●				●
40	Kihon sonota kata			●	●	●	●	●				●
41	Heian Shodan			●	●	●	●	●	●	●	●	●
42	Heian Nidan			●	●	●	●	●	●	●	●	●
43	Heian Sandan				●	●	●	●	●	●	●	●
44	Heian Yondan					●	●	●	●	●	●	●
45	Heian Godan								●	●	●	●
46	Tekki Shodan								●	●	●	●
47	Bassai Dai								●	●	●	●
48	Hangetsu									●	●	●
49	Kanku Dai								●	●	●	●
50	Kanku Sho											●
51	Ichi no Kata					●	●	●	●	●	●	●
52	Uke no Kata								●	●	●	●
53	Ni no Kata								●	●	●	●
54	Gosoku									●	●	●
55	Gosuku Yodan										●	●
56	Denkogetsu										●	●
57	Ippon Kumite					●	●	●				
58	Nihon Kumite						●	●				
59	Sanbon Kumite					●	●	●				
60	Sonota Waza					●	●	●	●	●	●	●
61	Tome Waza								●	●		
62	Sanbon Waza					●	●	●	●			
63	Shitsumon			●	●	●	●	●	●	●	●	●
64	Shudo										●	●
65	Kumite								●	●	●	●
66	Goshinjutsu										●	●

CHAPTER 17

Tournaments

Sport karate, unlike traditional karate-do, is a relatively new concept originally developed and practiced in Japan in the early 1960s. Its creators wanted to develop a safe and fair method of comparing the wits and technical abilities of karate students in combat-like situations. Their intentions excluded creating an Olympic type sport, or a crowd pleasing spectacle.

Today's tournament style sparring, or Sanbon Shobu–literally, three point victory defeat–is a much restricted and regulated version of the traditional Shinken Shobu, or fight to the death, used to test the martial skills of contestants in actual combat.

The practice of Shinken Shobu and challenge to the death was phased out completely before the beginning of the present century. Instead, the concept of the Shiai, or the test meeting, was introduced to compare the fighting skills of the challengers in a nondeadly, but still harmful, method of sparring practice. This type of some-holds-barred event was held in a special contest area known as the Shiai-jo under the supervision of an authoritarian contest judge, or Fukushin.

The rules of the shiai were simple. Known lethal blows were withheld while all other techniques were delivered with full contact and power. The shiai would end when one of the contestants was knocked out, forced out of the shiai jo, admitted defeat, or signaled his unwillingness to continue the match.

The main difference between sport karate and traditional karate-do is that sport karate draws only on a small portion of the arsenal of sparring techniques available in traditional karate-do. These techniques can be directed only at specific target areas assumed safe against moderate and/or controlled blows. Furthermore, sport karate does not concern itself with the "do" aspect of the art, which is considered by many the essence of traditional karate practice.

In traditional karate-do, the primary objective is overcoming self through daily practice of kata, kumite and waza. Sport karate aims mainly at proving superiority over others that, to the untrained mind, may seem contrary to the basic principles of traditional budo. Nevertheless, sport karate is a valuable athletic endeavor and a proven method of promoting karate and martial arts in the western world. This probably is the main reason sport karate also is part of the curriculum at IKA and other traditional schools.

Contemporary Sanbon Shobu was introduced by the Federation of All-Japan Karate-do Organizations (FAJKO) in 1965. The first official championship event under FAJKO rules–the All-Japan Karate-do Competition–was held in Tokyo in 1969.

As part of its scheduled activities, IKA organizes and sanctions annual karate tournaments at local, national and international levels through its tournament arm, the International Karate Association Tournament, Inc. (IKAT). IKAT is a nonprofit organization dedicated to the promotion and development of traditional karate-do.

The 1st and 44th annual All-Star IKA Karate Championships, incorporating improved FAJKO rules, were held in California in 1964 and 2007. Soke Kubota's ideas and recommendations have been instrumental in modifying these rules in favor of competitor safety and fairness.

IKA tournaments are regarded widely as one of the most important karate events of the year, both in the United States and abroad. They have become a celebration of Soke's contributions and dedication to the martial arts. IKA students from all over the world come to meet each other and guest karateka from other schools.

The Kubota World Cup is the flagship tournament of IKA and was held first in Canada in 1971. The World Karate-do Goodwill Championship, also organized and sanctioned by IKAT, was held first in Gifu, Japan, in 1996. The last IKA World Cup championship prior to the publication of this book took place in Warsaw, Poland, in 2007.

The main purpose of IKAT, besides promoting karate-do and reaffirming its ideals through tournament events, is providing a congenial environment for dissemination of information and exchange of ideas. IKAT founders firmly believe that a contest is merely a test of proficiency in sport karate and not a means of proving superiority over others.

The Kubota Cup is an international festival of karate and martial arts. Its activities include scheduled Dan ranking sessions, karate seminars, practical workshops, demonstrations, lectures, festivities

and championship events. Most importantly, it is an occasion for new and old friends to meet, have fun and exchange ideas.

World Cup educational events, which now have a large following, are well- attended and give trainees plenty of material to take away and work on after the event is over. Participation in IKA tournaments is by invitation only. Only recognized schools and individuals are invited to take part in these events.

Taking part in IKA tournaments, either as competitor, spectator, instructor or official, is always a fulfilling experience. All IKA students–regardless of age, sex, rank, or grade–are encouraged to get involved in as many activities as possible.

Table 7 contains a typical list of championship events, which may be subject to change without notice depending on the number of participants, local rules and regulations, logistics and other considerations.

A summary of the more important rules and regulations specifically designed for IKAT is presented below.

Contestants, their coaches, guardians, and supervisors must be familiar with these rules, regulations and the corresponding Japanese terminology.

RULES AND REGULATIONS

Usually, three distinct types of competition are held at major karate tournaments: Kumite, Kata and Weapons Kata. All three types of competitions are held in both individual and team categories, for both men and women of all ranks and ages. There are several categories within these areas, divided by age, gender and ranking. The following divisions, based on rank and age, are designed specifically to encourage greater turnout and participation by as many karateka as possible. Depending on the circumstances, organizers may exercise their rights to combine and/or alter these divisions. It is the duty of each competitor to check the specific divisions of each and every event days before the announced dates of the tournament.

IKA DIVISIONS

Beginners — All 7th, 8th, 9th, and 10th Kyus are considered Beginners

Intermediate — All 4th, 5th, and 6th Kyus are considered Intermediate.

Advanced — All 1st, 2nd, and 3rd Kyu Black Belts are considered Advanced.

Children — All 6 to 12 year olds are considered Children

Juniors — All 13 to 17 year olds are considered Juniors.

Adults — All those 18 years of age or older are considered Adults.

These categories are subdivided further into individual and team events. It can not be over emphasized that each participant should know his/her registration number, schedule of events, and time and place (ring or mat number) of each specific event.

All contestants should honor the code of conduct described in Chapter 4 and abide by the rules and regulations presented in this section. Contestants should also familiarize themselves with additional criteria announced by particular tournament organizers.

KATA COMPETITION

Competitors will use only Japanese/Okinawan katas. All beginners and intermediate level competitors must use either Heian, Pinan, Gekisai, Sanchin, Tensho, Tieshi-Shodan, Konchabo, or similar level katas. Brown and black belts may perform any advanced kata. Gosoku-ryu katas are considered as Japanese forms.

Kata scoring: All katas will be scored by a panel of three or five judges. When there are five judges, the high and low scores are dropped and the remaining numbers are added together. In the

event of a tie, the low scores are added back. If still tied, the high scores are added back. If still tied, the contestants must do another kata.

Team kata is scored the same way as individual kata. Usually, there are no limitations on the selection of members of team kata. A team consists of three or five performers. It may consist of men and women of all ages and ranks.

Nowadays, in some local and international kata championships, the performers also are asked to formally present the bunkai of the same kata. Usually, bunkais are performed in accordance with their classical interpretations. Ideally, the team bunkai is completed in the same length of time as the kata itself. It should start and end at the same point as the original kata.

New but relevant and meaningful interpretations also are accepted for scoring purposes. Presentation of new or undiscovered bunkai always is encouraged.

SPARRING CONTESTS

Sparring competition is only a means of assessing a student's emotional stability and technical skills in a combat like situation.

The following rules and regulations were devised to ensure safety and proper conduct during official kumite matches, and to remind the contestants that winning at all costs is contrary to the spirit of karate-do.

KUMITE (Sparring) – A mouthpiece and protective cup are mandatory for all male competitors. Female competitors also must wear a mouthpiece. A chest protector is optional. All competitors must wear cloth fistguards. Protective headgear is mandatory for competitors 17 years of age and under.

Headgear is provided or competitors can use their own if it is an approved design. Accepted techniques include Mae-geri, Yoko-geri, Ushiro-geri, Mawashi-geri, Tobi-geri, Ura-mawashi-geri, Fumikomi-geri (after takedown), Ashi-barai (followed by a scoring point), Jodan-tsuki, Chudan-tsuki, Gyaku-tsuki, Tate-tsuki, Shuto-uchi, Haito-uchi, Kentsui-uchi, Uraken-uchi, and Empi-uchi (no contact).

Competitors may be asked to wear red or white ribbons or belts to identify their side of the tatami.

Team kumite usually involves an odd number of competitors, from three to nine, on each side. Usually, there are fewer restrictions on the ranking and other classifications of members of team kumite.

MATCHES – The duration of the bout is two minutes or three Ippons. Waza-Ari (one-half point) is given only after the second Jogai. This rule is not universal and may vary from tournament to tournament and from place to place.

ENCHO-SEN (Extension) – In case of a draw at the end of two minutes, the bout is extended for one minute. The first contestant to score is declared the winner. If it is still a draw at the end of the one minute extension, the referee must give a winning decision by Hantei, or judgment. The method of decision making may differ in other organizations.

HANTEI (Judgment) – Hantei is based on a contestant's attitude, fighting spirit, strength, and superiority of tactics and techniques.

JOGAI (Outside Match Area) – A contestant who steps outside the ring is penalized by Jogai. First Jogai is a warning; second

Jogai is Keikoku, with Waza-Ari awarded to the opponent; third Jogai is Hansoku-Chui, with Ippon awarded to the opponent; fourth Jogai is Hansoku, with No Kachi awarded to the opponent.

ATENAI-YONI (Warning, Facial Contact)

MUBOBI (Lack of regard for one's own safety) – First Mubobi is Hansoku-Chui, with Ippon awarded to the opponent; second Mubobi is Hansoku, with No Kachi awarded to the opponent. Hansoku can be imposed if a contestant's reckless attitude causes injury.

KIKEN (Forfeiture) – This is a decision given when a contestant abandons the bout or is unable to continue due to injury.

SHIKKAKU (Disqualification) – Any discourteous behavior, either by a coach or contestants, can be penalized by Shikkaku, or disqualification from the entire tournament.

HANSOKU (Foul, No Kachi to the Opponent) – Contestant can win only two matches as a result of Hansoku, or opponent's foul. A second win by Hansoku will lead to the winner's withdrawal, even though physically fit to continue.

OTHER TERMS:

The following Japanese terms often are used during karate tournaments and contests:

Term	Meaning / Explanation
Ai-uchi	simultaneous scoring with no points given
Hiki-wake	contest is a draw
Chui	warning
Shiai-jo	contest area/(a flat square, 30 ft. x 30 ft.)
Waza-ari	half point
Ippon	one point
Kachite	winner/win/win by
Sanbon-shobu	three point match
Shimpan/Shushin	referee/judge
Jikan	time up
Tzuzukete	carry on/continue
Make	loss/loss by
Awase-waza	decision wins
Shitei	compulsory (kata competition)
Tokui	favorite (kata competition)

Fusensho	default/loss by default
Fusen kachi	win/victory by default
Torimasen	unacceptable (as in scoring technique)
Kanza	arbitrator

IKA members and teams from all affiliated dojos worldwide participate in many local and international competitions, sanctioned by different organizing bodies with different rules and regulations. Most world class organizations, including the IKA, also subscribe to WKF (World Karate Federation) rules and regulations for karate tournaments.

A partial summary of these rules and regulations is presented in the next section. Interested readers can access further information on the subject from the Internet.

PARTIAL WKF KUMITE RULES AND REGULATIONS

A short list of World Karate Federation Rules for kumite matches is presented here for the added benefit of IKA members. These rules may be subject to change, depending on local and national restrictions. Rules governing attire and protective gear may also vary from tournament to tournament.

KUMITE SCORING

Technical attacks that score points are limited to the head, face, neck, abdomen, chest, back, and sides.

3 points or Sanbon

Is awarded for technically acceptable attacks such as:

Jodan or upper level kicks.

Throwing or leg sweeping the opponent to the mat followed by a striking technique

2 points or Nihon

Chudan or mid-level kicks.

Punches to the back, back of head and neck.

Combination hand or hand and leg techniques.

Unbalancing the opponent and scoring.

1 point or Ippon

Chudan or jodan punch.

Chudan or jodan strikes.

PROHIBITED BEHAVIOR

Two categories of prohibited behavior carry appropriate penalties.

Category 1

Techniques with excessive contact force.

Contact with the throat.

Strikes to the joints, groin, instep, arms, and legs.

Attacks to face with open hand techniques.

Dangerous or forbidden throwing techniques.

Category 2

Feigning or exaggerating pain or injury.

Repeat exits from the competition area.

Self-endangerment by exposing self to opponent.

Failing to adequately protect self.

Avoiding engagement for zero-zero outcome.

Clinching, pushing, and seizing without attempting a throw or strike.

Dangerous and uncontrolled or uncontrollable techniques and attacks.

Attacks using head, knees, and elbows.

Talking to, or goading the opponent.

Failing to obey referee's orders.

Breaches of etiquette, and discourteous conduct towards the official.

CHAPTER 18

Basic Health and First Aid

The dojo is the extended home of the IKA family, and as such is a place of public gathering. If someone gets injured and/or needs medical attention, then anybody who is eligible or can be of any help should respond immediately. If one member of the family brings a flu virus home and is not careful about it, then sooner or later every other member of the family also will suffer from it. It is common knowledge that personal hygiene, environmental responsibility, and sensible behavior are the cornerstones of healthy living.

Acting responsibly will reduce or prevent injuries during practice and will prevent the spread of diseases in the dojo and elsewhere. This is why we take our shoes off, do soji, and wear clean white gis in the dojo. We use our own soap and towels at the showers. We abstain from bringing food, beverages, and pets into the dojo. Smoking is strongly discouraged and we all observe the no smoking and no loitering rules.

According to official sources, less than half of a percent of all sports injuries reported in the United States are related to martial arts practice. And less than half of this percentage is related to karate practice. This statistic covers more than 50 major sports, starting with cycling, soccer, and tennis to archery, curling, etc.

The percentage of injuries per sport in karate is considerably less than most popular American sports like hockey, basketball, football, baseball, etc.

All karate students are encouraged to learn the ABCs of basic first aid as presented in this chapter. They should all be familiar with such basic first aid concepts as mouth-to-mouth resuscitation, disinfecting, RICE, bandaging, taping, and providing comfort for the injured person. RICE is a four-part first aid guideline before rushing to a doctor's clinic. The word rice is a simple reminder of the four ingredients of basic first aid, i.e., Rest, Ice, Compression, and Elevation.

Long-term practice of karate, together with a holistic way of life, eventually will improve the immune system and increase the body's resistance to minor injuries. However this should not become a pretext for karateta to drop their guards against apathy, unruly behavior, and social responsibility.

The basic first aid guidelines presented in this section are very limited in nature and are related to what may happen in a typical dojo environment. Remember that the 911 call is always there to help us with emergencies.

ABCs OF FIRST AID

***A* stands for Assist.** We help someone who has been injured. In IKA, we show respect for our training partner. All of us have different levels of skill and different strengths. The idea is not to beat up your partner but to get the best training you can, whatever the circumstances. That is part of karate training, too.

Accidents happen. If you are involved in an accident, it is your responsibility to help the injured party. That means going at once to the injured person and doing what you can to treat the injury or finding someone who can help. In extreme circumstances, you may have to drive the injured person to the hospital.

***B* stands for Bleeding.** If an injury is bleeding, bleed it well by going to the sink and running water into it. This will cleanse the wound. Then, stop the bleeding by applying pressure. If bleeding is so severe that simple pressure will not stop it, seek medical attention. It is not a good idea for inexperienced individuals to apply tourniquets, as an incorrect application can do more harm than good.

Most of the people in karate dojos do not have blood diseases, such as AIDS. To contract AIDS, it is believed that infected blood must enter the bloodstream. The AIDS virus is very weak outside the body. Do not panic if you come in contact with blood while helping an injured person. Simply wash it off.

***B* also stands for Blisters.** Blisters are localized accumulations of fluid under the outer part of the skin. They usually are caused by repeated rubbing of the skin against a hard surface. Karateka usually get them under the big toe and or the ball of the foot, but you don't have to be a martial artist to earn one. If a blister becomes unbearable, you always can ask your doctor to drain it by puncturing the outer skin. The doctor usually punctures the blister on its outer edge, using a sterilized needle, after cleaning the site with alcohol.

C stands for Cool. If you have an injury, the best thing you can do first is to keep cool. Do not panic. Do not continue working an injured body part. Learn from Soke. When he had an injured shoulder, he trained with all parts of his body except the injured shoulder and arm.

Most severe injuries will take four to six weeks to heal completely. Less severe injuries will heal more quickly. Continued working of an injured body part can turn that injury into something more severe or chronic. Try instead to train without the body, by watching a lesson or doing kata as meditation. Soke is a master at this as well.

Muscle spasms also can be treated with ice and rest. Acupuncture often is extremely effective for muscle spasms and other injuries.

C also stands for Compression. Compression restricts bleeding and limits swelling. If properly applied, it can stabilize the wounded area locally. Bandaging and taping also can provide some degree of compression.

D stands for Dislocations. Dislocation is defined as separation of a bone from its joint. It can occur from a fall, uncontrolled leverage or a direct blow to the bone. The most common areas of bone dislocation in karate practice are the toes, fingers, knees, elbows, hips, and shoulders.

Symptoms of dislocations are pain, dysfunction, swelling, deformity at the joint, and tenderness upon touch. The first thing to do is to immobilize the injured part with a sling, pillow, or splint and have the injured person rest in a comfortable position (katate gis and pants make excellent slings and pillows). Call for emergency assistance. Non-experts should not attempt to restore a dislocation.

D also stands for Drugs. The best medications for fresh injuries are Arnica and ice, as mentioned above. Arnica is a nontoxic herbal preparation available at health food stores. Some people prefer aspirin or nonsteroidal, anti-inflammatory agents such as Advil or Motrin. If you use these medications, remember to take them with food or milk because they can tear up your stomach and cause ulcers. They also are not good for your kidneys, especially with long-term use, so drink lots of water. They also decrease the body's ability to stop bleeding. This effect is reversible in three to ten days after discontinuing use of the medication. These medications should not be taken with alcohol.

D also stands for Disinfect. We do this with simple soap and water. Diluted hydrogen peroxide is a good disinfectant for more severe wounds and also helps in the process of removing dead tissue from the site of the injury.

E stands for Elevate. It is best to raise the injured part of the body. This helps reduce swelling and assists the body in healing the area. If possible, the injured body part should be raised above the level of the heart so that excess fluids could run away from the injured part.

E also stands for Eye injuries. Eye injuries should be checked by a professional.

F stands for Fainting. If someone loses consciousness, the first thing you should do is make sure he/she is breathing and has a pulse. If the person has a pulse and is breathing, revive him/her by elevating his/her legs above the head. A cold cloth behind the neck also is useful for people who have fainted. Also see "U" below.

G stands for Get a doctor. We have several doctors and paramedics capable of handling medical emergencies at our headquarters dojo. Almost all other dojos have access to nearby health clinics and hospitals. Injuries and accidents more serious than those discussed in this section require a doctor's attention.

Breaks, dislocations and severe wounds should be handled, or at least checked by, a professional. Accidental bites also should be checked by a professional. Human bites have a great potential for infection. Even if a bite is not deep, the injured person may require medical care and a dose of antibiotics.

H stands for Health. If you expect your body to heal, you must nourish it with proper food and rest. A diet consisting of a balanced amount of protein and carbohydrates is best. For a really healthy system, food high in fat should be avoided. Our bodies are designed to run on 20 to 30 grams of fiber per day. Most of the protein in American diets comes from animals. This does not have to be the case. Nutritious protein can be obtained from beans, legumes (peas and lentils), and soy products.

Animal protein contains toxins and poisons in the form of pesticides, fertilizers, and hormones. If you do eat flesh, try to eat free-range chicken and turkey. Fish, particularly salmon and halibut, also is good for you. It may cost a little more to eat properly, but the long-term benefits will be well worth it.

Many stores in the United States and Europe carry healthful organic foods. There is a great deal of stress living in a large urban area. Many of our foods are processed and irradiated. For these reasons, it also is a good idea to take a multivitamin supplement to help your body process your food. Remember, though, that vitamins are not a substitute for eating healthful foods and maintaining a balanced diet. They are only partners in the process.

H also stands for Heat. Heat treatment after two days of ice treatment stimulates blood flow and speeds up the healing process. Intermittent moist heating appears to work better for some people than continuous dry heating.

***I* stands for Injuries.** Unfortunately, injuries are almost unavoidable in martial arts practice. However, according to the Consumer Product Safety Commission, the percentage of injuries in martial arts is far less than that reported for football or soccer or ice hockey. In general, two types of injuries are observed in karate practice: self-induced and that caused by others.

The majority of injuries encountered in karate practice are self-inflicted and mainly are due to lack of fitness, carelessness, and/or insufficient preparation. Muscle and ligament as well as joint-related injuries are the most common .The only way muscles and ligaments can be injured is when they are pulled beyond their natural strength and range. In medical parlance, there are three grades of overstress,;these are called strains:

Grade I, where less than 10 percent of the constituent fibers of the muscle is affected.

Grade II, where the range of injured fibers is between 10 and 50 percent.

Grade III, where the range of damaged fibers is more than 50 percent and could mean an extensive tear or complete muscle rupture.

The first phase of treatment of all muscle and ligament injuries is RICE; then, seek medical assistance.

The other sources of karate injuries are direct hits and uncontrolled falls, both of which are the result of poor sportsmanship, irresponsible behavior, and insufficient training. Such dangerous acts could result in bone fractures, joint dislocations, internal bleeding, and organ failure. The first line of action in such cases is to immobilize the injured person and immediately call an ambulance.

***I* also stands for Ice.** Putting ice on an injured and painful body part, be it due to tendonitis, bursitis, minor fractures, or other causes, is the best first aid action immediately after injury. The affected area should be kept under a sufficient amount of ice so that the injured person can feel its soothing effect. Make sure the ice is wrapped in proper material so that the skin does not suffer from ice burns.

Ice tends to shrink torn blood vessels and prevent excessive swelling. It will reduce pain and help the healing process. It is advisable to continue the initial ice treatment for two days, say twenty minutes at two hours intervals. Never put heat on a new injury.

***J* stands for Joints.** The human skeleton consists of bones that mostly carry compressive forces, muscles that only can sustain tensile exertions, and body hinges or joints. Joints occur at bony levers. Without joints, humans cannot move their limbs and karateka cannot execute techniques. Mobility and stability are the two most important functions of all joints.

Not all joints are equally stable and mobile. The shoulder joint is extremely mobile and can rotate in many directions, but it also is rather unstable. It easily can be dislocated. The hip is not very mobile but is the most stable joint of the body.

Joints are complex, yet sensitive structures, and as such have limited force carrying capacities and ranges of motion in specific directions. They are designed to remain stable during normal motion. Joint injuries commonly occur as a result of direct overloading, excessive rotation, undue torsion, impact, and regular wear and tear. In general, the first attempt in treating joint injuries consist of administering anti-inflammatory medication together with RICE, followed be expert examination.

K stands for Knees. The knee joint is the hardest working joint in karate practice. Practitioners are required to keep their knees bent all the time. It indeed is the most used and abused joint of the body. It is subject to more normal wear and tear than all other joints together. The knee joint is a trade-off between mobility and stability.

There are four major causes for knee pain: The knee cap and extensor mechanism, like quadriceps tendonitis (inflammation of the tendons), chondromalacia, (softening and wearing out of bone and cartilage), etc.; the inside part of the knee, stress fracture, bursitis, etc.; the outside part of the knee, like runner's knee, bursitis (inflammation of the bursa of the joints), etc.; and the inside of the joint, such as arthritis, meniscal tear, ligament problem, etc.

The most common symptoms of knee discomfort are swelling, pain, grinding, buckling, locking, and sliding kneecap. The immediate treatment is RICE, followed by a doctor's visit.

Long-term treatment may include rest, reduced activity, injections, use of anti-inflammatory drugs, orthotics, braces, surgery, and physical therapy. The best way to prevent knee injuries, besides being thoughtful, is to maintain a high level of physical fitness, especially in the muscle groups surrounding the knee joints.

L stands for Learning. Learn as much as you can about basic health and first aid. Learn about basic taping, bandaging, and immobilization. It always is desirable to know people who can perform mouth-to-mouth resuscitation. Know all there is to know about hospitals, clinics, and emergency services nearest to your dojo.

M stands for Medication. Almost all prescription drugs and medications, as well as a large number of over-the-counter remedies, have unpleasant and sometimes serious side effects. The most common side effects are body aches, dizziness, and shortness of breath. Almost all karateka, knowingly or otherwise, ignore the warning signs in favor of attending dojo. This could result in poor performance, falling, and other injuries. It would be to your and everyone else's advantage if you inform the officials of your temporary conditions.

M also stands for Mental. If you notice unusual behavior from any one, and feel a person is experiencing a mental problem, is affected by substance abuse, or simply is emotionally disturbed and unstable, do not intervene, but request assistance from the administration office.

N stands for Nerves. Nerve damage in karate practice usually is associated with dislocations, bone fracture, jammed toes and fingers, hyperextended joints, and spinal disc problems. Pain along the limbs, numbness, and tingling of the extremities all are signs of nerve problems. Serious nerve damage such as those caused by neck whiplash is not common in karate practice. However nerve damage is serious business and should be looked at by experts. Nerve damage is not easy to diagnose.

P is for Pain: Martial artists in general and karateka in particular are known for their high thresholds of pain and discomfort. Pain is an internal self-defense mechanism. Without pain, we would continue punching and kicking each other with fractured limbs and open wounds until we drop. It is unwise to ignore pain, even if it is tolerable. A minor pain could be a signal for a major underlying cause. Pain is a signal that something is not quite right.

P also stands for Pregnancy. Moderate, regular exercises have many physical as well as psychological benefits during pregnancy. Obviously, sparring, jumping, sudden moves, and overstretching are out of the question. Pregnancy may vary from case to case. It always is prudent to consult a physician before starting any exercise program.

R stands for Rest. It is unwise to continue practice on an injured limb before administering first aid and stabilizing the affected area. Providing rest and comfort for the injured person is the most important step in basic first aid.

S stands for Surgery. The human body is capable of curing and healing itself to some extent, but sometimes external intervention or surgery is unavoidable. Surgery is the last option to try to restore body function to a damaged limb.

If you are scheduled for a surgery, inform your dojo and ask your doctor for pre- and post-operation instructions. Some 25 percent of all karateka with more than thirty years of experience in active karate training eventually face one or two sports-related surgeries, which is the same number for ordinary folks who do not engage is sports at all.

S also stands for Shortness of breath and Stop. Shortness of breath is easy to detect. The victim will be the first to stop and complain about the condition. Shortness of breath or the feeling of being winded is a symptom that can represent anything from a lack of conditioning/physical fitness to the onset of a severe medical condition. Addressing the potential seriousness of this symptom is not within the scope of this book. Suffice it to say that if you or your partner feels short of breath, STOP. If the shortness of breath is accompanied by chest pressure or dizziness, a trip to the local emergency clinic would be in order. However, you must be cleared medically before taking on any physically demanding activity.

T stands for Therapy. If you have to have some type of sports surgery, then you must be prepared for a period of rest or hiatus, followed by different therapies. Being a karateka, you will be anxious to return to practice as soon as possible. Do your therapy and resume your workout routine, provided you can let the healing limb rest during training. Refrain from kumite practice.

U stands for Unconsciousness. Unconsciousness is not common in the dojo environment; however, with sparring situations and lack of control, it can occur. The symptoms are collapse, unawareness and unresponsiveness. The scenario will vary from a quick coming around to potentially more severe damage and prolonged unresponsiveness. Again, the purpose of this book is not to provide medical advice to the reader. A common sense response in this event is first to call for help by dialing 911. Next, with an unconscious person, the ABCs of CPR ALWAYS are appropriate. To become familiar with CPR, a basic CPR course given by an accredited American Heart Association provider is recommended. Briefly, in review, A is for airway. Open it by performing a jaw thrust, moving the jaw forward to allow air in, past the tongue, in the event that the person's breathing muscles are working. DO NOT move the person's head/neck in case there is a neck fracture sustained in the fall. Be careful of any possible fractures. B stands for breathing. Look, listen, and feel for spontaneous respiration. If it is present, then wait for help to arrive. If not, then pinch the nostrils together and give two breaths mouth-to-mouth, lasting about one second each. If the person still is not responding, we move to C. C is circulation. Check for a pulse by finding the windpipe in the neck and sliding fingers, not thumb, to one side or the other. The carotid artery rests near here on both sides, and hopefully a pulse will be detectable. A weak pulse may be more difficult to detect. If there is no pulse, then chest compressions should be started by stacking one hand upon the other and placing the hands slightly below the nipple line. Push down on the chest enough to see it depress about 1 to 2 inches. Do not bounce. Count out 30 compressions to two respirations at a rate of 100/minute. Stop while the person gives the breathing. Continue this until the person wakes up or help arrives. You can check for a pulse every few minutes by feeling for the carotid artery in the neck.

While unconsciousness is not common in dojo environments, it can happen because of head, back, neck, and vital point injuries. The symptoms are unawareness and unresponsiveness. Promptly seek medical assistance from an emergency service.

V stands for Vertigo. Vertigo is malfunctioning of the balance mechanism of the inner ear. It may be caused by many factors, including a direct blow to the head, an injury to the inner ear, or decreased blood flow to the brain. The symptoms of vertigo are dizziness, nausea, vomiting, and loss of balance. The best thing to do is to seek immediate medical attention and have the patient rest in a chair, or on the floor against a wall. Meanwhile the patient should be reassured that he or she is not actually spinning around and that he or she is not about to fall.

APPENDICES

APPENDIX A1
ON SOKE KUBOTA

This story is being retold in its original form without any modifications. The original article, which first appeared in 1964, contains many interesting and historical photographs that could not be reproduced here for technical reasons. The original copy of this and many other historically important articles may be accessed from Soke's private files.

Karateka Fights Thugs

The police car stopped abruptly and out came a small man. "Leave her alone!" he yelled.

"Mind you own business," came an answer from the dark alley, as a huge man kept beating a helpless woman.

Without hesitating, Takayuki Kubota, 5-foot-4 judoka, rushed toward the man, grabbed him and flipped him to the ground. He held him there until the police secured the man with a handcuff.

In few moments another call of disturbance was reported in the vicinity –four men were robbing and wrecking a teahouse. Kubota ran to the scene on foot and encountered the four thugs Single-handedly, he threw the four men out of the building with aikido techniques.

A week later Kubota accompanied the squad car to break up a dope ring. On this raid Kubota applied karate because some of the assailants were armed with knives and sticks.

Prodigious Takayuki Kubota at 29 is already ranked 7th Degree (shichi-dan) in karate, 5th Degree (go-dan) in aikido, 3rd Degree (san-dan) n judo, and 1st Degree (shodan) in kendo. Born in Kyushu, Japan he studied karate at an unusually young age of 5. Later he studied the other martial arts ad sport of judo, aikido, and kendo.

KARATEKA BECOMES CURIOUS

After he became a Black Belt in karate, Kubota, while still a teenager, became curious as to its power. But the guiding principles of karate forbid anyone to engage in actual physical combat except in self-defense. The insatiable curiosity to test his knowledge obsessed him from day to day. Finally he thought of an idea. Kyushu, the southern island of Japan, is largely a farm area and it was easy for Kubota to receive permission to kill hogs for the markets.

While the other farmhands employed heavy hammers to kill the hogs, Kubota just used his fists entering the pens and instantly killing, even the largest hogs, with a single blow from either hand.

Kubota's striking power clearly transcends the normal capabilities one would expect of a man of his small stature (145 pounds). During some of the exhibitions he has performed, he would smash as many as five bricks stacked one on top of another, and occasionally "shut" chop through sizeable tocks.

PATROLING THE STREETS OF TOKYO

Kubota may be the only man who voluntarily, without any payment, actually faces and subdues assailants singly and in groups. Often they are armed with knives and other weapons, but he is always unarmed. Even today, when time permits, he accompanies the police on their night patrols to maintain his proficiency in actual street-fighting-techniques. Some of the policemen became interested in karate and began to study under him after being impressed by Kubota's remarkable success in handling harden hoodlums and dope addicts in Tokyo.

Kubota spends most of his time in his dojo, located in Hamada, a suburb near Tokyo's main airport. He still participates wholeheartedly his advanced students as well as the black belt holders who desire to be promoted.

He emphasizes forms (kites) and free fighting (kunzite) in training. In addition, he concludes each training period by teaching "was a" to the American students. This is a situational type of training where students are shown to defend themselves from specific attacks.

Unlike the basic sparring, which he also teaches, one student defends against another, and vice-versa. On occasion, he will teach either a karate, aikido, or judo technique to defend against certain type of attacks.

PROFICIENCY IN THREE STYLES

In his childhood, Kubota lived in Okinawa for a year where he studied the "Goju-Ryu" style of karate. Although he is proficient in, at least, three different styles of karate, he favors the "Shotokan" method.

Kubota leads a Spartan life and constantly experiments to increase his power and to resist sickness. He often takes cold showers in winter and believes in sleeping with only a light blanket during the cold season.

APPENDIX A2

REFERENCES AND SUGGESTIONS FOR FURTHER READING

The following books and periodicals were used as sources of reference for the preparation of this book. These publications also are recommended as approved literature for further reading and karate studies. This list is by no means complete. It is, however, a good starting point for those who wish to broaden their knowledge of karate-do and traditional martial arts.

Books

- Guide to Becoming a Better Karateka, by Kengo Isamu Manako, International Karate-do Association, 1982
- Karate-do Kyohan. The Master Text, by G. Funakoshi, Kodansha International, 1973
- Comprehensive Asian Fighting Arts, by D. F. Draeger & R. W. Smith, Kodansha International, 1969
- The Way of the Warrior, by H. Reid & M. Grouche, The Overlook Press, 1995
- Manual of Karate, by E. J. Harrison, Sterling Publishing Co., 1975
- Zen in the Martial Arts, by J. Hyams, J. P. Tarcher Co., 1979
- Bushido: The Warriors Code, by I. Nitobi, Ohara Publications, 1975
- Karate-do Nyumon, by G. Funakoshi, Kodansha International, 1974
- An Introduction to Karate, by K. Singleto
- Optima Publishing, 1989
- A Dictionary of Martial Arts, by L. Frederic, Charles E. Tuttle Co., 1988
- The Overlook Martial Arts Dictionary, by E. Farkas & J. Gorcuran, Overlook Press, 1983
- Stretching, by B. Anderson, Sheter Publication, 1980
- Encyclopedia of Modern Body Building, by A. Schwarzenegger, Simon and Schuster, 1985
- The Wellness Encyclopedia, University of California, Berkeley,

Houghton Mifflin Co., 1995
- Dynamic Karate, by M. Nakayama,
  Kodansha International, 1986
- Close Encounters, by T. Kubota, Dragon Books, Westlake, Calif.
- Karate Masters Volume 1, by Jose M. Fraguas,
  Empire Books, Los Angeles, Calif., 2001
- Idiot's Guide to Karate, by Hassel and Otis,
  Alpha Books, 2000
- The Secrets of Shotokan Karate, by R. L. Rielly,
  Tutle publishing, Tokyo, 2000
- The Advanced Shotokan Karate Handbook, by G. Sahota,
  Sahota Publishing, England, 1997
- [21] Shotokan Karate, by K. Enoeda & C. J. Mark
  Paul H. Crompton Ltd, London, 1975
- The Karate-do Manual, by PMV Morris,
  Barnes & Noble, New York, 1979
- Sports Health, by W. Southmaid and M. Hoffman,
  The Body Press, New York, 1981.
- Karate Jutsu, by Gichin Funakoshi,
  Kodansha International, Tokyo, 2001.

APPENDIX A3

CLASSES AT HEADQUARTERS

The official timetable presented in this section summarizes the weekly schedule of IKA karate training sessions offered at the headquarters dojo. The schedule has been designed specifically to provide the most convenient selection of practice periods for all categories of students. It also has been arranged in such a way as to allow all students to meet the attendance and training requirements of the curriculum under the tutelage of the best available instructors. All instructors are appointed directly by Soke himself.

This schedule has been in effect without major changes for many years. However, it may be subject to minor changes without notice. IKA membership is divided into three main groups. Children (CHLD) under 10 years of age are grouped together in specially scheduled classes. The Juniors (JRS) group is structured for students aged 11–15. Students 15 years of age and older are considered adults (ADLT).

Karate training for all groups is divided into three levels: beginners (BEG) intermediate (INT), and advanced (ADV). White through purple belts are considered beginners.

TIME	MON	TUE	WED	THU	FRI	SAT
8:00AM			MIXED		MIXED	WEAPONS
9:00AM						INT/ADV
10:00AM						BEG/CHILD
11:00AM						INT/CHILD
12:00PM		MIXED		MIXED		
4:00PM	INTRO		INTRO		BEG/CHILD	
4:30PM		BEGINNER	INT/CHILD	BEG/CHILD		
5:00PM					ADV/JRS	
5:30PM	Jr. KATA/KUMITE	KATA/ADV		INT/CHILD		
6:00PM			ADULT BEGINNER		BEGINNER	
6:30PM	ADULT/BEG	ADULT BEG/CHILD		ADULT BEG/CHILD		
7:00PM	INT/ADV			INT/ADV		
7:30PM	INT/ADV	INT/ADV				

Green belts are considered intermediate. Brown and black belts are advanced. Mixed classes are best suited to advanced and intermediate level students. Beginners, with permission from Soke, may participate in mixed sessions. Kata and kumite classes are intended only for qualified intermediate and advanced level students. Only advanced students with Soke's permission may participate in weapons classes.

Information regarding private classes, defensive tactics courses, special and traditional weapons training, seminars, and other unscheduled classes may be obtained directly from the administration desk at the headquarters dojo or by calling (818) 541-1240.

APPENDIX A4
IKA KARATE TRAINING AND STUDIES

NONTECHNICAL & THEORETICAL		PHYSICAL & TECHNICAL	
GENERAL KNOWLEDGE	IKA SPECIFIC	STUDY & READING	TRAINING PRACTICE
Respect & Etiquette	Dojo Kun	Karate Studies	Components of Kihon
History of Karate	History of IKA	Basic Sciences	Basic Skills / Kihon
Karate Masters	Takayuki Kubota	Counting & Numbers	Stances & Postures
History of Shotokan	History of Gosok	Shitsumon	Kihon Katas
Essence of Karate	The Insignia	Basic Terminology	Shotokan Katas
Tournaments	Titles & Ranking	Offense Philosophy	Gosoku-ryu Kata
Basic Health	Testing & Certification	Defense Philosophy	Bunkai
Basic Vocabulary	IKA Administration	Teaching	Basic Sparring
Physical Fitness	Dojo Schedules	Seminars	Kumite
Other MartiatArts	IKA Martial Arts		Self-defence

APPENDIX A5

IKA – AFFILIATED DOJOS

ARGENTINA	ECUADOR	MACEDONIA	SOUTH AFRICA
ARMENIA	EL SALVADOR	MEXICO	SPAIN
ARUBA	FRANCE	MOROCCO	SWITZERLAND
AUSTRALIA	GERMANY	NEPAL	THAILAND
AUSTRIA	GREECE	NEW ZEALAND	TRINIDAD
BARBADOS	GUATEMALA	NORWAY	TURKEY
BELARUS	HOLLAND	NOVA SCOTIA	UKRAINE
BELGIUM	HONG KONG	PAKISTAN	UNITED STATES
BRAZIL	HUNGARY	PALAU	VENEZUELA
CANADA	INDIA	PERU	VIETNAM
CHILE	INDIES	POLAND	ALASKA
COLOMBIA	IRAN	PHILIPPINES	HAWAII
CROATIA	IRELAND	ROMANIA	PUERTO RICO
COSTA RICA	ISRAEL	RUSSIA	ST. THOMAS
CUBA	ITALY	SARDINIA	
EGYPT	JAPAN	SAUDI ARABIA	
ENGLAND	LUXEMBURG	SERBIA	

HEADQUARTERS INSTRUCTORS

SOKE TAKAYUKI KUBOTA

Soke-Dai James Caan

Shihan Val Mijailovic
Shihan Boban Petcovic
Shihan Hank Hamilton
Shihan Paul McCaul
Shihan Leonard Kamer
Shihan Adam Pearson
Shihan Ted Bratakos
Shihan Tatsuo Hirano
Shihan Rod Kuratomi
Shihan Mike Berger
Shihan Gordon Pfiiffer
Shihan George Sinan
Shihan Mark Grigorian
Shihan George Rolon
Shihan Norvell Carrere
Shihan Mark Gudja
Shihan Antonio Antonetti
Shihan Marcial Soto
Shihan-dai Danny Kahan
Shihan-dai Sami Asmar
Shihan-dai David White
Shihan-dai Judy Marx
Shihan-dai Kirk Stites
Sensei Victor Chico
Sensei Mike Miller

NOTES

www.ingramcontent.com/pod-product-compliance
Lightning Source LLC
Chambersburg PA
CBHW081345080526
44588CB00016B/2384